Implementing SOA Using Java™ EE

The Java™ Series

Visit **informit.com/thejavaseries** for a complete list of available publications.

Publications in **The Java™ Series** are supported, endorsed, and written by the creators of Java at Sun Microsystems, Inc. This series is the official source for expert instruction in Java and provides the complete set of tools you'll need to build effective, robust, and portable applications and applets. **The Java™ Series** is an indispensable resource for anyone looking for definitive information on Java technology.

Visit Sun Microsystems Press at **sun.com/books** to view additional titles for developers, programmers, and system administrators working with Java and other Sun technologies.

Addison-Wesley Cisco Press EXAM/CRAM IBM Press QUE PRENTICE HALL SAMS | Safari Books Online

Implementing SOA Using Java™ EE

B. V. Kumar
Prakash Narayan
Tony Ng

Addison-Wesley

Upper Saddle River, NJ • Boston • Indianapolis • San Francisco
New York • Toronto • Montreal • London • Munich • Paris • Madrid
Cape Town • Sydney • Tokyo • Singapore • Mexico City

The publisher offers excellent discounts on this book when ordered in quantity for bulk purchases or special sales, which may include electronic versions and/or custom covers and content particular to your business, training goals, marketing focus, and branding interests. For more information, please contact:

U.S. Corporate and Government Sales
(800) 382-3419
corpsales@pearsontechgroup.com

For sales outside the United States please contact:

International Sales
international@pearson.com

Visit us on the web: informit.com/aw

Library of Congress Cataloging-in-Publication Data:

Kumar, B. V. (Balepur Venkatanna), 1959-
Implementing SOA using Java EE / B.V. Kumar, Prakash Narayan, Tony Ng.
p. cm.

ISBN 978-0-321-49215-9 (pbk. : alk. paper) 1. Service-oriented architecture (Computer science) 2. Java (Computer program language) I. Narayan, Prakash, 1960- II. Ng, Tony. III. Title.

TK5105.5828K95 2010
004.6'54--dc22

2009041877

Pearson Education, Inc
Rights and Contracts Department
501 Boylston Street, Suite 900
Boston, MA 02116
Fax (617) 671 3447

ISBN-13: 978-0-321-49215-9
ISBN-10: 0-321-49215-3

Text printed in the United States on recycled paper at Edwards Brothers in Ann Arbor, Michigan.

First printing December 2009

Editor-in-Chief
Mark Taub

Acquisitions Editor
Greg Doench

Development Editor
Songlin Qiu

Managing Editor
Kristy Hart

Project Editor
Anne Goebel

Copy Editor
Apostrophe Editing Services

Indexer
Lisa Stumpf

Proofreader
Karen A. Gill

Publishing Coordinator
Michelle Housley

Cover Designer
Alan Clements

Senior Compositor
Gloria Schurick

To my mother—Mrs. M. N. Lakshmidevamma

—Dr. B. V. Kumar

To my parents—Mr. K.N. Krishnamoorthy and Mrs. Sharada Krishnamoorthy

—Prakash Narayan

To Kaitlyn, Tyler, and Sophia

—Tony Ng

Contents

Forewords

Robert Brewin

Recently, seasoned analysts like Anne Thomas Manes have said that SOA is dead and that it has failed to deliver its promised benefits. There have been opposing viewpoints to this. ZDNet blogger Joe McKendrick hosted a panel discussion on "Avoiding SOA Disillusionment," and the panelists concluded that any perceived disillusionment stemmed from lack of planning and measurement on the part of the Enterprises and not from a failure of SOA. In fact, Enterprises that have been working with SOA practices and methodologies remain bullish on the approach and recognize that SOA continues to hold promise as a model for integration and helping to tactically reduce costs in tough times. The promise of SOA is that it offers an architectural approach to support the proliferation and adoption of reusable services. This is an approach that companies should adopt to streamline their development processes and improve the quality and maintainability of their code.

At Sun, we developed the Java Platform, Enterprise Edition (Java EE) as an industry standard, and it forms the ideal foundation upon which developers can implement Enterprise-class SOA and next generation web applications. I am pleased to see this book by Kumar, Narayan, and Ng, which takes a practical approach to implementing SOA with Java EE. The focus is on real implementation techniques, leveraging the GlassFish Application Server and NetBeans IDE. By taking this approach, the authors have demystified SOA from an alphabet soup of Web Services standards and shown how readers can implement SOA in their Enterprise readily and easily. In addition to explaining the concepts of SOA and the concepts of Java EE, the authors dive deep into implementing SOA with

Java EE and show how services can be delivered within different tiers of an Enterprise architecture.

Architects, developers, managers, other IT professionals, educators, and students will benefit from different aspects of this book from concepts to architecting to implementation, configuration, and tuning. I trust that you will find this book beneficial and enlightening.

Robert Brewin
Chief Technology Officer, Software
Sun Microsystems

Raj Bala

Now more than ever, concepts like availability, leveragability, scalability, expandability, extendibility, and security permeate every discussion on technology architecture. As companies become more aware of harvesting maximum sustainable value from technology investments, the architecture fraternity has always cried loud for how the fundamentals matter. Architectural integrity is measured by all the "itys" that I mentioned in my first sentence, and it is heartening to see how the answers have been around and, in fact, getting better.

Service oriented architecture (SOA) as a fundamental fix to future problems has evolved to newer and more advanced frontiers. Saddling on ever-perfected technologies such as Java EE, SOA is becoming more appealing and compelling than ever before.

At Cognizant, we have been developing and delivering Enterprise solutions using SOA. And it is my privilege to write a Foreword for a book for one of our own—Kumar is a coauthor along with Prakash and Tony. The book carefully unravels the vast topic of service oriented architecture through a definitive and illustrative approach. It segments web services across First Generation Web Services for services composition, Second Generation Web Services for wiring these services into the process/workflow of the enterprise, and WS-* for addressing the nonfunctional needs of the Enterprise application. This book will also double-up as an effective implementation guide on the advanced features of the new Java Platform, Enterprise Edition and indicate how different APIs, such as JAX-WS and JAXB, of the new platform help in different aspects of service orientation for the Enterprise application.

This book should be extremely relevant to a variety of stake holders including architects, senior enterprise developers, and application integrators. This book is also a great reference material for students of computer science, software, and systems architecture.

From academics to architects, practitioners to pedants, students to specialists, coders to CXOs, this book could be a vital source of SOA inspiration—of how to build great architecture without compromising on the "itys."

Raj Bala
VP and Chief Technology Officer
Cognizant Technology Solutions

Acknowledgments

I would like to acknowledge and thank Cognizant immensely for encouraging and supporting this collaborative work with Prakash and Tony, which was initiated two years ago. Special thanks are due to Frank (CEO) and Chandra (president and MD) for their encouragement for this collaborative work. Thanks are due to Raj Bala (VP and CTO) and Dr. Appa Rao (VP, GTO) for their continuous encouragement and support during the course of authoring this book. I am highly indebted to Viswakumar (AVP, Projects) for his incessant help and support of this collaborative work.

Support from my wife Sujatha Kumar, my daughter Nayana Kumar, and my son Govind Kashyap has been tremendous throughout the course of this book, and I sincerely acknowledge their continued support on this project for the past two years.

We owe our sincere appreciation to Ramesh Srinivasaraghavan and Arijit Chatterjee of Adobe (India) for their timely help in shaping the companion website for this book. We also admire Sujit Reddy and Shyam Prasad of Adobe (India) for helping us with the content and design of this site.

—Dr. B. V. Kumar

I would like to thank Chris Atwood and Octavian Tanase at Sun for their support and encouragement throughout this project. Special thanks and love to my family—Jayanthi, my wife and Akshay, Madhuri, and Rohan, my children—for always being there for me and supporting my endeavors with vigor. I was fortunate to work with a great team of coauthors: B. V. Kumar and Tony Ng. Each brought their expert-level skills to make this a rewarding experience. Thanks to Gopalan Suresh Raj, Binod P. G., Keith Babo, and Rick Palkovic for their seminal paper, "Implementing Service-Oriented Architectures (SOA) with the Java EE 5 SDK," which inspired me to explore the subject further and get involved in writing this book. This book is all about implementation. The basis for this book is the NetBeans IDE. The team that I worked with—Todd Fast, Chris Webster, Girish Balachandran, Nam Nguyen, Rico Cruz, Jiri Kopsa, Ajit Bhate, PCM Reddy, and Hong Lin (among many others)—have all contributed in helping make the NetBeans product a great success.

On the editorial and production side, thanks to Greg Doench, Michelle Housley, Anne Goebel, and the rest of the editorial staff at Pearson for their guidance.

—Prakash Narayan

I would like to thank Jeet Kaul and Tom Kincaid for their encouragement and support, Bill Shannon and Eduardo Pelegri-Llopart for their guidance, and the entire GlassFish team who worked on the Java EE platform and SDK.

—Tony Ng

About the Authors

Dr. B. V. Kumar, currently the director and chief architect at Cognizant Technology Solutions, has an M Tech from IIT Kanpur and a Ph.D. from IIT Kharagpur. He has more than 19 years of experience in the field of information technology at various levels and in organizations such as ComputerVision Corporation (Singapore), Parametric Technologies (Seoul, S. Korea), and Sun Microsystems (India). Prior to joining Cognizant, Dr. Kumar was the principal researcher and technologist at Infosys Technologies and was responsible for the research and development activities and new initiatives at the SETLabs. Dr. Kumar has been working on the Enterprise technologies for more than 7 years, focusing on J2EE and web services technologies. As a chief architect and director at the Global Technology Office of Cognizant (India), Dr. Kumar is managing IP and asset creation, technology evangelization, and community development and project support. Dr. Kumar has filed for two patents in the IP space and published many technological papers in international journals and conferences. He has coauthored *Web Services—An Introduction* and *J2EE Architecture*.

Prakash Narayan is the CTO and cofounder of Micello, Inc. Micello is an early-stage startup in Silicon Valley focusing on delivering high-value data to users at the point of consumption by providing the information within a map of the indoor location. Prior to founding Micello, Prakash was at Sun Microsystems, where he was one of the founders of Zembly—a social network for developers to build services, widgets, and social applications. Immediately before Zembly, Prakash had responsibility for Java EE and SOA tooling in NetBeans.

Prakash holds an MS degree in computer science from Indian Institute of Technology, Delhi, and a BS degree in electronics engineering from Birla Institute of Technology and Science, Pilani, India.

Tony Ng is the senior director of engineering at Yahoo!, where he is responsible for Yahoo! developer platforms and technologies including Yahoo! Application platform (YAP), Yahoo! Query Language (YQL), and Yahoo! Developer Network (YDN). Before joining Yahoo!, Tony was the director of engineering at Sun Microsystems, where he managed development of the Java EE platform and GlassFish application server. Tony is a coauthor of *J2EE Connector Architecture* and *Enterprise Application Integration*. He holds an MS degree in computer science from Massachusetts Institute of Technology and an MBA degree from the University of California, Berkeley.

Part I

Overview

1

Introduction

Enterprises are in a state of flux. New business requirements are challenging enough to drive innovations in information technologies. Such advancements are pushing enterprises to newer business challenges. Significant innovations always impact architectural requirements. This has transformed enterprises from a state in which there was no concept of architecture to a state in which a significant amount of architectural planning is the most important step in an enterprise solution. Although the functionality of enterprise applications drove the requirements of the enterprises in an earlier era, the nonfunctional parts are now controlling the enterprise architecture requirements. The multifarious nature of enterprise businesses has necessitated that businesses reorient the architecture to enable automation. This is advantageous to the enterprises and their partners and collaborators in the long run.

Service Oriented Architecture (*SOA*) is the latest architectural buzzword to take the enterprises by storm. Business requirements for the enterprises are changing more rapidly than ever and are posing several challenges that put tremendous pressure on enterprise stakeholders to push businesses to hunt for long-lasting solutions. Although there are no silver bullets architecting (or rearchitecting) the enterprise solution to implement, SOA seems to promise a lasting and, perhaps, even futuristic solution to the enterprises. But, is SOA the newest trend? If we look at the historical trends in architectural evolution, we can see that the attempts for service orientation in the architecture existed but never were recognized by that terminology. In the following sections, we explore the evolution of the term SOA and explain its impact on enterprises.

Products and Services

Initially, enterprises depended on traditional means of conducting business transactions, including marketing and promotion of products and services. Although the traditional ways of merchandising products and services were simple, the innovative and creative ways pursued by many of the enterprises were powerful enough to sustain business in a competitive environment. The life cycle of a product or a service merchandising involved these simple steps:

- Creation of products or services and ways to merchandising
- Discovery of products and services by customers
- Vendors and customers confluence and negotiation
- Sale of products and services
- Maintenance of products and services until the completion of the life cycle

Software-Driven Services

Both products and services were referred to with respect to merchandising as the viewpoint. Notice here that the products are tangible in nature, whereas the nature of services is mostly intangible. Technical training, maintenance and safekeeping, installation of machinery (or hardware), delivery of goods or packages, and so on are a few of the examples of "services." Services are rendered and used as a part of the process or workflow in almost all the enterprises. The requirement of services[1] as a part of the process/workflow is gaining more importance. The growth of information technologies across the industries appears to have fueled the requirement and the delivery of services in a profound manner. Services as a business are becoming an attractive business proposition for many enterprises.

The business of services delivery has several advantages, including that they can be delivered or used directly or indirectly. A *direct service* is tangible in nature. A courier service could be considered tangible, whereas a stock-quote service might not be considered tangible. Also, any service could be simple or complicated in nature. A simple service can be a precise, single-step task, whereas a complex service can be composed of several simple services, which can be associated with tangible and intangible implications. A *courier service* might also use a *courier-tracking service*, in which the services of software are used to track routing and other details of package delivery. The growing importance of IT in general, and soaring demand for tangible and intangible services, has increased the demand for software-driven services businesses. Software-driven services have played an important role in enabling the delivery of services in various enterprises. Many enterprises have actively leveraged their business using software-driven services. Supply-chain, retail, banking and financial services, education, manufacturing, pharmaceuticals, health care, and so on are examples of a few of the industry verticals that have continuously leveraged the software-driven services as a part of their process/workflow.

When software-driven services are used to deliver or utilize services, there are additional implications, based on the nature and the use of software. A service delivered using a mainframe system can be isolated within the stand-alone system environment. Likewise, service delivery on a client/server system can transpire anywhere within the *local area network* (*LAN*). On the other hand, delivering a software service on the Internet can occur beyond the LAN or larger networked environments such as the *wide area network* (*WAN*) or *metropolitan area network* (*MAN*). As the requirement of the software-driven services delivery grows, the complexity of the delivery of services also increases. It is important to understand the nature and role of the "service" or service process, the "client" or client application, and the client using the service.

A software-driven service can be defined as a server process (a program executing on a system) that fulfills the client request by performing a specified task on the server system. Examples include an application that can retrieve the most up-to-date information about a particular stock trade, or an application that can provide a real-time traffic report on any freeway the user requests. Among the other things, the server process involves the host operating system, file server, and other related applications. Note that the server process will usually be running as a daemon process and will always be waiting for a request.

The client can be either a user or a computer application. The client applications are of two varieties. One application displays the queries to the human user and obtains inputs in real time. Such client applications are usually associated with *Graphical User Interfaces* (*GUI*), which are designed to collect the user inputs. The other client application automatically accesses and uses the services without any human interaction. These are full-fledged applications and can handle all possible situations. Such clients help in automating the process/workflow.

When the server process receives the request from a client application, it accepts and analyzes it and generates a suitable response that is communicated back to the client. The request and response between the client and server is synchronous and uses the same protocol for communication. This is analogous to two people communicating using a common language.

Prior to the advent of the Internet and World Wide Web, systems and software architectures were designed to offer services to the clients over the LAN/WAN of the company's intranet. Server processes and client applications were developed on identical operating systems (and programming environments) and deployed on compatible systems. However, if such services are developed and deployed over different hardware and operating environments, they cannot communicate. Ensuring compatibility between such heterogeneous systems, although not impossible, became vendor-dependent. The emergence of the World Wide Web and Internet, and the popularity of *Hypertext Transfer Protocol (HTTP)* as a lightweight communication protocol, changed the software-driven services scenario profoundly. A standard web browser could be used as an effective client on the intranet and the Internet. Initially, the web and Internet were exclusively used by universities, research academies, and military research establishments. Proliferation of the web and Internet into the business arena and the acceptance of the same as a suitable business medium by the enterprises provided a tremendous boost to the Internet, while acceptance of HTTP[2] as a business communication protocol also gained momentum.

The service delivered by the server process to the client application (browser) is in HTML. The content of the services can be one of three forms: static information, dynamically generated information, or a combination of static and dynamically generated information. Although the static information can be repurposed, dynamically generated content indicates the availability of most up-to-date information. Businesses and enterprises typically require a suitable mix of both.

Web Services

Web services are available on most of the desktops all over the world, and on *Portable Digital Assistants (PDA)* and mobile phones. The most prominent advantage the web has provided businesses is the availability and accessibility of software-driven services on the Internet. Scale and distribution of customers also present unique opportunities for the businesses to expand, although scale and distribution also bring along many challenging issues for the businesses. Because the advantages outweigh the disadvantages, business and industries are increasingly depending on the web and Internet for growth. Growth and proliferation in the *Business-to-Consumer (B2C)* enterprises can be seen as the immediate result of the Internet revolution.

The advent on the Internet and web did not bring the same kind of growth to *Business-to-Business (B2B)*.The predominant problems could be attributed to factors such as disparate systems, incompatible applications, and a proprietary communication protocol. In fact, the medium of communication was identified as the predominant stumbling block in the realization of business automation. When two or more organizations needed to agree on B2B proceedings, they would be confronted with a complicated scenario and dogged with serious integration and interoperability issues. Interoperability is the key to business automation and promotes effective business automation among partners and collaborators.

Interoperability is the capability of an application to communicate with any other application, regardless of the hardware on which the application is deployed, the operating environment on which the application is executing, or the programming language used to develop the application. In other words, applications deployed on disparate systems should communicate and interchange enterprise information. Web services technology promises interoperability among a variety of business applications deployed on disparate systems. Web services also promise to fully leverage the web and Internet to make interoperability possible beyond geographical boundaries. The unveiling of *Extensible Markup Language (XML)* in the mid-1990s introduced the possibility of interoperability through the use of text-based mark-up language. XML can be used to represent any business-related information. It has the capability to make the information exchange independent of networking, operating system, or deployment platform, thus enabling the interoperability of the business information. XML is the foundation language, supporting a number of advanced dialects (or standards), often referred to as *vocabularies*. There are more than 450 such vocabularies, representing different industry vertical requirements.

Web services applications can be used to implement synchronous or asynchronous services. Realize web services do not refer to one single technology, application, or specification but a combination of several technologies and specifications based on XML. These are the advanced vocabularies (or standards) on top of basic XML. The three vocabularies considered most important with respect to web services are *Simple Object Access Protocol (SOAP)*, *Web Services Description Language (WSDL)*, and *Universal Description, Discovery and Integration (UDDI)*.

According to Gartner Group, a web service can be defined as

> *...the software components that employ one or more of the following technologies—SOAP, WSDL, and UDDI—to perform distributed computing. Use of any of the basic technologies—SOAP, WSDL or UDDI—constitutes a web service. Use of all of them is not required....*

Utilizing services through the web services route essentially involves three categories of players, as shown in Figure 1.1. They are *service provider*, *service requester*, and *service broker*. A provider would be an industry, business, or company capable of creating and providing software-driven services. Similarly, a requester would be a company or a business that would like to use the service. On the other hand, the broker would be a place, entity, or system that helps the requester to discover the provider.

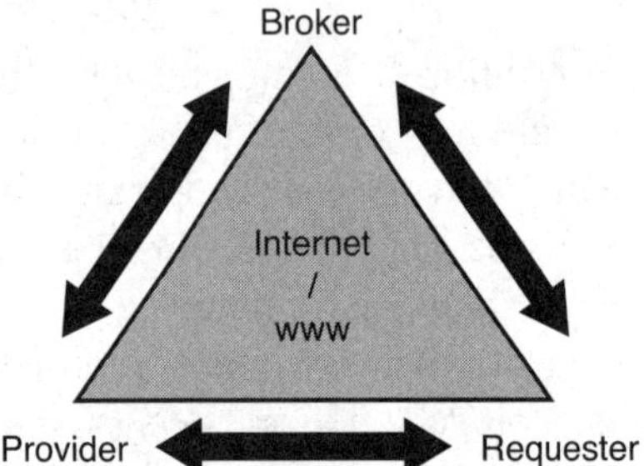

Figure 1.1 The first generation web services

The arrows in Figure 1.1 indicate the interactions between the three participants. The interactions between the provider and broker are essentially the services *publication*. The interaction between the requester and the broker is the task of *searching* for the services and the services provider. Finally, the interaction between the provider and requester is called the *bind*.

Although the role of the service provider and the service requester is simple and straightforward, the role of the broker requires additional clarification. The broker's role is to enable both the provider and the requester to come together to discover and understand each other, discuss, and negotiate. The requirement of the broker and his services might no longer be required after the provider and the requester agree to transact between themselves. The provider and/or requestor, typically, don't need to visit the broker after they agree with each other on the terms and conditions of services transaction. However, the need for the broker's services can arise only when there is a change in the services and services-related information. This situation is likely when the provider of the service prefers to notify the changes in the registry.

SOA

SOA is a way of architecting the enterprise application as a set of cooperating services that all the enterprise users want. The enterprise user can be a human user or a client application. Let's consider an enterprise application such as an online pet store. An online store, for example, can offer a variety of items that the remote clients can purchase. When a Submit button is pressed to finalize the purchase, several other services swing into action, as shown in Figure 1.2. For instance, the inventory service launched checks the inventory status of all the selected items. The shipping service can be invoked to initiate the shipping of different materials. A tracking service can then be invoked to generate the tracking number to locate the shipped order. The entire process, from the initial order to delivery, can be managed by the interactions between several cooperating programs.

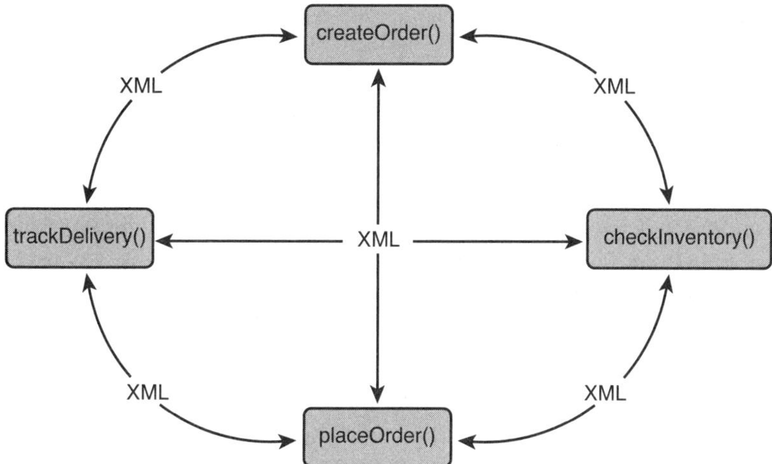

Figure 1.2 Services and interaction among services forming SOA

SOA is all about designing programs as a set of cooperating services—services that can interact with each other through the Internet and Web. The term "service" is essentially the business service. An enterprise application, designed using SOA, is composed of several services. These services are, usually, loosely coupled in nature so that new services can be added or existing services can be modified (or even retired) quickly, based on the dynamic nature of the business situation. Such organizations can be more competitive and are therefore more likely to survive and thrive in the business world.

In a nutshell, an enterprise application created with SOA would be a set of service components distributed in a network. These service components communicate, through messaging standards, with the end users and with each other using the web services standards recognized across the computing environment. The services providers can, sometimes, publish services-related information known as *service exposure*.

Still, the concept of SOA is not entirely new. It existed anonymously even before the advent of object-oriented languages.[3] Let's explore some early approaches to SOA. One of the earliest attempts to implement service oriented architecture was the *Distributed Computing Environment* (*DCE*), which preceded the Internet and Web. With DCE, you could implement services in different locations (sometimes in different cities) and on different types of systems and operating environments. Client applications could request different services from anywhere in the network with no thought to where the service was accessed from. Later approaches in SOA included *Distributed Component Model* (*DCOM*) from Microsoft. A cross-platform approach called *Common Object Request Brokered Architecture (CORBA)*, from *Object Modeling Group* (*OMG*), included the IDL approach. The request for services by one user or application from another application or service can be brokered, enabling applications in different operating environments and using different databases to communicate effectively. However, all three earlier approaches[4]—DCE, DCOM, and CORBA—were not blessed with Internet or HTTP.

The two approaches for creating SOA and then using web services to implement it are the *top-down* approach and the *bottom-up* approach. In the top-down approach, you define the overall business in terms of its processes, how they flow, and how they are separated out as services. In the bottom-up approach, you can start with a few of the services and, later on, integrate them into the application that the enterprise is already using. Some architects advocate a middle ground so that both the business folks and IT engineers work out a pragmatic approach that gradually develops into a real-world business picture, while evolving the applications into components using web services. Whichever approach is used, it is important to know what the main standards are and which products are needed to build the service components that make the enterprise truly service oriented, agile, and dynamic.

HTTP played an important role in the proliferation of B2C transactions and plays an important role in B2B transactions. Another standard called the *Simple Object Access Protocol* (*SOAP*) piggybacks on HTTP carrying the information in the form of a message, which can be synchronous or asynchronous in nature. Furthermore, in an enterprise scenario, existence of a combination of synchronous and asynchronous message exchange patterns is not uncommon. Another industry-standard advanced XML vocabulary called *Web Services Description Language* (*WSDL*) (pronounced "Wisdel") enables you to describe the services an enterprise might offer. These services can be listed in a directory or registry known as the UDDI. The UDDI registry is like electronic "yellow pages" for worldwide services.

These standards are referred to as *First Generation Core Standards* for web services and SOA. As shown in Figure 1.3, these three standards form the cornerstones for the web services and SOA implemented using web services. These standards essentially form the nuts and bolts of web services and SOA. Recently, the industry consortium has contributed a new addition to these web services standards. This new standard is called the *Web Services Interoperability*, or *WS-I*.

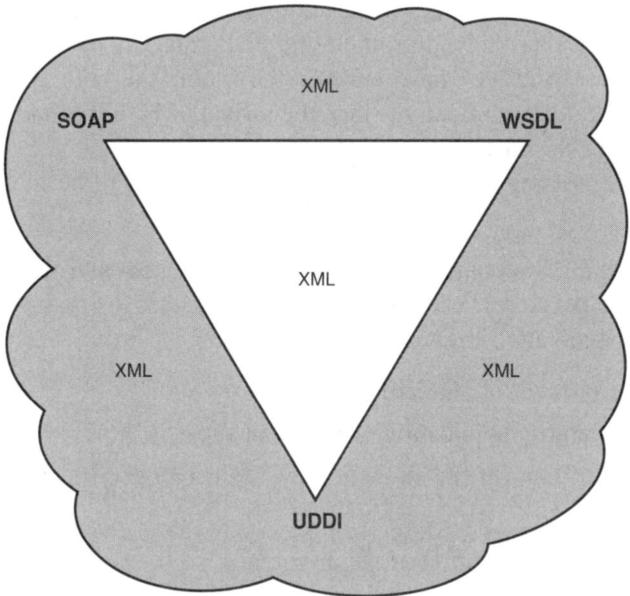

Figure 1.3 The first generation web services: SOAP, WSDL, and UDDI

The first generation web services are the essential part of the web services. Although this is necessary for any web services-based SOA, it is not sufficient. Advanced standards and frameworks are necessary for a satisfactory implementation of services oriented architecture. Additional advanced web services specifications and standards are evolving. Prominent among them are WS-Security, WS-Reliable Messaging, WS-Addressing, and so forth. Collectively, these web services standards are referred to as WS-* (pronounced "WS Star").

Products and IDEs are available that help organizations implement web services-based SOA through one of the three approaches: *top-down*, *bottom-up*, or *mid-way*. For bottom-up web services, there are two general development environments or operating system platforms. For a Windows-only platform, there is .NET from Microsoft Corporation. For Windows, Linux, and other UNIX-based systems, there is the J2EE[5]-based solution.

SOA implementations are becoming increasingly popular among enterprises. According to the Gartner Group, due to the growing preference of software as a service, business process management (BPM) and cloud computing are helping drive service oriented architecture adoption.

Web Services and SOA Opportunities

The arrival of web services heralded a significant milestone in the history of information technology. The Internet and the World Wide Web helped the B2C category of the organizations to thrive. The development of new XML standards and advanced vocabularies has helped promote the B2B category of the organizations. Transactions over the web have become the norm, and both B2C and B2B have gained tremendous momentum since the arrival of HTTP. SOA seems to be the new mantra for the enterprises to face and survive the impending business challenges. Implementing SOA using web services seems to be the most appropriate way.

Consider the following B2B scenario, for example, when a customer purchases pet food from an online pet store. When the customer completes the online transaction, the enterprise application triggers a chain of events:

- Charging the customer's credit card
- Notifying the inventory application of the retail store
- Informing the distributor if the inventory level falls below critical level
- Updating the appropriate databases
- Contacting the sales application of the distributor
- Notifying the Courier Tracking Service for initiating the dispatch
- Communicating with the Courier Tracking Service for tracking the location of the package
- Updating the manufacturer's database about the sale
- Notifying the manufacturer's guarantee and warranty applications

Note that this chain of events could take place on different systems, belonging to different business entities that could be situated in geographically different locations. The business relations among these entities could be widely different, ranging from manufacturer to supplier to trading partner to collaborator, and so on. The events can be sequential or parallel and can happen in a synchronous or asynchronous mode. It is worth noting that different applications belonging to different businesses can communicate with each other in an interoperable fashion.

This scenario is complicated. The implementation of the same can be done in one of the following ways: manual, vendor dependent (proprietary), or a SOA implementation using web services. Although the manual implementation is slow, error prone, and nonscalable, using a proprietary solution can severely hamper the business due to vendor-locking. Moreover, the solution could be expensive, and such solutions are often nonextendable. Implementing SOA using web services for such situations could not only enable this scenario to transpire smoothly, but also provides the business with a simple, extensible option.

Demand for SOA implementation using web services has been on the rise in many enterprises worldwide. Recent surveys have projected an increased adoption rate of web services among several industries. Among several vertical industries, *Supply Chain Management (SCM)*, *Customer Relation Management (CRM)*, retail, banking and financial services, telecommunications, utilities, pharmaceutical, health care, and so on have SOA implementation at the top of their IT agenda. The outlook on adoption of web services among these industries indicates a moderate but matured way of adoption—from evaluation to prototype, all the way to mission-critical application deployment.

Summary

As businesses evolve, the demand for the services continues to grow among all the related partners and collaborators, and the need for business automation among these partners and collaborators is on the rise. The technology behind XML-based web services is ramping up to meet these needs.

In the next chapter, we analyze the progression of enterprise architecture through the study of two important conceptual approaches: server-side architectural progression and client-side architectural progression. Here, you understand how the convergence of these architectural progressions has resulted in the evolution of architecture that promotes loosely coupled and interoperable applications.

Endnotes

1. The term *service* here essentially indicates software service.
2. HTTP is a request/response protocol. The way this protocol works is as follows: A web server would be deployed on a server system, and this system would be hosting one or more web applications. These applications would be in a daemon state and would be listening for HTTP requests from clients on a specific port. When the request from a client is received on the designated port, the request is intercepted by the corresponding web application, processed, and the results are generated. This is called the HTTP response. This response is then communicated back to the client on the same port.

3. What's the relationship between service orientation and object orientation? You can think of object orientation and service orientation as complementary. The enterprise applications are essentially object oriented in nature, and the services are essentially the functions or methods associated with the objects and/or components deployed in the enterprise application. Functions from different objects and classes form a service (or a set of related services). In practical situations, object-oriented programming is applied in environments because all the objects were on the same platform rather than distributed across the networks. This is referred to as a tightly coupled arrangement. The SOA approach assumes, from the beginning, that any service is a component, and it can be located anywhere on the network. When you get to the place where the service actually is, it is possible that the code executes the service, irrespective of the programming language used. Therefore, SOA is often described as architecture for service components that are loosely coupled.
4. In Chapter 2, "Evolution of IT Architectures," we delve more into these technologies.
5. J2EE was rechristened as Java Platform, Enterprise Edition (or Java EE) in 2006 by Sun Microsystems.

2

Evolution of IT Architectures

Businesses and enterprises were the earliest adopters of computer technology outside military and government establishments. Large enterprises invested in various parts of the businesses—from Point-of-Sale (POS) terminals to mainframe computers. Initially, the mainframes provided Centralized Model architecture to manage business data and processes. The concept of software architecture started to evolve when enterprises and other businesses started adopting small and medium computers and networking them to share resources. The need for decoupling of the systems and software applications in smaller networked environments resulted in the emergence of what is considered the most important of architectures: client/server. Many of the architectures that evolved later were influenced by clients and servers. The evolution of distributed architectures can be considered a sophisticated extension of client/server architecture. Clearly, the Internet and World Wide Web caused a shift in the nature and ways of business transactions taking place today. These challenges and opportunities have caused the architecture to be governed by nonfunctional requirements of the enterprises. Some of the important nonfunctional requirements include performance, reliability, availability, and security.

Enterprise businesses are continuously evolving, and the information technology requirements for the enterprises and organizations continue to drive the *information technology (IT)* evolution in a recursive manner. On the one hand, business requirements have driven IT research and development efforts. On the other hand, introduction of newer systems, devises, protocols, programming languages, and so forth, has always helped business to proliferate and prosper. A peek into the chronological view of the history of the evolution of IT shows us many examples. A qualitative analysis of chronological events provides a good understanding of the background of the emergence of web services technology and *Service Oriented Architecture* (*SOA*).

The field of IT is not about hardware and software in isolation. It is about dependent and interdependent development efforts of both hardware and software by industries, educational institutions, research, establishments of the military and space research, and so on. Other factors such as inventions and introduction of newer devices and systems, protocols, programming languages, and specifications and have also influenced the field of IT. A chronological analysis of this is referred to as *progression*. In this chapter, we have adopted an approach that is termed the *Conceptual Architectural Progression*. The architectural progressions mark some noteworthy eras that indicate the existence and sustenance of important architectures. Two conceptual architecture progressions can be visualized: *Server-Side Architecture Progression* and *Client-Side Architecture Progression*.

The Server-Side Architecture Progression

We first explore the chronological progression on the server side of IT. Some significant events in advancement on the server side called *eras* include the following:

- Mainframe era
- Client/server era
- Distributed era
- Internet era

Figure 2.1 presents the conceptual view of the progression of server-side enterprise architectures along the time line. Notice that all the predominant architectures evolved are overlapping and coexisting with each other. Mainframe computer systems dominated in the mainframe era but still exist even in the Internet era. None of these architectures have vanished completely. This could be attributed to return on investment, allegiance, dependency on vendor, and so forth. It is important to note that newer technologies need to be integrated with older existing systems. These older systems are often referred to as *legacy systems*. Examples of the legacy systems in the enterprises and their integration with the newer distributed/Internet architecture can be found in many enterprises across the world.

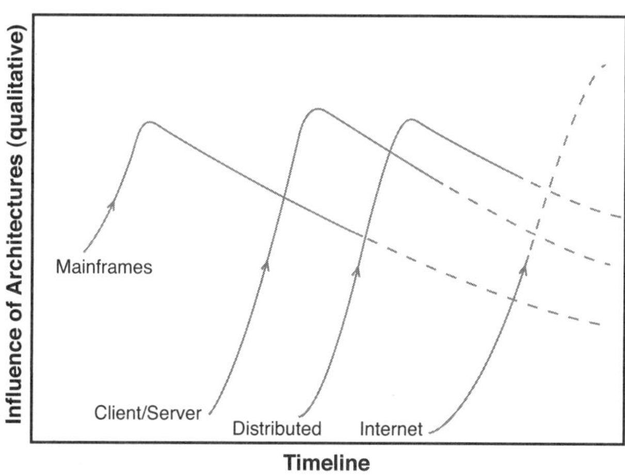

Figure 2.1 Progression in server-side architectures

Progression of Mainframe Architecture

Initially, mainframe computers dominated the IT scene. Companies such as IBM and Digital[1] dominated the IT scenario for a long period of the IT history. Mainframe systems thrived for a fairly long period; this time frame is referred to as the Mainframe era. Mainframe systems were big and expensive and affordable by only large- and medium-sized corporations. These systems predominantly represented the hardware muscle.[2] Mainframe systems are essentially single-tiered systems; architecture was referred to as the Centralized Model, and the software applications were executed on the CPU of the mainframe. This system was connected to several terminals that acted as a conduit for input/output between the mainframe system and the user. These mainframe systems were also connected to other peripherals such as printers, tape drive units, card readers, and so on. It is worth mentioning here that some of early versions of mainframe systems did not even have consoles or terminals. Card readers or tape drivers were often used for submitting the batch jobs,[3] and printers were used as the output from the systems.

Figure 2.2 presents the centralized model of mainframe architecture. The mainframe system is shown connected to several terminals.

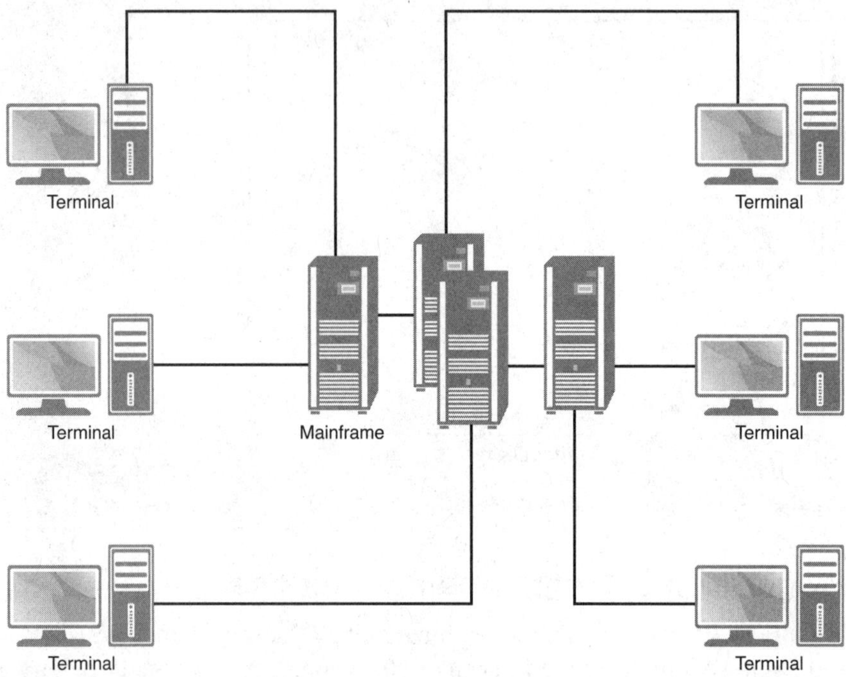

Figure 2.2 Centralized model of mainframe architecture

The mainframe systems supported a primary memory in which the application was loaded into the memory for executing. The secondary memory of these systems stored the applications from the users. However, these applications were completely tied to the mainframe systems and could be used only within the hard-wired limits of the mainframe systems in which they were developed. Many mainframe vendors sold utility applications along with the mainframe systems that were made available to all the users of the mainframe systems.[4] These utility applications were provided in the form of subroutines.[5] The subroutines were essentially mathematical algorithms encoded into a suitable programming language such as FORTRAN. A collection of such mathematical subroutines was termed a library. Any individual interested in using this service needed to call the appropriate subroutine from his programming environment. Organizations such as the *Numerical Algorithms Group (NAG)*, *International Mathematics and Statistics Library (IMSL)*, and so on provided subroutines on a variety of mainframe systems. These subroutines provided a variety of services predominantly for business, scientific, and engineering computations. IBM Corporation provided several business-related subroutines that could be used by the appropriate applications for carrying out business tasks such as sorting, indexing, arranging and so forth. The mainframe systems have been the backbone of many large enterprises for a long time, and many applications developed on these mainframe systems are still considered relevant today.

Progression of Client/Server Architecture

The client/server term corresponds to a model of computing in which client applications running on a desktop or personal computer access information on remote servers or host computers. The client portion of the application is typically optimized for user interaction, whereas the server portion provides a centralized access and multiuser functionality. The client/server architecture appeared on the horizon in the late 1970s.

The development of client/server architecture closely followed the appearance of smaller and inexpensive computers such as microcomputers, minicomputers, and workstations. As against the mainframe systems, these smaller systems were affordable by *Small and Medium Business (SMB)*. The possibility of networking such smaller systems within the organization provided a basis for the dawn of two-tier architecture. In this architecture, the application (and data) and the user interfaces could handle two different systems in a distinct way. While the server system could host application and data, the client system could handle user interaction. Figure 2.3 provides the simplistic architectural concept of client/server.

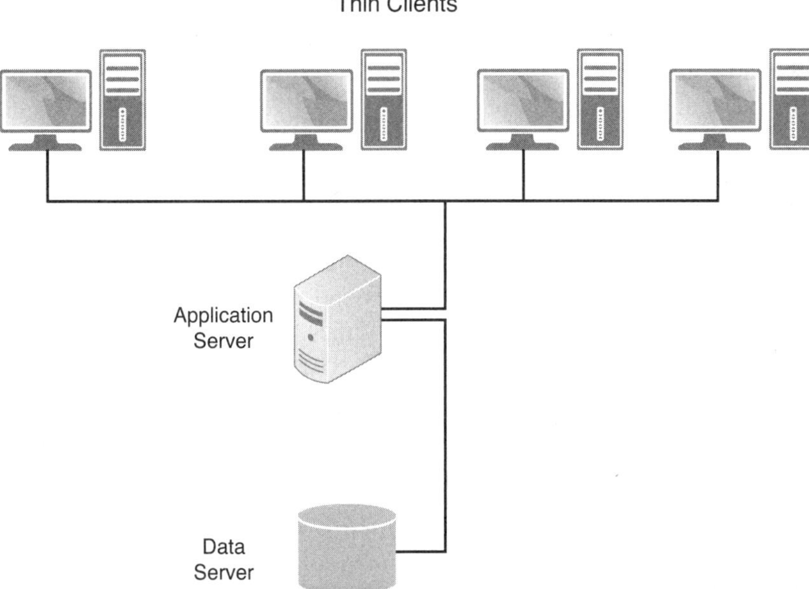

Figure 2.3 A simplistic representation of client/server architecture

In the mid-1980s desktop computers heralded a revolution in the history of computers. These popular systems, known as *personal computers (PC)*, could be afforded by individuals and professionals alike. The proliferation of PCs provided an ideal client environment for the client/server architecture within the premises of the organization because it could help the user access information on the desktop. The networked environment of such computers provided useful business computing facilities at an affordable cost to the SMB. The affordability of small computers coupled with the success of the client/server architecture that allowed everyone in the organization to access the data in a simplistic way soon gave way to SMBs adopting client/server architecture.

The success of the client/server environment might be attributed to many reasons including

- The architecture was simple.
- User interface-related applications were executed on the client systems.
- Data resided on the server, and data access applications were executed on the server system.
- The business logic applications could be executed on the client and server.
- The server also provided sharing of resources to all the clients.
- The professionals and individuals took initiative.
- The business schools, academic schools, and research institutions were enthusiastic.

The client/server environment provided an ideal environment to creative individuals who could develop a plethora of programs and applications. Contributions from the individuals and professionals, a relatively short application development cycle, the availability of a variety of applications, the cost of the system, and so on contributed enormously to the sprawling growth of desktop computers across the business world.

The success of the client/server architecture encouraged many large organizations to diversify their system resources and reduce dependency on inflexible and expensive systems such as mainframes. By allowing desktop systems, minicomputers, and mainframes to coexist, the client/server architecture encouraged the large enterprises to distribute specific tasks to appropriate systems. For instance, more powerful systems, such as minicomputers, were identified as servers to hold the data, whereas less powerful systems in the network provided a perfect client environment.

Progression of Distributed Architecture

The distributed architecture provides an environment in which applications (or programs) can be divided and distributed among many systems in a networked environment. These bits of applications execute on their individual systems, and the results are then combined to produce the final result. Such distributed systems, working together, can often outperform large mainframe systems. Note that in distributed architectures, no individual application (or process) has any privileged role, and one process does not depend on another.

Distributed architecture, therefore, enables multiple computers to be networked and applications to be deployed in a distributed fashion. Distributed architecture thus provides multiple tiers for the computational environment. Thus, the distributed architecture is not fundamentally different from the client/server architecture. The client/server architecture might just be a subset of the distributed architecture, in which there are just two tiers: client tier and server tier. This architecture might be considered a natural and logical progression to client/server architectures. In fact, the emergence of distributed architecture is often attributed to accommodate a large number of systems in the network. The operating environments on these distributed systems provided basic services such as resource sharing, printing, terminal and file transfer, and so on. Some popular distributed architecture includes *System Network Architecture (SNA)* from IBM, *Distributed Network Architecture (DNA)* from DEC, and so forth.

It is important to note that although the distributed architecture models proposed by individual vendors worked fine in isolation, serious issues arose when the enterprises needed to integrate two or more such distributed networks. This was particularly true in large enterprises that had deployment from multiple vendors in different divisions/departments. This disparity and incompatibility led to the industry movement toward open systems and saw the emergence of popular communication protocols such as *Transport Communication Protocol/Internet Protocol* (popularly known as *TCP/IP*). Growth of distributed architecture entailed the following four important aspects with respect to applications and services:

- Remote procedure calls
- Remote database access
- Distributed transaction processing
- Messaging

Among these, *Remote Procedure Call (RPC)* and *messaging* represent powerful mechanisms that can help achieve integration among different vendor networks. The next two sections discuss how RPC and messaging help in the development and deployment of services on distributed architecture.

Remote Procedure Call (RPC)

The RPC model of distributed network communication was proposed by Birrel and Nelson in the mid-1980s and was standardized by Schroeder and Burrows in the late 1980s. This model enabled systems in a network to communicate in a distributed architecture environment. Figure 2.4 provides a graphical representation of how the RPC model works in the distributed environment. Different vendors have implemented RPC in different ways. Notable of them are Sun Microsystems, Object Management Group, Microsoft, and so on. In the next section, we present some concise information on three of the important implementations of RPC.

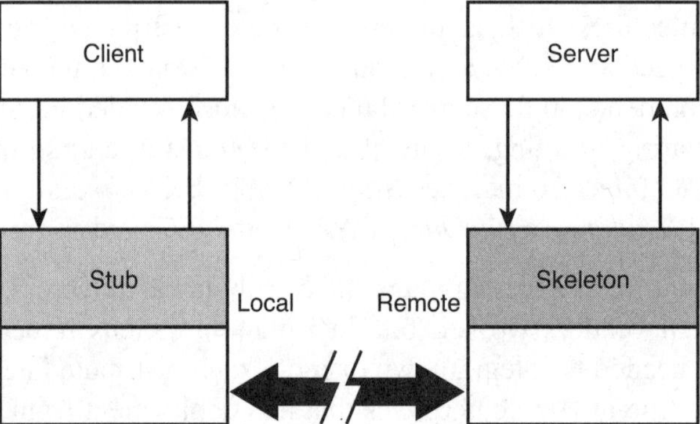

Figure 2.4 Remote procedure call communication semantics

Sun Microsystems's implementation of RPC is Sun RPC. The *Remote Method Invocation (RMI)* implementation of RPC, particularly, is known for its contribution as the foundation for enterprise Java technologies. This technology was introduced in the late 1990s. This implementation of RPC ensures that the Java applications deployed in a distributed environment communicate in an interoperable manner, using *Java Remote Method Protocol (JRMP)*.

Common Object Request Broker Architecture (CORBA) from *Object Management Group* (*OMG*) is a generalization of RPC. The OMG model included several improvements on the object and on the primitives of the RPC model. CORBA enables development of applications and services that are interoperable and can communicate with other disparate applications. This architecture was essentially developed by OMG to bring about portability and interoperability of applications across different hardware platforms and operating environments.

The basis of Microsoft's *Distributed Component Object Model (DCOM)* essentially emerged from the Component Object Model *(COM)* introduced in the mid-1990s. The COM technology enables the development of software components, as per COM specifications, for integrating the applications on the network. In a distributed environment, such components can interact in an interoperable fashion. DCOM is built on the object RPC layer, which in turn, is on top of DEC RPC[6] to support communication among remote objects. Other advanced technologies from Microsoft, such as *Object Linking and Embedding (OLE)*, *ActiveX*, and *Microsoft Transaction Server (MTS)*, are built on top of COM and DCOM technologies.

Messaging

All the communications discussed in previous sections referred to a synchronous or blocking mode of communication. Messaging, on the other hand, introduces asynchronous communication into distributed architecture. Messaging technology introduces message servers, which can deliver to (or receive messages from) applications. MQSeries from IBM, MSMQ from Microsoft, and SonicMQ from Progress software are some of the popular implementation of messaging technologies. Messaging technology is often termed Messaging Middleware or *Message Oriented Middleware (MOM)*. MOM is essentially a software implementation on client/server or distributed architecture systems that reside on the client side and the server side. This enables the client/server or distributed systems to communicate asynchronously, thereby increasing the flexibility of the distributed architecture.

Basics of Messaging Messaging technologies enable the sending or receiving of a message (or data) between two or more applications networked in a distributed architecture. Messaging middleware forms an important infrastructural tier to enable asynchronous communications. Messaging technology provides a "loosely coupled" infrastructure in the distributed environment. Loose coupling of the infrastructure enables the client and server to be unaware of each other. Most importantly, the client and server applications need not be connected to each other at the same time.

Messaging systems are involved in the messaging middleware. The message from the sender[7] is received by a messaging system. This system submits the message into a queue. The queuing of the message ensures the message is delivered to the recipient immediately or at a later time. The sender does not wait for an acknowledgment and response from the recipient. The sender might (or might not) receive the response from a middleware messaging system about the delivery of the message to the recipient. This phenomenon is called *asynchronous messaging*.[8] Semantics of the messaging phenomenon that involves messaging systems are shown in Figure 2.5.

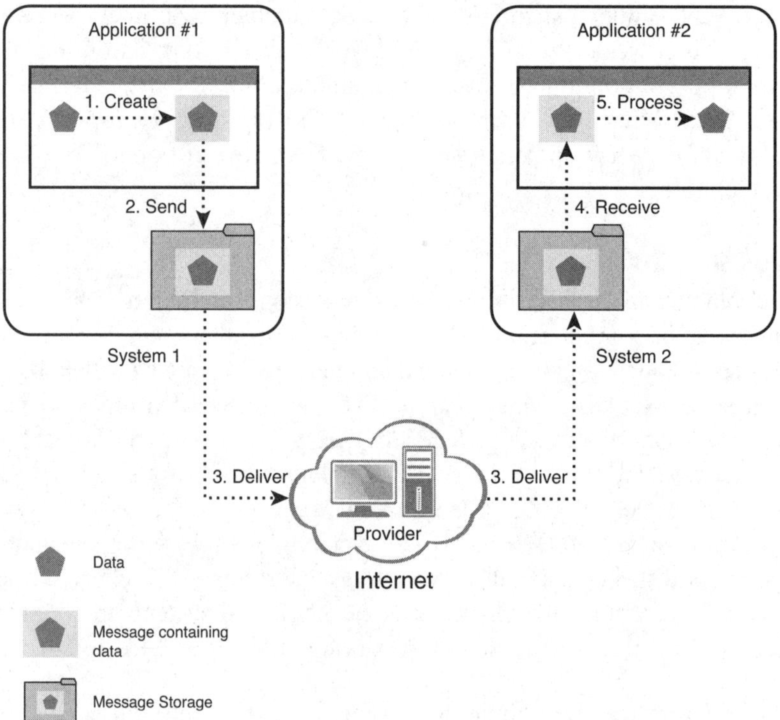

Figure 2.5 Semantics of asynchronous messaging technology

Messaging technology has been a reliable and efficient infrastructure of e-business. The potency of the messaging technology arises from its capability to interconnect applications that run on disparate systems, disparate operating environments in different environments, and in an asynchronous fashion. MOM involves a specialized hardware and software combination that coordinates the communication among multiple applications for sending and receiving messages in an asynchronous manner. MOMs in large enterprises are designed to respond to a variety of events, exchange messages in a wide variety of formats, and deliver the messages reliably and quickly.

Messaging technology can be tuned to work in a variety of communication models. The two most important models are the *Synchronous Communication Model* and *Asynchronous Communication Model*. In the Synchronous Communication Model, the sender and recipient must be executing in their respective runtime environment, and the communication between these two applications is blocked until the exchange of messages is completed in a prescribed manner. This type of messaging exchange can be compared with that of a synchronous RPC communication model. In the Asynchronous Communication Model, the sender and recipient do not need to execute at the same time on their respective runtime environments. The sender can send messages "at will," and the message will be delivered to the recipient whenever the recipient goes online to the system.

Messaging Models In the enterprise application scenarios, two of the prevalent messaging models (or messaging domains) are *Point-to-Point (PTP)* and *Publish/Subscribe (Pub/Sub)*. Both are capable of providing a synchronous or asynchronous communication mode of message exchange. The semantics of the PTP messaging model are shown in Figure 2.6. The PTP model works on a one-on-one message delivery mode. The sender intends to send the message to only one designated recipient. To implement this model, message queues are used for enabling the message delivery mechanism. The PTP model becomes unviable if the sender intends to send the same message to a large number of recipients. The viability of this model is further affected if the number and the addresses of recipients are unknown.

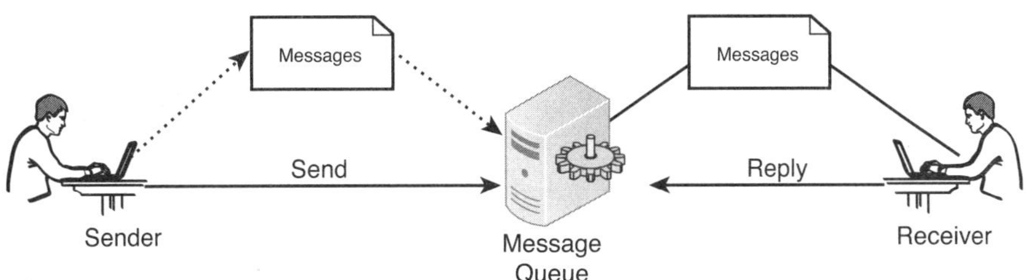

Figure 2.6 Semantics of Point-to-Point or PTP messaging technology

The semantics of the Publish/Subscribe model are shown in Figure 2.7. The Pub/Sub model is an excellent message delivery model appropriate for multiple senders and multiple recipients. The number of senders and recipients does not need to be fixed. Senders would publish messages based on a topic on a channel, and interested recipients would subscribe to the channel to receive the message. Within the messaging infrastructure in this model, channels are used for publishing messages. Senders connect to the channels when required to publish the message, and recipients subscribe to one or more channels to receive the messages.

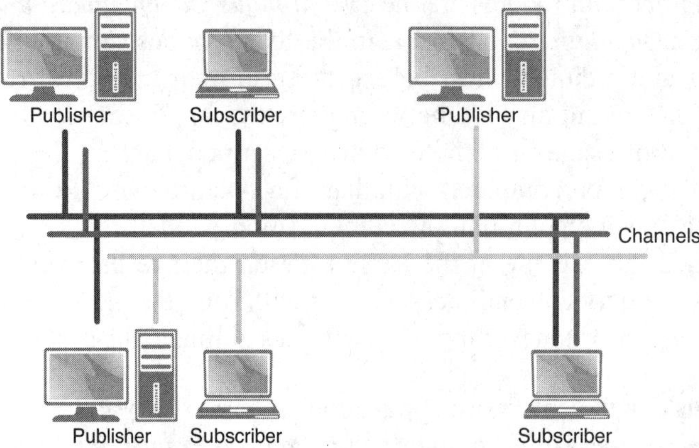

Figure 2.7 Semantics of Publish/Subscribe (or Pub/Sub) messaging model

Internet and World Wide Web

It is appropriate at this time to introduce the web architecture and the profound effect it had on the enterprises, particularly those involved in electronic commerce. The pre- and post-web architecture scenarios portrayed here indicate the reasons for the popularity of the new architecture.

E-Commerce in the Pre-Internet Era

The concept of E-Commerce, particularly the B2B variety, first existed as *Electronic Data Interchange*[9] *(EDI)*. This technology was designed to exchange a variety of business documents such as purchase orders and invoices among partners and collaborators in electronic format. Before the evolution of the Internet and World Wide Web, EDI was implemented only by a few large organizations, primarily because EDI technology was cumbersome, expensive, complex, and, often, error prone. Moreover, EDI technology demanded more expensive infrastructure, such as *Value Added Networks (VAN)*, for implementation and functioning.

E-Commerce in the Post-Internet Era

The Internet and World Wide Web brought fundamental changes to the way enterprises and business, large or small, interact. The Internet has rendered TCP/IP as the default protocol for communication and has introduced the concept of a new type of client called the *browser client*. In the web architecture, the web server could serve as the application and data server. The browser-based clients connect to the web server through a typical set of firewall and proxy servers that provide security to the web and application servers. Figure 2.8 presents how, in a typical web architecture, web servers connect to a large number of browser-based clients on the desktops.

The arrival of the Internet and World Wide Web has brought about fundamental changes in how many organizations and enterprises work and transact. The Internet has ensued previous unknown marketplaces, from across the globe to the doors of the organizations, and has made globalization possible even to the SMB. The Internet and the World Wide Web, together, have triggered changes in the ways of accessing and sharing information. They have influenced the nature and concept of all types of E-Commerce-oriented organizations: *Business-to-Business (B2B)*,[10] *Business-to-Consumer (B2C)*, and *Consumer-to-Consumer (C2C)*.

The Internet revolution along with the proliferation of personal computers and desktops brought the retail shops to the desks of individual customers. This led to the propagation of a large number of online business establishments, particularly in the B2C area. Internet banking, online shopping, cyber training, online stock trading, and so on are some of the areas in which the web influences the ways businesses are changing.

Although the Internet and World Wide Web brought enormous success to several lines of enterprise businesses, they also presented some critical problems. Two of the problems encountered, which are of concern even now, are

- Limitation in the bandwidth for accessing
- Partial failure of the systems and applications

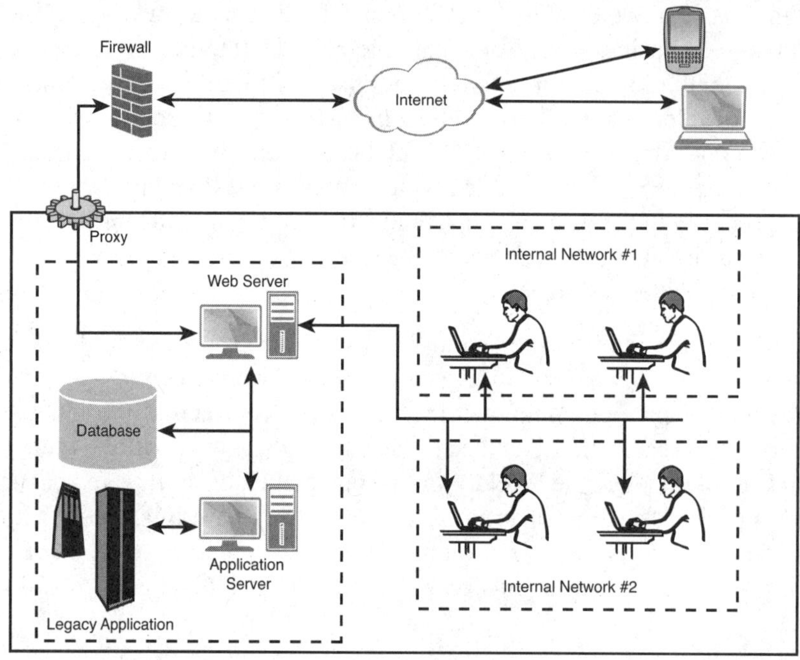

Figure 2.8 An overview of web architecture

Client-Side Architecture Progression

In this section we address the chronological progression on the client side of IT. Several events, or eras, can be marked as significant in the advancement on the client side of the architecture. Some of the significant eras are

- Terminals
- Thick clients
- Thin clients
- Browser clients
- Mobile clients

Figure 2.9 presents the conceptual progression of the client-side architecture. Notice that there are many similarities between the server-side architecture progression and the client-side architecture progression. Also notice that there are some striking differences.

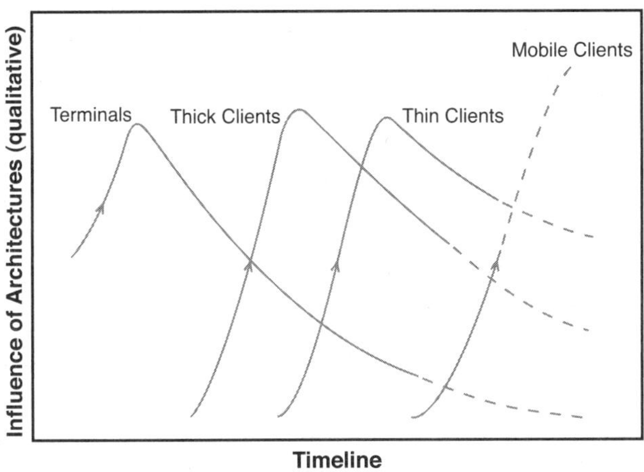

Figure 2.9 Client-side architecture progression

The client- and server-side progressions share similar characteristics, and most of these clients still coexist in many organizations. However, worth noting is that the terminals, as clients, are rapidly diminishing. Devices, such as mobiles and *Portable Digital Assistants* (*PDAs*), are appearing on the horizon and are assuming significant importance as clients.

Before the first tangible client appeared on the horizon, mainframes were accessed essentially by I/O systems. Batch jobs were submitted to the mainframe systems through card readers or spooled tapes. Interactive *Cathode Ray Tube (CRT)* terminals were introduced as clients to the mainframe systems, and these CRTs were referred to as *terminals*.

Terminals as Clients

Terminals were the first among the clients that appeared during the Mainframe era, although the CRT terminals cannot be strictly categorized as clients. They can be considered the extension of I/O to the mainframes. In the Centralized Model of the mainframe architecture, these terminals were hard wired to the mainframes systems. These CRT terminals were very expensive, and due to inherent problems, these clients were not scalable in nature. Terminals such as

VT100 belong to this category, in which each keystroke generated an interrupt that was conveyed to the CPU. Moreover, such CRT terminals could support only textual data. More intelligent CRT terminals, such as 3270 from IBM, could perform more sophisticated tasks than VT100. These terminals had a page-based interaction model, in which the program could download a page description with input fields. Such page-based models even contained associated validation rules (numeric, alpha-numeric, required, and so on). The keystrokes that entered the data in the input fields yielded no communication/interaction between the 3270 terminal and the CPU. However, when the full page was submitted, the server process would swing into action.

Thick Clients

The client/server era witnessed the appearance of desktop systems. These desktop systems were essentially the microcomputers, workstations, and personal computers. These desktop systems were equipped with all the peripherals, such as terminals, keyboards, mouse, and more. They also possessed a limited amount of processing power. These computers, therefore, were suited as the best candidates as clients in the client/server era. Unlike the VT100 type of CRT terminals, these clients systems were not dumb. These clients could be equipped with software applications that could process user input. And, unlike the terminals of the Mainframe era, the software applications on the client systems could display to the user in text and graphical format.

These desktop systems, together with software applications, were referred to as thick clients. These client systems could carry out many client-side operations, such as data validation, graphical processing, and such at the client system itself. Often, these clients, also called "fat" clients, could display graphics and images. These clients were capable of supporting GUI-based applications on the client side and frequently carried out either full or partial business-logic processing at the client side.

Thin Clients

Thin clients are a result of the natural progression of the thick clients. Like thick client systems, thin client systems processed and validated the user inputs. However, these thin clients, designed to be lightweight applications, focused less on the business logic processing. Instead, these thin clients performed the general user interface and limited input data processing on the client side, pushing the majority of the processing task to the server side.

Browser Clients

The advent of the Internet and World Wide Web saw the appearance of browser clients. Browsers are those application programs that execute on the client system. These applications are capable of interpreting HTML and presenting it to the client. The browser software also enables the user to browse for information, enabling the user to search, view, print, and save the data. These programs, using HTTP as the communication protocol, communicate with the web server systems using a suitable port. Initially, these browsers were capable of only text processing. The introduction of the graphics-based browser Netscape Communicator, by Netscape Communication Corporation, popularized the use of both HTTP and HTML and formed the basis of browser-based clients. Together, Netscape Communicator and Internet Explorer, from Microsoft Corporation, even revolutionized the term *browser*. As the popularity of the browser application increased, the capability and functionality of the browser applications increased as well.

Browsers are capable of instantiating *Java Virtual Machine (JVM)* inside the browser environment and enable the java applets to run securely. They can also support graphics applications such as Flash Player, Shockwave Player, and supporting scripting languages, such as JavaScript. Note that these scripting languages can perform a limited amount of business logic-related activity.

Mobile Clients

Devices such as mobile phones, Pocket PCs, and PDAs, whether wired or wireless, are not only capable of performing their intended functions but can also access information from the Internet and can perform important business transactions such as banking, stock trading, online shopping, and more. These clients, although limited in size,[11] are useful to the user who is on the move.

Mobile clients are essentially the applications running on mobile devices such as mobile phones and PDAs. Although they are designed like any other client applications, their display power and functionality are severely limited due to client-side restrictions for memory, processing power, and real estate.

Service Oriented Architecture and Web Services

Clearly, the Internet and World Wide Web provided new opportunities for growth and globalization, particularly for E-Commerce-based enterprises involved in B2C and B2B organizations. The B2C types of businesses benefited from lightweight protocols such as HTTP, markup languages such as HTML, proliferation of desktop computers, and so on. However, the opportunities for automating the B2B transaction among the business partners and collaborators remained to be fulfilled. Prior to the Internet era, the enterprise applications developed were tightly coupled in nature and were not designed for portability or interoperability. For successful B2B ventures among the partners, it was critical that the collaborators use a common communicating medium. For a fruitful automated business transaction between consumers and partners, enterprise applications need to be architected in a way that they are loosely coupled and interoperable in nature. Furthermore, the distinction and the differences between the business definition of the service and the IT definition of the service needed to be minimized (or even removed). This led to SOA.

SOA can be defined as architecture that enables linking resources on demand. In SOA, information and resources are made available to all the participants in the enterprise as independent services that are enabled to be accessed in a standard way. Independent services and loose coupling form the mantra of SOA. This architecture enables more flexible coupling of services and resources than traditional enterprise architectures. Because this is advantageous to the enterprises, consumers, and partners, businesses prefer that the applications be architected (or rearchitected) in SOA terms and be suitably implemented. In other words, businesses should identify the resources and services, group them as a collection of services, and allow them to be accessed by the required participants. This new architecture ensures flexible and simplified delivery of services to all the required participants. Proven technologies such as CORBA from OMG, *Java2 Enterprise Edition (J2EE)* of Sun Microsystems, .NET from Microsoft Corporation, and such might be used to design and deploy enterprise applications based on SOA.

Web Services

Although an enterprise solution can be architected in SOA terms, this architecture can be developed and deployed in many ways. Designing and implementing the XML-based web services using SOA, however, seems to be the best value proposition for any enterprises that provide or use services. SOA implementation using web services has the potential to be loosely coupled and is in the unique position of delivering services (or a collection of services) in an interoperable manner. XML provides a simple and extensible way of data representation and promotes the exchange of information. However, this calls for all agreeing partners to represent the data in a predefined XML format acceptable to all parties involved.

Let's assume, for instance, all the banking business ventures agree to collaborate. They also agree to use XML to exchange the relevant information. Furthermore, consider that all these banks agree to use the same set of XML elements to represent the appropriate set of information. For example, let's assume that the international bank code number will be represented by the `<BankCode>` element, and all the banking business ventures agree to use this element for representing the bank code number in all their transactions, wherever this data is involved. Using any other element to represent the bank code would result in the violation of agreements, and this could lead to partial or complete breaking of transaction between the involved banks. This scenario is presented in Figure 2.10.

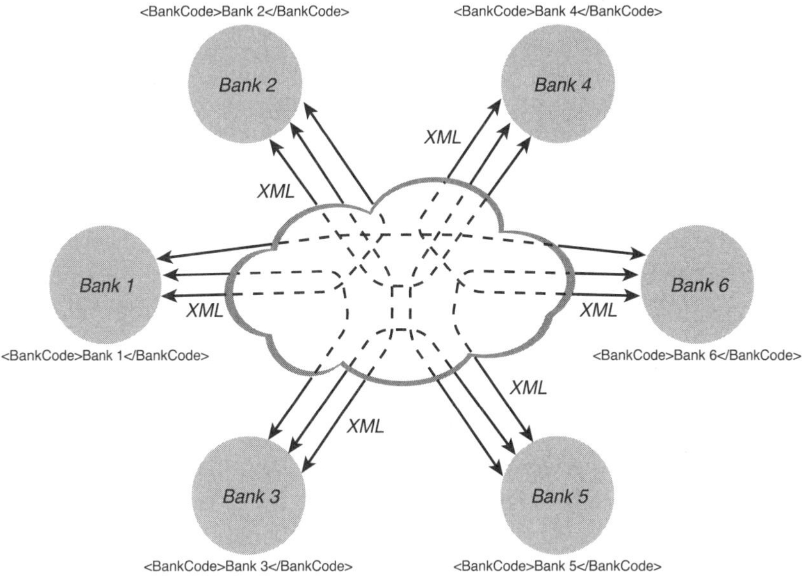

Figure 2.10 Role of XML technology in web services scenario

This represents a B2B opportunity on the web for all banking-related organizations bound by a common business interest. These banking organizations could be located in different areas using disparate systems and applications for banking transactions. Note that all the concerned partners use an XML-based route to interchange the data for transaction. The <BankCode> XML data is exchanged to identify itself during the transaction and is also indicated in Figure 2.10.

Arrival of SOAP, WSDL, and UDDI Infrastructure

Although XML provides a suitable interoperable medium of information interchange, it is insufficient to be useful in its "as is" form. However, the idea of XML as interoperable data triggered experiments and research among several organizations and individuals to effectively build a lightweight infrastructure for an efficient information exchange. Creating distributed applications that deliver the data on the RPC model using XML as the data was one approach. One of the early accomplishments in this area was achieved by Dave Winer of Userland Software. Microsoft joined Userland Software in promoting this effort, as the idea of XML-RPC had great potential, and together, a new protocol called *Simple Object Access Protocol*[12] (*SOAP*) was initiated. This event is recognized as a momentous milestone in the history of interoperability. Because the initial work on SOAP by Userland Software and Microsoft was considered narrow in its approach to interoperability, IBM joined the bandwagon by proposing changes in the SOAP specifications. These changes widened the scope of SOA, promoting SOAP as a predominant way of message interchange using web services. This joint proposal led to the creation of SOAP version 1.1 specifications (and SOAP 1.1 with Attachments specifications), and so the Web services revolution began. IBM's strategic involvement in SOAP resulted in the combination of SOAP with the Java environment. The combination of these two technologies was seen as the best blend for developing and delivering web services-oriented applications. It also promised a seamless, cross-platform interoperability among loosely coupled applications that deliver SOA-based enterprise solutions.

Two other important developments occurred around the same time that led web services closer to a significant milestone. They are the initiatives on *Web Services Description Language*[13] (*WSDL*) and *Universal Description, Discovery and Integration*[14] (*UDDI*). The UDDI initiative by IBM and Microsoft was an effort to bring in the registry for publication and discovery of services to support the efforts on web services. Ariba, IBM, and Microsoft pioneered the WSDL initiative. WSDL and UDDI, together with SOAP, formed the basis of lightweight infrastructure for delivering basic web services.

Summary

The progression of enterprise architecture has been analyzed through the combination of two conceptual approaches: server-side architectural progression and client-side architectural progression. The convergence of these architectures has resulted in an architecture that provides loosely coupled and interoperable applications, and this is essentially Services Oriented Architecture (SOA). Although there are ample technologies that can deliver SOA, an SOA implemented using XML-based web services is considered the best for any enterprise. An architecture that is based on the principles of SOA and implemented through Web services brings about the intended interoperability among the partners and collaborators of related business.

In the next chapter, we describe how the combined effect of the Internet revolution coupled with the introduction of newer languages, technologies, specifications, and tools resulted in a paradigm shift the way enterprises do business. We also describe how that recursively affected the need for change in the enterprise architecture—service orientation.

Endnotes

1. Digital Equipment Corporation (DEC) was acquired by Compaq in 1998. Compaq discontinued the mainframe business after the acquisition. Later, Hewlett-Packard acquired Compaq in 2001, predominantly for PC business interests.
2. The Mainframe era was a hardware-predominant system. Software was just considered the by-product of the hardware systems.
3. All the mainframe computers accepted the tasks as jobs. In IBM mainframe systems, Job Control Language (JCL) is still used for submitting batch jobs to the mainframe computers.
4. Security, sharing, and so on to the extent that the enterprises focus today were of limited concern in the Mainframe era.
5. The predominant languages used in the Mainframe era were FORTRAN and COBOL. FORTRAN stands for Formula Translation and COBOL stands for Common Business Oriented Language. The functional aspects of these languages were termed subroutines in those days.
6. DEC RPC is the RPC model proposed by the Digital Equipment Corporation.
7. The terms "sender" and "recipient" referred to here are essentially the message-oriented applications. A sender is an application that sends the message to a recipient through a messaging system. The recipient is an application that receives the message from a messaging system.
8. Although we refer to the messaging technology as asynchronous, it is possible that the messages are delivered synchronously. Under such circumstances, MOMs work in a synchronous fashion for delivering the message. However, this synchronous delivery of the message should not be confused with the RPC mode of communication.
9. According to the International Data Exchange Association (IDEA), Electronic Data Interchange (or EDI) is defined as the transfer of structured data by agreed message standards from one computer system to the other by electronic means.

10. The advent of XML in the mid-90s gave life support to the EDI-based B2B industries. XML-based EDI enabled enterprises to exchange the documents with other organizations using a disparate EDI message format (EDI-XML) without calling for extensive changes to their internal systems.
11. The display part of the devices such as mobiles and PDAs is often referred to as real estate.
12. Chapter 4, "Messaging Oriented Services and SOAP," focuses on the technology and the specification of SOAP.
13. Web Services Description Language (WSDL) technology and specifications are dealt with in detail in Chapter 5.
14. Similar to SOAP and WSDL, the UDDI technology belongs to the first generation web services technology. Chapter 6, “Registries and UDDI,” is dedicated to providing a descriptive treatment of the UDDI specifications and services.

3

Evolution of Service Oriented Architecture

The requirement of service orientation for the enterprises first emerged with the advent of the Internet and World Wide Web. The IT world has since witnessed numerous paradigm shifts, as newer technologies such as XML and Java impacted enterprise solution requirements. The business of "service delivery" started gaining momentum among the enterprises and their collaborators. But the IT definition of the term "service" was not aligned with that of the business definition, and this cohesion was crucial for the enterprises to remain competitive in the dynamically changing market conditions. Evolution of business components such as Enterprise JavaBeans, as a part of J2EE technologies, on the one hand, and the emergence of core constituents of web services such as SOAP, WSDL, and UDDI, on the other, provided the opportunity to draft service definitions in alignment with the business requirements. Furthermore, the eventuality of loosely composing these services and binding them with the business process of the enterprise resulted in the arrival of Service Oriented Architecture *(*SOA*).*

The idea of SOA is not completely new. Different forms of service orientations were previously attempted and implemented as enterprise solutions by many vendors on different businesses and enterprises during the era of client/server. These architectures were implemented as enterprise solutions with different degrees of success, but they were never known or termed as SOAs during those eras. Regardless, none of these attempts could be considered successful implementation of SOAs. Before the arrival of XML and other web services, SOAs, (though not referred to as such), were implemented as a solution, without snazzy name and fanfare. In this chapter, we first explore the concept of service orientation and then analyze how the emergence of different architectures' combined paradigm shifts in enterprise technologies led to the evolution of web services and SOA.

Services Oriented Architecture—The Description

SOA can be described as a unique style of architecting and designing the enterprise solution using business services throughout the life cycle—from concept to retirement. SOA also enables for provisioning the IT infrastructure of the enterprise so that disparate applications[1] can exchange data as a part of the business process.

Business services can be defined as a set of actions or tasks an organization provides to different service stakeholders. Some of the service stakeholders are customers, collaborators, clients, employees, and so on. Consider that whereas an SOA can be defined as an approach to building IT systems, the business services are considered the key organizing principle for aligning IT systems for business needs.

The key point here is *business services* and *alignment of IT infrastructure* as per business services and business process requirement. Service orientation, therefore, enables the architects to focus on the description of the business problem rather than any development or execution environment of the enterprise solution. Because these two are delinked, a business solution that is architected as per SOA would be loosely coupled, flexible in nature, and allow implementation of dynamic needs of the enterprise business requirements.

It is important to notice here that the description of SOA does not mention the requirement of web services technologies as a prerequisite. Technologies such as CORBA or J2EE can still be efficiently and effectively used to implement the enterprise solution so that enterprise architecture is service oriented. However, what is crucial in the context of service orientation is the possibility of separating the *service interface* from the *execution environment*. An SOA that is appropriately implemented provides a scope in which it is possible to mix and match the execution environment.

Early Architectures

Earlier approaches to building enterprise solutions essentially focused on functional aspects of the enterprise problem. These approaches tended to directly use the specific implementation environments, such as object orientation, procedure orientation, data or information orientation, message orientation, and so on to solve business problems. This resulted in enterprise solutions that were often tied to features and functions of a particular environment technology. Some of the popular technologies that evolved were *Information Management Systems (IMS)*, *Customer Information Control Systems (CICS)*,[2] *Common Object Request Brokered Architecture (CORBA)*, *Component Object Model/Distributed Component Object Model (COM/DCOM)*, and *Message Oriented Middleware (MOM)*.

Enterprise architectures have evolved tremendously since the Mainframe era or the Centralized Model of mainframe architecture. The progression in architectures such as client/server architectures, distributed architecture, or web architectures discussed in Chapter 1, "Introduction," are generic in nature. Specific architectures on mainframe systems, such as IMS, CICS, CORBA, and DCOM, have evolved as environment-specific distributed architectures. You need to analyze some of these technologies and their contribution to the evolution of enterprise architectures.

IMS

IMS is one of the earliest technologies to lay the foundation for more advanced data accessing technologies such as DB2 and Universal Database. IMS was developed by IBM in the late 1960s to manage data for NASA's Apollo Moon Landing project. This technology was later released as the world's first commercially sold Database Management System. IMS technology's data management was based on the earliest data model called the Hierarchical Data model. This premier database and transactional management system was implemented to handle many commercially critical, online operational and on-demand business applications and data that enabled information integration, information management, and scalability.

The IMS technology essentially is composed of two subsystems: a Database Manager called IMS DB and a Transactional Manager called the IMS TM. We explore briefly these two subsystems in the next section.

IMS as Database Manager

The IMS DB is basically a large system Hierarchical Database Management System. When introduced, IMS DB was an enormous success, and many large organizations employed IMS DB for managing the enterprise information. Subsequent research and development efforts by IBM resulted in the revolutionary way of handling the data. The *Relational Database Management System* (*RDBMS*) by E. F. Codd in 1971 prompted IBM to introduce a radical product called the DB2. Following the introduction of DB2, IBM intended to replace the Hierarchical Data Management System with relational databases and replace IMS DB with DB2. However, IBM was not entirely successful in replacing IMS because a number of major IMS-based organizations were not interested in replacing the otherwise stable and satisfactorily running IMS-based applications. As a result, IBM continues to develop newer products and packages around the IMS technologies that help those organizations that continue to maintain IMS-based legacy products on their mainframe systems.

IMS as Transactional Manager

The IMS TM is a robust transactional management system that primarily functions on the IBM mainframe systems. This Transaction Manager was initially designed as an interactive system that interacts with an end user, through a combination of 3270 screens and VTAM communication mode to process business transactions. In coordination with IMS DB, IMS TM technology uses a messaging and queuing methodology to implement the transactions in the business processes.

When the user initiates a transaction through a 3270 screen, the IMS Control Program receives a transaction identification number and stores it on a message queue. The Transaction Manager, thereafter, invokes a scheduler on the queued transaction to initiate the business process. The message processing region of the IMS TM then retrieves the transaction from the IMS message queue and processes the same. The processing could involve reading/writing/updating the information on the IMS DB.[3] Based on the system design and the architecture of the enterprise application, the IMS TM could respond and return an output message to the user who initiated the transaction on the 3270 terminal.

CICS

CICS from IBM is a transaction server that runs primarily on IBM mainframe systems under operating environments such as z/OS. CICS is now available for other operating environments such as OS/2, AIX, Microsoft Windows, and Linux. The z/OS implementation of CICS is, by far, the most popular and significant implementation of the CICS technologies.

CICS is a transaction processing system designed for both batch and online business transactions. On large IBM mainframe systems, CICS technology supports a large number of transactions in a given time. The CICS technology has enabled IBM to retain a dominant position in the mainframe-oriented enterprise computing. Initially CICS applications were written in COBOL. Presently, CICS applications can be created using a variety of modern programming languages, such as PL/I, C, C++, REXX, and Java. CICS is one of the world's most durable software products on the IBM mainframe system. Supported by a variety of applications and tools, CICS is known for its reliability, security, and performance, particularly on IBM mainframe systems. Thanks to the aggressive marketing by IBM and rich research and development efforts in the United States and the UK, many of the Fortune 500 giants that invested into these systems during the Mainframe era continue to rely on core parts of enterprise applications based on CICS technologies.

The CICS applications programs are basically screens, popularly known as 3270 screens.[4] The initiation of a CICS program signals the initiation of a transaction, and the system initiates a transaction identification number. The CICS screens are sent as "maps" or "pages" using a programming language such as COBOL. The end user, on the other end of the system, inputs data that is made available to the CICS program by receiving a map. CICS screens essentially contain textual information. The textual information is presented to the end user in different formats. This includes highlighted text, colored fonts, or even blinking text.

CORBA

CORBA is not that different from the RPC technologies introduced in Chapter 2, "Evolution of IT Architectures." Developed and supported by *Object Management Group* (*OMG*), CORBA technology can be considered a generalization of RPC technology and includes several improvements on the data objects and on the data primitives. The purpose of this technology and architecture was to enable the development of distributed applications and services that can interoperably communicate with other disparate applications over the network. The CORBA architecture was essentially developed to bring about a discipline to implement portability and interoperability of applications across different hardware platforms, operating environments, and disparate hardware implementations. CORBA technology uses a binary protocol called *Internet Inter-ORB Protocol* (*IIOP*) for communicating with the remote objects.

DCOM

A bit of background is required here. In the mid-1990s Microsoft Corporation introduced a technology popular as the COM.[5] This technology enabled the development of software modules called *components* for integrating applications over the client/server architecture. To build these components, developers must adhere to the COM specification so that the components can operate interoperably within the network. The DCOM technology, introduced sometime in late

1990s, enabled interaction among network-based components to bring in the *Distributed Communication Environment* (*DCE*). DCOM technology is essentially built on an object RPC layer, which in turn is on top of DEC RPC to enable the communication among the remote objects. DCOM technology uses a binary protocol, termed *Object Remote Procedure Call* (*ORPC*), for distributed communication among remote objects. Technologies such as *Object Linking and Embedding* (*OLE*), ActiveX, and *Microsoft Transaction Server* (*MTS*) are some of Microsoft's technological advancements built on COM and DCOM technologies.

Paradigm Shifts

We previously indicated that the field of information technology has witnessed many paradigm shifts.[6] These paradigm shifts are affecting the enterprise businesses in many ways—specifically in how they conduct business and communicate. These paradigm shifts can be primarily attributed to technological innovations in the field of hardware, software, and operating and networking environments. Some of the paradigm shifts[7] that are of importance to the enterprise businesses are

- Internet and World Wide Web
- Java and Java 2 Enterprise Edition
- Extensible Markup Language
- Web Services—XML-RPC and SOAP
- Influence of the Internet and the World Wide Web

The arrival of both the Internet and the World Wide Web ushered in a paradigm shift to the enterprises, specifically in the way business transaction takes place. You might be aware that extensive research and development work sponsored by the Department of Defense[8] resulted in the foundation of what is now the Internet. The evolution of the web, in fact, ensured fundamental changes in the way B2C and B2B partners interact. More revolution than evolution, the Internet and World Wide Web has enormously grown, thanks partly to the contribution from several companies, organizations, academic and research institutions, and even the individual professionals all over the world. On the technology front, the web has not only rendered TCP/IP as the default business protocol, it also has brought forth a new type of client called the *browser client*.

Java and Java 2 Enterprise Edition

Prior to the arrival of Java, the software development for any enterprise application needed to be developed on many programming environments, on different hardware and operating environment. Frequently a software application would need to be developed and delivered on multiple hardware platform and operating environments so that functionally they delivered repeatable results. Developed by Dr. James Gosling of Sun Microsystems, Java technology was introduced in 1995. The arrival of Java as a programming language ushered in yet another paradigm shift in the world of software development. A Java Virtual Machine would behave the same way on any platform, and therefore, applications developed using Java programming language would behave reliably and consistently on any platform. Java programming has brought about acronyms such as *WORA* (*Write Once Run Anywhere*), *WORE* (*Write Once Run Everywhere*), and *WORD* (*Write Once and Run on any Device*).

Java and J2EE technologies have witnessed tremendous growth over the past decade and Java, in particular, has been the most widely employed programming environment in the world today. Java is easily considered the most successful programming language. Some of the features and attributes that popularized the Java platform are object oriented, platform independent, portable, secure, robust, multithreaded, and more.

One of the prime reasons for the widespread industry adoption of this environment could be because the environment has been the product of the industry movement toward the requirement of portable and interoperable applications that can work over the web. Other contributing factors include reliable web component technologies, such as Servlet and *JavaServer Pages* (*JSP*), and distributed components such as *Enterprise JavaBeans* (*EJB*) that can enable the developers to deploy these components in a variety of container/component environments. These components essentially use a binary protocol called Java Remote Method Protocol (RMI over IIOP) for communicating with remote objects.

Since its introduction over a decade ago, Java has grown from the status of a mere programming language to a full-fledged platform on a variety of systems and environments,[9] including devices such as PDAs, mobile phones, set-top boxes, rings, cards, chips, and so on. A community called the *Java Community Process* (*JCP*) now governs the development of this language. Most of the industry leaders and key players in the IT field participate in shaping the development of this remarkable technology.

Extensible Markup Language

John Bosak of Sun Microsystems is credited with the revolutionary work on *Extensible Markup Language (XML)*. The idea of XML essentially emerged from the other nonexpendable markup languages such as *Generalized Markup Language (GML)* from IBM, *Standardized Generalized Markup Language (SGML)* from ISO, and *Hypertext Markup Language (HTML)* from ECRN. XML's popularity essentially stems out of its extensible capability. One of the biggest contributions of XML is its capability of interoperability.

The development of XML resulted in its adoption by a variety of industries—both vertical and horizontal. This has resulted in the creation of a large number of XML vocabularies that cater to the interoperability needs of different industries. The biggest contributions of XML for enterprise solution needs are the SOAP, WSDL, and UDDI technologies. Part II, "Service Oriented Architecture Essentials," discusses this in detail.

Web Services—XML-RPC and SOAP

Introduced by Dave Winer, XML-RPC is an RPC protocol that is text based. As the name indicates, the XML-RPC protocol enables the exchange of XML data between remote objects. The idea of transporting XML as a payload over transport protocols such as HTTP has resulted in laying the foundation of web services such as SOAP and WSDL. Initial work on XML-RPC resulted in a simple and portable way of making text-based RPC in a distributed environment. This pioneering work resulted in the opening of a new perspective in the history of middleware technologies. Further work in this direction resulted in a new message-oriented protocol called SOAP and brought the interoperability one step closer to business automation.

Arrival of Web Services and SOA

Earlier in this chapter we highlighted the Remote Procedure Call and its influence in the distributed communication technologies such as CORBA, DCOM, and J2EE. The protocols used in these technologies, IIOP, ORPC, and RMI/IIOP, respectively, are the binary protocols used for communication between remote objects over the corporate networks. This laid the foundations for a radically new protocol and resulted in the development of extensible vocabularies such as SOAP, WSDL, and UDDI. These extensible languages are referred to as *First Generation Web Services*. These languages provide fundamental level support for enterprise applications and enable them to be web service-oriented at the functional level. However, for enterprises, nonfunctional requirements take priority over functional requirements. The web services extensions that attempt to meet the nonfunctional aspects of enterprise requirements are referred to as the

Second Generation Web Services extensions, and we explore them briefly in the following sections.

First Generation Web Services

As you may recall from Chapter 1, the three pillars of web services are SOAP, WSDL, and UDDI. These technologies are advanced vocabularies of the XML and use other supportive XML vocabularies such as Namespace and *XML Schema Definition* (*XSD*). Each of these web services vocabularies address different aspects of enterprise information interchange in an interoperable manner.

SOAP

This new text-based messaging technology enables applications to exchange information in the form of messages. The messages can be interchanged in a synchronous or asynchronous manner. The design of SOAP message structure is such that the messages can be interchanged between applications through RPC invocation or through MOM technologies.

WSDL

WSDL enables description of the service through the use of a set of specialized XML elements. The service description includes the data types interchanged (this is programming language-independent), name of the service, parameters passed, transport protocol used, and so on. WSDL also enables several related services to aggregate into a service suite.

UDDI

UDDI is a specification and service that helps businesses provide a platform in such a way that the service requesters can discover service providers, zero in on appropriate partners, and enable an agreed-upon business automation. UDDI, like WSDL, uses advanced XML vocabularies to define the business and service information in an elaborate manner. As a service, UDDI registries enable the service requester to store all necessary information regarding business and service information that is suitably categorized as per industry standards.

The Second Generation Web Services

Enterprise solution requirements might be categorized into functional requirements and nonfunctional requirements. Nonfunctional requirements govern the architectural and design aspects of any enterprise solution. There are many nonfunctional requirements, and one enterprise's nonfunctional requirements list and priorities would be different from another. Some of the nonfunctional requirements that are common to most of the enterprises are

- Security
- Reliability
- Availability
- Quality of service
- Business process
- Choreography

Several web services extensions and frameworks have been proposed by various industry consortia, and there is more than one web service extension proposed by competing industry consortia. These extensions and frameworks address one or more nonfunctional enterprise requirements Although there is a general consensus among the industry consortia on some of the web service extensions, this is not the case for all web service extensions.

Some of the important web services extensions are

- WS-Security Specifications and Frameworks
- WS-Addressing Specification
- WS-Reliable Messaging Specifications
- WS-Business Process Execution Language
- WS-Choreography Definition Language
- WS-Metadata Exchange Specifications

SOA Using Web Services

We have already discussed how the arrival of XML and related technologies brought in a paradigm shift for enterprise solutions. The core web services technologies provided a sound foundation for the functional aspects of the services, its description, and invocation. The second generation web services extensions, on the other hand, brought the nonfunctional requirements into the web services fold. Together, web services technologies provide several key features and advantages that the earlier technological solutions could not. Interoperability, for example, enables a clear separation of the service interface from the execution environment. Therefore, SOA implemented using web services technologies is likely to provide a leading edge over any other technological implementation.

Using web services, it is easier to change service compositions of the enterprise application and implement the changes at a lower cost. These features help the enterprise project developers to quickly respond to the dynamic requirements of the enterprise business needs.

Benefits and Challenges with SOA

SOA with web services as an implementation route brings a host of advantages to the enterprises. This doesn't necessarily mean that service orientation of the enterprise architecture is void of any disadvantages. Some of the significant pros and cons associated with SOA are as follows:

Benefits

- Rapid integration of enterprise applications—departments and partners
- Efficient business automation
- Enhanced corporate agility
- Faster time to market for new products and services
- Reduced IT costs for the corporate long-term investment
- Improved operational efficiency of the business processes
- Better ROI

Challenges

- Identifying the need for SOA
- Significant investment in resources on rearchitecting the core IT assets
- Identifying the right kind of governance model for the enterprise
- Mind share for the right kind of professionals and stake holders
- Legacy system issues—some legacy applications cannot be service oriented

Notice here that the issues and challenges for SOA relate more to the cultural aspect of the problem than the technological or business aspects. Of course, issues such as integration of unsupported legacy systems to service orientation remain as bottlenecks to the implementation of SOA.

SOA Implementation Technologies

Web services implementation of SOA has many crucial advantages over any other implementation strategies. Presently, there are two predominant solutions that help in web services implementation of SOA: Microsoft's .NET technologies and Sun Microsystems's Java Platform Enterprise Edition[10] technologies.

Microsoft's .NET Technologies

The .NET product suite from Microsoft enables enterprises to build enterprise-class web SOAs. The .NET product suite is largely a rewrite of Windows DNA,[11] which constitutes Microsoft's previous platform constituents for developing enterprise applications. The new .NET Framework replaces these technologies and includes the web services layer.

The .NET Environment

The .NET technologies offer language independence and language interoperability. This is an interesting aspect of the .NET technology. Accordingly, a .NET component can be written, for example, partially in different programming languages and implemented as part of the web services solution. The .NET technology converts this composite language component into an intermediary neutral language called *Microsoft Intermediate Language* (*MSIL*). This MSIL[12] code is then interpreted and compiled to a native executable file.

The .NET Framework also includes a runtime environment called the *Common Language Runtime* (*CLR*). This environment is analogous to the Sun Microsystems *Java Runtime Environment* (*JRE*).

The .NET Server Services

Microsoft has packed a number of servers as part of the .NET platform called The .NET Enterprise Servers. These servers provide vital services for hosting enterprise-class applications. Some important servers included as part of the .NET Servers are SQL Server, Exchange Server, Commerce Server, Cluster Server, Host Integration Server, and BizTalk Server.

Sun Microsystems's Java Enterprise Edition Technologies

The Java Platform, Enterprise Edition (Java EE) is a progression of the Java environment to the server side of the application software paradigm. J2EE, unlike Microsoft's .NET, could be termed a defacto industry standard and has resulted in a large industry initiative called the *Java Community Process* (*JCP*). The participants of this community include the "who's who" in the IT and related industries—IBM, Oracle, Nokia, BEA, and so on. The spirit of Java as well as the other related technologies, such as Java EE, was to free the customers from the dependency of products and tools from vendors.

Java Foundation

The launching of Java as a programming language took the industry by storm in 1995. As previously indicated, the Java programming environment provided unique features that no other programming language provided: portability, platform independence, and so on. The core feature is the *Java Runtime Environment* (*JRE*) that can be made available on any hardware or operating environment. The application is developed using the Java programming language and compiled into platform-independent *bytecodes*. This bytecode can then be deployed to run on JRE that is installed on any compatible system.

Java EE is the server-side extension of Java. The applications are not just Java objects but are also appropriate server-side components. For creating web applications, components such as Java Servlets and *JavaServer Pages* (*JSP*) are used and deployed on web servers, and these web servers run on JRE. Likewise, for creating enterprise applications, components such as *Enterprise JavaBeans* (*EJB*) are developed and deployed, optionally with web applications, in application servers. Again, these application servers also run in JRE.

Web Services Using Java Enterprise Edition

The evolution of Java EE has been steady. Java EE technologies are consistently improving with each version. These improvements are essentially driven by *Java Specification Requests* (*JSR*), and once again, this is the JCP initiative. The arrival of XML and the related advanced vocabularies has resulted in immediate adoption into the Java environment. Simply put, this is because Java, as a portable programming language, and XML, as portable information, are an excellent combination for any environment. Further, the arrival of web services, in the form of SOAP, WSDL, and UDDI, has resulted in the creation of appropriate APIs.

Java EE applications can be executed on the web and on application servers. Appropriate components are developed and assembled to create enterprise applications. The Java EE servers and containers provide all the necessary "service plumbing" support for the web and application server.

Java EE architecture supports the following tiers: presentation tier, business tier, and data tier (or EAI tier). Not all of them are essential, and depending on the enterprise requirement, even one of the tiers can enable the application to be identified as a Java EE application. If the presentation tier is present, Java Servlets and JSP can be designed and deployed to create the web application. The Servlets can also be configured to be the services (or clients of) web services application. If the business tier is present, EJB can be developed and deployed as part of the enterprise application. The EJBs can be Session EJBs and Entity EJBs. Although session EJBs can handle session management, Entity EJBs address persistence activity. Alternatively, session EJBs can participate in the web services interactions. Business partners can connect with the presentation tier and business tier of J2EE applications through web services technologies.

Summary

The concept of Service Oriented Architecture is not entirely new. SOA essentially promotes the separation of the service interface and the execution environment. SOA also promotes the alignment of IT infrastructure to meet the business service requirements. Although SOA can be implemented in a number of ways, utilizing web services provides several advantages, particularly because web services bring enterprise application closer to business automation. Two of the most popular technologies for implementing SOA through web services are Microsoft's .NET and Sun Microsystem's Java Platform, Enterprise Edition.

In the next part, we devote our attention toward the building blocks of SOA technology. Three elements included here are the derivatives of the extensible markup language, namely SOAP, WSDL, and UDDI, and business process-related XML vocabularies such as BPEL and CDL. Advanced elements of web services address aspects such as security, reliability, quality of services, and so on.

Endnotes

1. Different applications are exchanging the data, while participating in business processes, regardless of hardware platform, operating environment, or programming languages underlying these applications.
2. Often pronounced as "kicks."
3. The IMS DB now supports relational database management systems such as DB2 and Universal DB.
4. Pronounced "three two seven zero" screen or terminal.
5. Most of the technologies invented/introduced by Microsoft Corporation are invariably on the Windows/Intel combination. Often this combination is referred to as Wintel: Windows and Intel.
6. The term paradigm shift was first used by Thomas Kuhn in his famous book *The Structure of Scientific Revolutions*, in 1962, to describe the process and result of a change in basic assumptions within the ruling theory of science. It has since become widely applied to many other realms of human experience and the field of information technology as well. Paradigm shift can also be defined as a significant change from one fundamental view to another. Such changes are usually accompanied by discontinuity.

7. We are essentially focused on the field of enterprise solutions here. Scope of information technology is really wide, and paradigm shifts as applied to this scope, as per the interpretations of different experts, could be different. For example, as per the essays of Bioss Sari, the following three events mark the paradigm shifts in the field of information technology:
   - Invention of the microprocessor and its impact on the computer industry
   - Paul Baran's invention of the distributed network and packet switching
   - The future of computing and the end of the silicon era
8. DARPANet and ARPANet are the two revolutionary projects sponsored by the U.S. Department of Defense. DARPANet is the origin of ARPANet project. The aim of the DARPANet project was to exchange military information among analysts, scientists, and researchers located at different geographical locations of the United States. The ARPANet project was launched by DOD sometime in the late 1960s. The network infrastructure for this project was created by the U.S. Defense Advanced Research Project Agency (ARPA). The idea of ARPANet was to set up an experimental wide area network within the United States to survive the military exigencies.
9. Java technology from Sun Microsystems was initially developed as a programming environment for devices. However, when it was launched, it was launched as a "portable" programming language. However, the language grew in several directions, including the devices.
10. Sun Microsystems has rechristened the J2EE as the Java EE. This change is not just in the name. There are fundamental changes in the way web services are created as a part of web applications or enterprise applications. These aspects are discussed in detail in Chapter 9, "Java Platform, Enterprise Edition Overview."
11. Windows DNA includes many technologies that are part of Microsoft's products today. They include Microsoft Transaction Server (MTS) and COM+, Microsoft Message Queue (MSMQ), and the Microsoft SQL Server database.
12. This IL code is language-neutral and is analogous to Sun Microsystem's Java bytecode.

Part II

Service Oriented Architecture Essentials

4

Message Oriented Services and SOAP

SOAP is a web service extension of Extensible Markup Language (XML). *This simple, powerful protocol promises multifarious advantages to the enterprise processes for delivering service (or exchange information). SOAP efficiently piggybacks on* Hypertext Transfer Protocol (HTTP), *and, as a result, can help enterprises exchange information on the Internet. The enormous success of SOAP as a protocol of choice can be attributed to its simplicity and elegance. The SOAP message, in its present version, can carry textual and binary information. Although the textual information can be enclosed in the body of the message, the nontextual information can be carried as a MIME attachment. A SOAP message can be exchanged between any two communicating partner applications in a synchronous or an asynchronous mode.*

SOAP is an XML-based messaging protocol and a specification. This protocol is designed to be simple and extensible in nature. It helps interacting applications to exchange information in a distributed environment and in a decentralized manner. The most interesting aspect of this protocol is that it can transport the data over the "wire," and it specifies a set of rules for the interacting application on the target system to initiate a response action after the data is delivered. We can compare this protocol with other similar wire protocols: *Internet Inter-ORB Protocol* (*IIOP*) for CORBA, *Object Remote Procedure Call* (*ORPC*) for DCOM, and *Java Remote Method Protocol* (*JRMP*) for RMI. However, these protocols are binary in nature.

SOAP is, by design, a simple, lightweight, and transport-independent protocol. This design essentially enables transportation of SOAP on another protocol of choice. With the advent and popularity of the Internet and World Wide Web, HTTP has become the choice of SOAP as a transport agent. One of the main reasons for the popularity of SOAP over HTTP is the capability of latter for a distributed data exchange over the web.[1]

SOAP Conventions

To cater to the needs of distributed data exchange, the SOAP specification defines four important conventions. They are *message envelope*, a set of *encoding rules*, *remote procedure call* (*RPC*) *convention*, and *binding* with underlying transport protocol. In the following sections, we define and describe these conventions.

Message Envelope

The SOAP message envelope defines a convention that describes the contents and packaging of the SOAP message. It also defines how to route and process the SOAP message as part of the message exchange between two applications.

Encoding Rules

Sets of encoding rules provide a convention of mapping the application information to XML. These encoding rules are based on a standardized XML Schema definition and, as such, closely model most of the standard data types and constructs supported by most of the popular programming languages. Moreover, these encoding rules strictly enforce guidelines that help in the creation of properly formatted information. Some of the significant guidelines are

- Use of the correct SOAP Namespace convention by all the elements and attributes encoding the message
- Exclusion of the use of *Document Type Definition (DTD) Processing Instructions* (*PI*) and DTD as part of the message
- Use of the `<Header>` element of the SOAP message along with the appropriate attributes, and so on

RPC Convention

Remote procedure calls are essentially the request-response-oriented calls. When a request for the message is made, along with the request, the data is serialized and transported to the target application. Similarly, the message received as a response from the target system is deserialized and processed. The SOAP specification defines rules for carrying out RPCs. The RPC convention addresses how data is routed through the request call and receives the result through the response.

Binding

Recall, SOAP is designed independent of any transport protocol. In principle, a SOAP message can be exchanged over any transport protocol, without disturbing the structure and content of the message. When a SOAP message is built, the binding to the underlying transport protocol needs to be explicitly indicated in the SOAP message itself. The tools generating the SOAP message take care of binding the message to the transport protocol. Although SOAP, by design, is transport protocol-independent, enterprise applications prefer to bind SOAP messages to HTTP. This is because HTTP is increasingly considered the defacto transport protocol by the enterprise world. However, the reasoning for making SOAP transport protocol independent is future-proofing the SOAP for message interchange. In essence, if a better and more elegant transport protocol were to appear on the enterprise communication horizon, SOAP would be ready to piggyback on this new protocol as well. Some of the SOAP examples presented in this chapter indicate the use of HTTP as the transport protocol.

Anatomy of SOAP

Recall that SOAP was designed to be simple, lightweight, elegant, and extensible. In this section, we cover the anatomical treatment of SOAP in the next two subsections and then address some of the important issues in the SOAP request and response mechanism vis-á-vis the structure of the SOAP message.

Basic SOAP Model

The structures we present here are representative of the essence of SOAP 1.1 with attachments specifications and SOAP 1.2 specifications. Prior to the discussion on the basic SOAP model, we would explore the message structure used in the conventional postal system.

In this system, messages are written on one or more sheets of paper, and the message is addressed to a particular person. The message on the paper is essentially the content or body part of the conventional message system. Some of the messages can optionally carry one or more attachments. The attachments can be in the form of photographs, audio tapes, and such. Although normal posts are delivered to the addressee as is, some of the special categories of mail such as "Registered" or "Certified" provide services such as security and reliability to the conventional message system. The target person's name and address on the envelope is the recipient of the message, and the message is meant to be opened and acted upon only by the recipient.

In the SOAP message system, the message structure is not all that different from that of the conventional message system. Although the structure is almost identical, some differences are obvious and imminent. Figures 4.1 and 4.2 represent the essence of the SOAP message system. Although Figure 4.1 represents the overall SOAP structure that consists of the textual and the nontextual part of the message system, Figure 4.2 focuses on the textual details of the SOAP message structure.

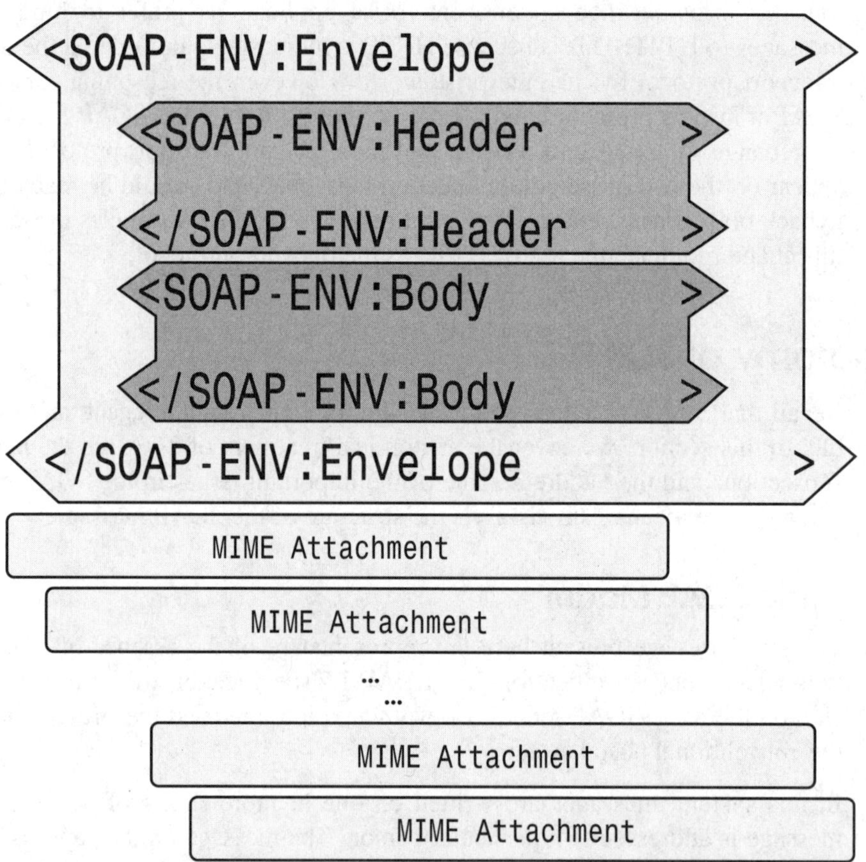
<SOAP-ENV:Envelope >
<SOAP-ENV:Header >
</SOAP-ENV:Header >
<SOAP-ENV:Body >
</SOAP-ENV:Body >
</SOAP-ENV:Envelope >
MIME Attachment
MIME Attachment
...
...
MIME Attachment
MIME Attachment

Figure 4.1 SOAP structure—The complete overview

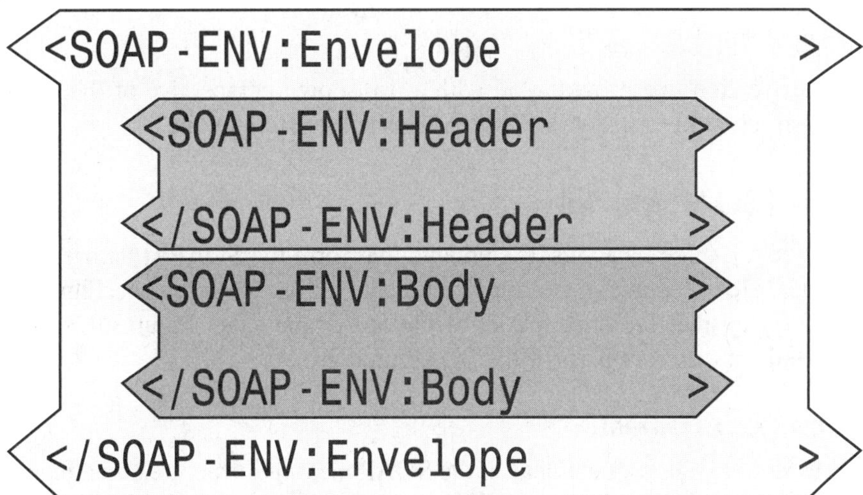
<SOAP-ENV:Envelope >
<SOAP-ENV:Header >
</SOAP-ENV:Header >
<SOAP-ENV:Body >
</SOAP-ENV:Body >
</SOAP-ENV:Envelope >

Figure 4.2 SOAP structure—The textual message part

According to the SOAP specification, there are two parts in the message structure. The first part is referred to as the Primary MIME. This part is of type text/xml, and the second part is referred to as MIME attachments. In a single SOAP message, there can be any number of MIME attachments. The main part of the SOAP message system is the text/xml part. This part defines an element called the `<Envelope>` element. This element houses two important elements: a `<Header>` element and a `<Body>` element. As per the SOAP specification, we have the following important rules in place.

- In any SOAP message, the `<Envelope>` and `<Body>` elements are mandatory.
- In any SOAP message, the `<Header>` element can be optional.
- In case, both `<Header>` and `<Body>` elements are present in the SOAP message; then `<Header>` appears first along with its contents, and then the `<Body>` element and its contents appear.
- The `<Header>` and `<Body>` elements can contain one or more entries.
- The entries inside the `<Header>` element are called the *header entries*.
- The entries in the `<Body>` element are called the *body entries*.

The SOAP message `<Body>` is designed to carry textual information. This is often referred to as *payload*. However, if nontextual information is to be transported, SOAP 1.1 with attachments and SOAP 1.2 specifications enable the binary data to be carried as MIME-encoded attachments. However, note that the binary contents are sent only as part of the `<Envelope>` element and not the `<Body>` element.

In the next section, we provide you with a drill-down perspective of the SOAP message structure in terms of its XML entries and related details.

Detailed SOAP Model

Recall there are three basic XML elements that form the SOAP structure. They are the `<Envelope>` element, `<Header>` element, and `<Body>` element. Figure 4.2 would be our prime reference model of the SOAP message. Figures 4.3 to 4.5 reveal details of different parts of the SOAP model.

The <Envelope> Element

This is essentially the root element in the SOAP message structure and a mandatory element as per the SOAP specification. This acts as a container element for the entire SOAP message. Figure 4.3 reveals the overview of the `<Envelope>` element and its contents.

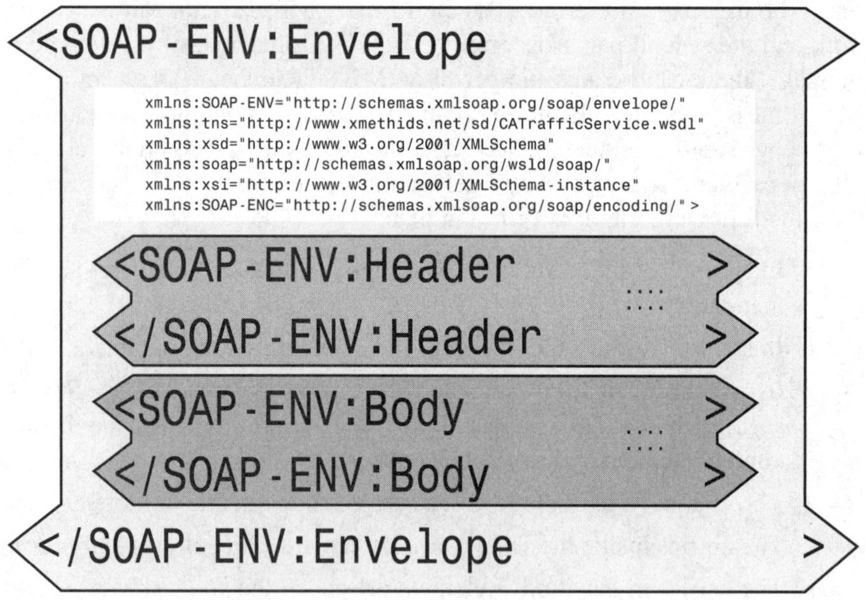

Figure 4.3 SOAP structure—The envelope details

Notice here that the `<Envelope>` element makes extensive use of the Namespaces convention. Similar Namespace conventions are used in the child elements of the `<Envelope>` elements. The prefix SOAP-ENV used in this example (and elsewhere in the text) is associated with the Uniform Resource Identifier (URI) `http://schemas.xmlsoap.org/soap/envelope`. This element uses an important attribute `encodingStyle`.[2] This attribute can appear in the `<Envelope>` or other elements that appear inside the `<Envelope>` element. If this attribute is incorporated into any of the body entries, for example, then the encoding declared by this attribute is applicable to that element and all the child elements that appear inside the corresponding body entry. However, if SOAP encoding is used, the `encodingStyle` attribute usually appears in the `<Envelope>` element. Details of SOAP encoding are covered in the next section.

The <Header> Element

The `<Header>` element in the SOAP message structure is optional. However, it hardly would be the case in the enterprise application real-life scenario. This is a powerful element that can assist in architecting distributed enterprise systems that are robust and flexible in nature. This element supports one or more header entries. The header entries are the most significant part of the `<Header>` element in the SOAP message structure.

The header entries in the SOAP message are designed for providing services to the payload that is transported by the `<Body>` element. Notice here that, by providing a `<Header>` element and its entries, the services (for the payload) are separated from the payload. For example, when no services are required for the payload, there is no requirement for the header entry and the corresponding `<Header>` element. However, when a payload requires one or more services, appropriate header entries need to be incorporated in the `<Header>` element to provide the intended services.

In an enterprise situation, a payload requires one or more services during the transport of the message. Some of the distinctive services that header entries can provide are transaction, authentication, authorization, and so on. In Figure 4.4, we provide the details of a typical `<Header>` element with header entries. In this figure, these entries are annotated for the purpose of clarity. The header entries might be designed in such a way that the application on the target system disregards the entry unless it understands the extension. This is a unique design aspect of the SOAP message structure. This design enables services to evolve over a time frame in a flexible manner.

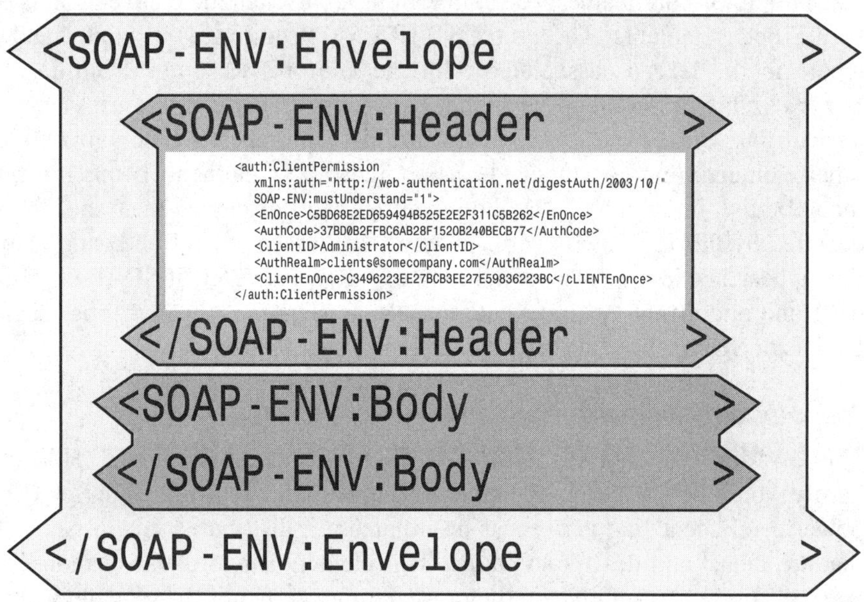
<SOAP-ENV:Envelope >
<SOAP-ENV:Header >
<auth:ClientPermission
xmlns:auth="http://web-authentication.net/digestAuth/2003/10/"
SOAP-ENV:mustUnderstand="1">
<EnOnce>C5BD68E2ED659494B525E2E2F311C5B262</EnOnce>
<AuthCode>37BD0B2FFBC6AB28F1520B240BECB77</AuthCode>
<ClientID>Administrator</ClientID>
<AuthRealm>clients@somecompany.com</AuthRealm>
<ClientEnOnce>C3496223EE27BCB3EE27E59836223BC</cLIENTEnOnce>
</auth:ClientPermission>
</SOAP-ENV:Header >
<SOAP-ENV:Body >
</SOAP-ENV:Body >
</SOAP-ENV:Envelope >

Figure 4.4 SOAP structure—The header part details

The header entries are meant for the SOAP intermediaries and not the application on the target system. Delivering a payload in an enterprise situation might require one or more services; therefore, the SOAP message hops on as many numbers of intermediary systems as it can. It is also important that the header entries are appropriately understood by the intermediary system so that the necessary services are rendered to the payload. To enforce this, two main attributes are used as part of the header entries. They are `mustUnderstand` and `actor`.[3, 4]

The mustUnderstand Attribute This attribute accepts a value of either 1 or 0. If the value for this attribute for a particular header entry is set to 1, the next target system in the SOAP message path must understand the header entry and act upon it. A value of 0 for this attribute indicates the converse. In Figure 4.4, we presented a sample header entry that exemplifies the use of a typical `mustUnderstand` entry in the `<Header>` element. If this target system cannot understand this header entry, for which the `mustUnderstand` attribute is set to 1, a SOAP `<Fault>` is generated and thrown back to the sender of the SOAP message. Issues such as `<Fault>` handling will be covered later in the chapter.

The actor Attribute[5] Recall that the presence of header entries in the `<Header>` element denotes that service extensions are used in the transport of the payload. The presence of a header entry with the attribute `mustUnderstand` set to 1 indicates that the SOAP message needs to *hop* in the SOAP message path before reaching the target system. It is, therefore, possible to create a *chain* of such intermediaries (or more appropriately endpoints), providing services to the SOAP message in an extensible way. The `actor` attribute in the header entries indicates the next intermediary target in the message path. The value of the `actor` attribute is the URL of the next endpoint in the SOAP message path. Note that the absence of the `actor` attribute in the header entry indicates that the next endpoint is the ultimate recipient of the payload.

The <Body> Element

Although this element carries significant importance, it is surprisingly simple and lightweight in nature. This is a mandatory element in the SOAP message structure. It bears the payload of the SOAP message that will be processed by the ultimate target endpoint. The payload is the textual information, and it can actually be an RPC call that is carrying an invoice, a purchase order, or even a document or any XML message. To reveal the dexterity of the `<Body>` element, we provide two different examples of the SOAP usage scenarios. Figure 4.5 is an example of a SOAP message carrying an RPC method invocation payload. Notice here that the payload contains the method name and the method parameters. In the present example,[6] the body incorporates a single method `getTrafficStatus()`. This method accepts the parameter `hwycode`, which is of type `String`. RPC message exchanges are, as referred elsewhere, called *Request—Response* Exchanges.

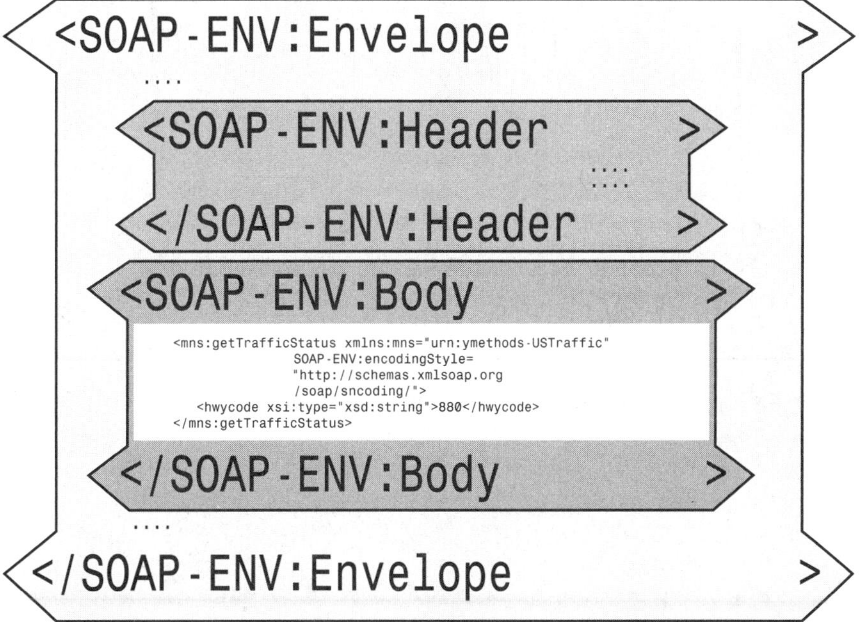

Figure 4.5 SOAP structure—The body part carrying the RPC payload

Figure 4.6 is another example of a SOAP message, which carries a purchase order as a payload. All the details of the purchase order are encoded into the body of the message: client name, shipping address, billing address, description of the purchased materials, total amount, tax, the total receivable amount, and so on. Such messages can be exchanged between two trading partners, and such exchanges are referred to as *Conversational Message Exchanges*.

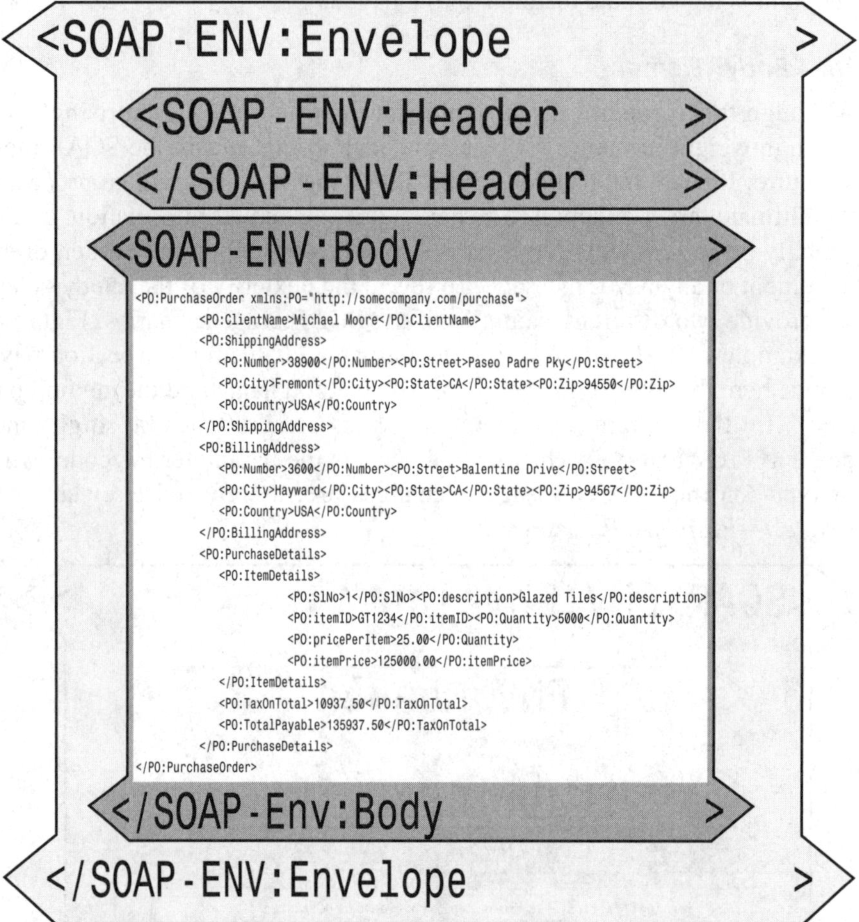
<SOAP-ENV:Envelope >
<SOAP-ENV:Header >
</SOAP-ENV:Header >
<SOAP-ENV:Body >
<PO:PurchaseOrder xmlns:PO="http://somecompany.com/purchase">
<PO:ClientName>Michael Moore</PO:ClientName>
<PO:ShippingAddress>
<PO:Number>38900</PO:Number><PO:Street>Paseo Padre Pky</PO:Street>
<PO:City>Fremont</PO:City><PO:State>CA</PO:State><PO:Zip>94550</PO:Zip>
<PO:Country>USA</PO:Country>
</PO:ShippingAddress>
<PO:BillingAddress>
<PO:Number>3600</PO:Number><PO:Street>Balentine Drive</PO:Street>
<PO:City>Hayward</PO:City><PO:State>CA</PO:State><PO:Zip>94567</PO:Zip>
<PO:Country>USA</PO:Country>
</PO:BillingAddress>
<PO:PurchaseDetails>
<PO:ItemDetails>
<PO:SlNo>1</PO:SlNo><PO:description>Glazed Tiles</PO:description>
<PO:itemID>GT1234</PO:itemID><PO:Quantity>5000</PO:Quantity>
<PO:pricePerItem>25.00</PO:Quantity>
<PO:itemPrice>125000.00</PO:itemPrice>
</PO:ItemDetails>
<PO:TaxOnTotal>10937.50</PO:TaxOnTotal>
<PO:TotalPayable>135937.50</PO:TaxOnTotal>
</PO:PurchaseDetails>
</PO:PurchaseOrder>
</SOAP-Env:Body >
</SOAP-ENV:Envelope >

Figure 4.6 SOAP structure—The body part carrying the purchase order payload

SOAP Encoding Details

The information exchanged between systems in an enterprise might travel as part of the header entries and body entries. SOAP Encoding is a way to represent such information in the SOAP required format so that the serialization/deserialization at both ends of the SOAP message path are in synchronization with the information exchanged. Because no default encoding schema exists, the enterprises need to use a standard encoding schema to appropriately represent the data. SOAP Encoding is an encoding schema that can be used on a wide variety of data. Enterprises might use this for encoding the data, although it is not imperative to use SOAP Encoding for encoding SOAP messages. SOAP specification enables other data models, alternative encoding, and unencoded data as part of the message exchange scheme. As previously indicated, the encoding scheme is identified by the `encodingStyle` attribute, and the SOAP encoding scheme provides XML Schema-based encoding to represent types of data. Any data types that can be used as part of SOAP message can be divided primarily into two types: *Simple Type* and *Compound Type*. Details regarding these data types are presented briefly in the next subsections.

Simple Type Encoding

The information represented by the Simple Type can be either a *built-in data type* or a *Derived Data Type*. A built-in Data Type in the SOAP Encoding is a data type that is defined by the XML Schema, whereas a Derived data type is a data type that is derived from the Simple Types. Some of the built-in data types such as `int`, `float`, `string`, and so on are listed in Table 4.1.

Table 4.1 Simple Data Types

No.	Data Type	Element	Example
1	Integer	`<int>`	`<int>`**`25`**`</int>`
2	Floating point number	`<float>`	`<float>`**`32.75`**`</float>`
3	String	`<string>`	`<string>`**`Naples`**`</string>`

In Table 4.2, we list some samples of Derived data types. The top box provides the definition of three data types, namely <script>, <number>, and <amount>. They respectively correspond to the <string>, <int>, and <float> data types.

Table 4.2 Sample of Derived Data Types

No.	Derived Type	Associated Primary Type	Example	Usage
1	premiumAmount	float	<xs:element name=" premiumAmount" type="xs:float"/>	<premiumAmount> **3457.75** </premiumAmount>
2	zipCode	string	<xs:element name=" zipCode" type="xs:string"/>	<zipCode> **95444** </zipCode>
3	totalEmploy-ees	int	<xs:element name="totalEmployees" type="int"/>	<totalEmployees> **12500** </totalEmplyees>

Examples of usage scenarios of these data types are provided in Table 4.2. The <premiumAmount> derived data type is derived from the `float` data type. Likewise, we have the <zipCode> derived data type representing the `string` type and the <totalEmployees> derived data type representing the `int` type, respectively.

Complex Type Encoding

`Struct` (or Structure) or `Array` data types are referred to as the Complex Type data types in SOAP Encoding. The `Struct` or "Structure" data type can be constructed using a combination of Simple and Derived data types. Construction of such a Complex data type is exemplified in Table 4.3. In this example, the Simple Type data types are `string`, `int`, and `float`. The Derived Type data types are <name>, <age>, <salary>, and <address>. Using these data types, we construct the <employeeInfo> data type, which is a Complex Type data type.

Table 4.3 Complex Data Type Usage

Simple Type	Derived Type	Construction of Complex Data Type
int	age	<xs:element name= "employeeInfo"…..> <xs:sequence> <xs:element name="name" type="xs:string"/> <xs:element name="age" type="xs:int"/> <xs:element name="address" type="xs:string"/> <xs:element name="salary" type="xs:float"/> </xs:sequence> </xs:element>
float	salary	
string	name	
string	address	

The `<employeeInfo>` is a Complex Type data type that includes other types of data types. This data type is a sequence of Derived data types – `name` (of type `string`), `age` (of type `int`), `address` (of type `string`), and `salary` (of type `float`) and in that order results in the construction of the `<employeeInfo>` Complex Type data type. To exemplify the usage of this type of data type, we have included the following examples in Table 4.4.

Table 4.4 Example Usage

No.	Example Usage
1	<emp:employeeInfo xmlns:emp="http://somecompany.com/emplyee/"> <name>**Uma Adams**</name> <age>19</age> <address>**12, 3rd Street, San Francisco, CA, 93456**</address> <salary>**23450.00**</salary> </emp:employeeInfo>
2	<emp:employeeInfo xmlns: emp="http://somecompany.com/employee"> <name>**Bryan Basham**</name> <age>**24**</age> <address>**2880, Beta Dr, New Jersey, NJ, 43456**</address> <salary>22570.00</salary> </emp:employeeInfo>
3	<emp:employeeInfo xmlns: emp="http://somecompany.com/employee"> <name>**Anita Dominic**</name> <age>**21**</age> <address>**3890, Kepler Dr, Menlo Park, CA 95656**</address> <salary>**19450.00**</salary> </emp:employeeInfo>

`Array` is another Complex Type data type that is frequently used in enterprise applications. Based on the needs to represent the appropriate business data, you can construct arrays of `<string>`, `<int>`, `<float>`, and so on that represent the arrays of simple type data. One can also construct the array of Complex Types such as `Structs`, and so forth.

SOAP Binding to the Transport Protocol

Recall the structure of the SOAP message has been designed in such a way that there is no explicit dependency on any transport protocol. In fact, it is a conscious design decision to keep SOAP independent of a transport protocol. Although any transport protocol can be chosen to send SOAP messages, HTTP has emerged as the preferred transport protocol of choice for transporting SOAP. That said, transporting SOAP over other transport protocols such as SMTP, FTP, and so on is not uncommon in many enterprise scenarios.

HTTP is the unanimous choice of transport protocol in the E-Commerce markets such as *Business-to-Customer* (*B2C*), *Business-to-Business* (*B2B*), and *Customer-to-Customer* (*C2C*). The Internet revolution has indeed propelled the use of HTTP as the most preferred transport mechanism. HTTP is also a natural fit as the transport protocol for the SOAP messages because it is the request-response-oriented protocol of choice in the present-day E-Commerce business scenario. In fact, service invocation using the request-response pattern is still the most widely accepted choice in the enterprise B2C and B2B scenarios.

Interaction Using the SOAP Protocol

When a piece of information is exchanged between two applications using the SOAP protocol, the applications that produce, consume, and understand the same should be bound by the SOAP specification. The exchange of information can be affected either through synchronous communication or asynchronous communication mode. In synchronous communication mode, the interchange of information takes place in a request/response fashion. The asynchronous communication mode enables interchange of information between two or more applications that use the message queuing route. The SOAP protocol is designed in such a way that applications communicating synchronously or asynchronously can use the SOAP protocol.

Message Exchange Model

The process/workflow in any enterprise involves a number of communications exchanges among multiple applications. Applications involved in the workflow using the SOAP protocol in such an enterprise scenario can perform one or more of the following main activities:

- Applications producing SOAP messages and binding them with the transport protocol. These applications are called the *Initial Senders* (or *senders*).
- Applications consuming SOAP messages to complete part of or a whole workflow activity. These applications are called the *Ultimate Receivers* (or *receivers*).
- Applications playing the role of media between the above two activities. These applications/systems are referred to as *Intermediaries*.

Figure 4.7 presents the SOAP message exchange model, illustrating the different roles played by these systems/applications. A clear understanding of this model helps designers and architects of the enterprise solutions design and architect applications that communicate using the SOAP protocol.

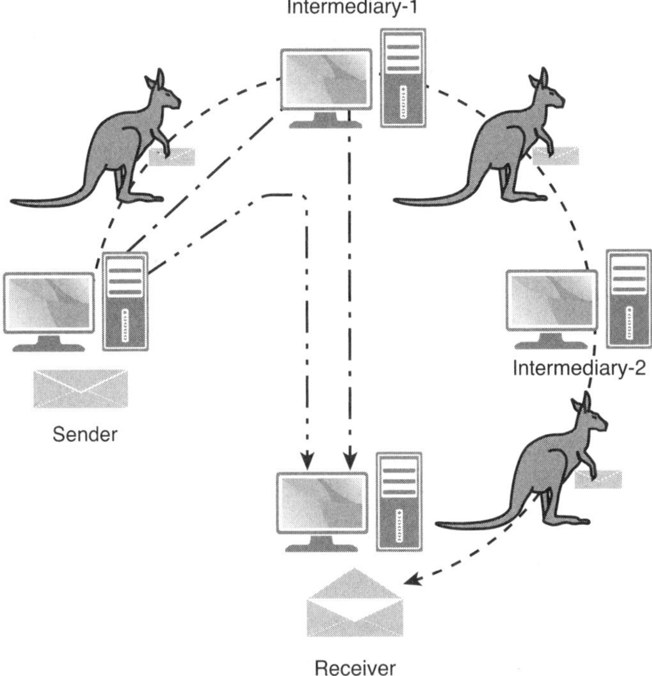

Figure 4.7 The SOAP message exchange model

Initial Sender

An application that creates the SOAP messages is referred to as the Initial Sender (or Initial SOAP sender). An Initial Sender application creates the SOAP message according to a particular SOAP specification adopted by the enterprise for its web services-based applications. The Initial Sender marked "*Sender*" in Figure 4.7 initiates the workflow when the SOAP message is created and transported to the next stage in the communication network.

Ultimate Receiver

An application that acts as the logical endpoint for a particular workflow in this message exchange model is called the Ultimate Receiver, or Ultimate SOAP receiver. Reaching the Ultimate Receiver signals the arrival of the final endpoint of the communication model. The Ultimate Receiver is the consumer of the SOAP message. This receiver, marked *Receiver* in Figure 4.7, is designed to receive and process the SOAP message. This application is designed in such a way that the received SOAP message is as per the appropriate SOAP specification and then the message is processed. The processing of the result on the Ultimate Receiver system can involve the execution of a specific application. The parameters required for running this application is extracted from the `<Body>` element of the SOAP message. Upon the successful initiation of the message, the result can be returned to the Initial Sender as a SOAP message. If the application does not run to successful completion on the ultimate receiver system, a suitable error/exception is generated in the SOAP format and sent back to the Initial Sender.

Intermediary

The Intermediary, or a SOAP Intermediary, is an application that enables the SOAP message to hop from point to point. Remember, between the Initial Sender and Ultimate Receiver applications, there could be zero or more Intermediaries. These Intermediaries play the role of both sender and/or receiver; however, under such circumstances, they are not referred to as Sender or Receiver. In Figure 4.7, the systems/applications marked Intermediary-1 and Intermediary-2 act as the Intermediaries for the applications marked Sender and Receiver. Unlike the Initial Sender and Ultimate Receiver applications, Intermediaries do not act on the `<Body>` content of the SOAP message. Intermediaries essentially act upon the information encoded in the appropriate `<Header>` element of the

SOAP message. Based on the `<Header>` content, an Intermediary can initiate a particular service required for the workflow. Typical services that can be offered by an Intermediary might include authentication, authorization, encryption, and so on.

The workflow path representing the Initial Sender, Ultimate Receiver, and Intermediaries together form the SOAP message path. The SOAP message path in an enterprise scenario is highlighted as a thick line in Figure 4.8. The Initial Sender that composes the SOAP message, the Ultimate Receiver that is the endpoint that consumes the message in the `<Body>` of the SOAP message, and the three intermediaries join together to form the SOAP message path.

SOAP Response and the Error-Handling Mechanism

Creating a SOAP request is hardly an issue in an enterprise situation because this is an initiation of the workflow in the communication network. However, when the SOAP message hops along the SOAP message path, a variety of issues can interfere with the typical workflow. There might be problems at one or more Intermediaries, or there might be a problem at the Ultimate Receiver endpoint.

The errors/exceptions at the Intermediaries could be due to problems at the Intermediary system or the appropriate header entry. Similarly, errors/exceptions could be encountered at the Ultimate Receiver endpoint of the SOAP message path. This could be caused by information in the `<Body>` element or a problem with the system processing the SOAP message content.

SOAP specification is designed to smoothly handle a variety of errors likely to occur in any enterprise situation. The error/exception handling and reporting back of the error/exception in SOAP are, by design, simple and extensible. When a situation results in an error condition, an appropriate error/exception information is generated on that system and sent back to the sender as another SOAP message. The error/exception information is encoded into an element called `<Fault>`. This element is a body entry of the SOAP response generated due to the error/exception situation at that endpoint. Detailed structure of SOAP `<Fault>` is illustrated in Figure 4.8.

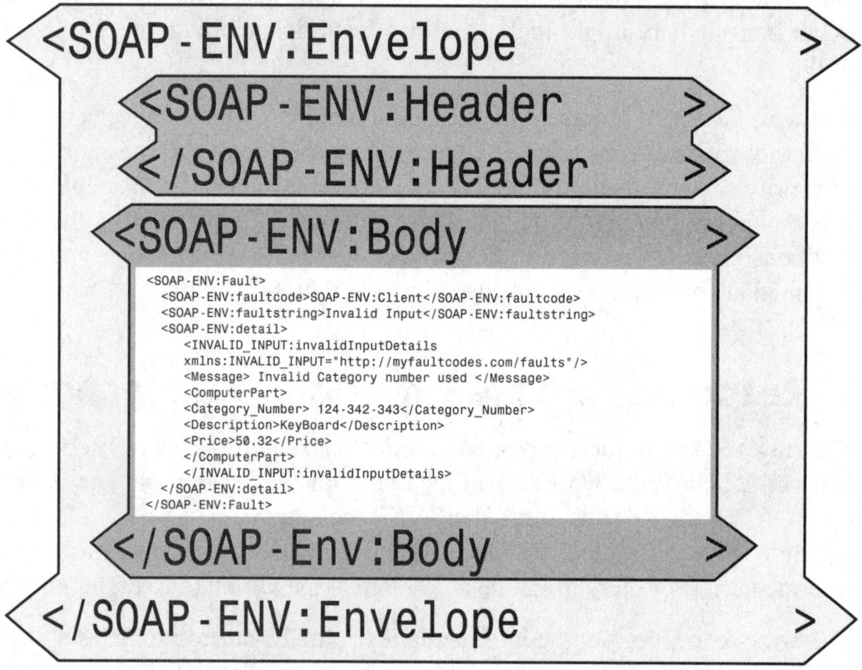

Figure 4.8 SOAP structure—The <Fault> reporting mechanism

The SOAP <Fault>

The error/exception information is coded into the <Body> element of a SOAP message, when the system encounters one during the traversal of the SOAP message along the SOAP message path. The name of this body entry is <Fault>. This element supports four subelements. They are <faultcode>, <faultstring>, <faultactor>, and <detail>.

The SOAP <faultcode>

The <faultcode> element recognizes the error condition. This element enables the systems/applications engaged in the web services workflow to discover and identify the occurrence of an error. SOAP specifications provide four default values that the enterprises use for identifying the type of errors. They are `VersionMismatch`, `MustUnderstand`, `Client`, and `Server`.[7] Enterprise systems can either use the default values or design and use their own fault codes. The latter ones are termed the *user-defined fault codes*.

The SOAP <faultstring>

The `<faultstring>` element provides a textual representation of the error/exception information reflected by the `faultcode`. Because the value of this element is in a textual format, the error/exception conditions are in the human-readable form, and as a result, the `faultstring` values can be browsed by system administrators and other stakeholders in the web services systems.

The SOAP <faultactor>

The `<faultactor>` element reports the location where the error/exception condition occurred along the SOAP message path. The value of this element would be a URL of the system/application that initiated the SOAP fault.

The SOAP <detail>

This element is designed to supplement the information for the error/exception condition that transpired in the SOAP message path. The value of this element can be a descriptive textual message, indicating the error occurred, and its likely location. It can also contain remedial suggestions for system administrators or others.

SOAP Version Differences and Dependencies

Since its introduction, the SOAP specification has undergone many changes, and the industry has responded collaboratively, contributing to the improvement of the specification.

SOAP Versioning

Since its inception, inventors and the industry participants have revised the SOAP specification a number of times. The pioneering work on XML-RPC initiated by Userland Software and Microsoft Corporation resulted in the introduction of SOAP as a protocol. This protocol is recognized as a significant milestone in the technological footsteps of interoperability. The initial work, SOAP 0.8, was considered close and narrow in its approach. However, when IBM joined the fray and proposed crucial changes in the SOAP structure and contents, the scope and utility value of SOAP was broadened. The new changes wrought in the openness in SOAP and widened the scope of SOA, and they promoted SOAP as a predominant way of message exchange. This resulted in the creation of SOAP version 1.1 specifications (and SOAP 1.1 with MIME attachments, a subsequent improved version). IBM's involvement in SOAP is considered a strategic step. This step also resulted in the combination of SOAP and

Java—a clear strategy for enterprise web services and SOA. The combination of SOAP and Java is seen as the best fusion for developing and delivering web services-oriented applications. This combination has been seen as an important milestone because it promises to deliver seamless, cross-platform interoperability between loosely coupled enterprise applications. This combination has indeed influenced many other specifications—J2EE in particular—in a significant way.

New SOAP Version

In April 2007, the World Wide Web Consortium (W3C) announced the latest specification for SOAP. The new specification is now referred to as *SOAP 1.2 (Second Edition)*. This revision was a consolidation of the work from many by the W3C. The new specification is a four-part document. Part 0 is the *Primer (Second Edition)*, Part 1 is the *Messaging Framework (Second Edition)*, Part 2 is the *Adjuncts (Second Edition)* and Specification Assertions and Test Collection *(Second Edition)*. The Primer is a document intended to provide easily understandable material on different features of the new specifications. The Messaging Framework is a detailed document on the new messaging framework. This part defines, using XML technologies, an extensible messaging framework including basic SOAP message structure and advanced concepts, including message exchange patterns, binding to a variety of underlying protocols, and so on. The Adjuncts document covers information on more detailed concepts such as SOAP encoding, HTTP-specific binding, and such. Advancement in the new specifications is the use of the *XML Infoset*, as against SOAP 1.1 with attachments using the normal XML 1.0 specifications. The XML Infoset is well formed and conforms to the XML Namespaces. This time, the Namespaces for Envelope and encoding schemas are different. These differentiations enable the SOAP processors to distinguish the documents properly and easily.

SOAP Elements

The `actor` attribute has been replaced by the `role` attribute. As a result, two new predefined roles are available: *None* and *Ultimate Receiver*. If the value of `role` is set to None, the header blocks should never be processed. On the other hand, if its value is set to Ultimate Receiver, only the final recipient can process the body content.

Changes are introduced to improve and enhance the fault processing. A new hierarchical fault processing has been introduced. As a result of this improvement, a hierarchical list of SOAP codes and associated supporting information can be included in every SOAP `<Fault>` message. Each SOAP `<Fault>` code can identify the corresponding `<Fault>` category at an increasing level of detail, as per the new <Fault> processing system. The new default <Fault> codes are `VersionMismatch`, `MustUnderstand`, `DataEncodingUnknown`, `Sender`, and `Receiver`. Although `DataEncodingUnknown` is newly introduced, Sender replaces the `Client` and `Receiver` replaces `Server` from SOAP 1.1 with attachments specification.

SOAP Binding

SOAP messages as per SOAP 1.1 with attachments specifications specify a single binding to HTTP for the communication protocol; whereas in SOAP 1.2 specifications, messages provide an abstract binding framework for binding the SOAP message to the transport protocol. Furthermore, SOAP 1.2 specifications also provide a concrete binding to HTTP and nonnormative e-mail binding.

SOAP Encoding

SOAP Encoding in SOAP 1.2 specifications is similar to SOAP 1.1 with attachments specifications but simpler. According to this encoding schema, multireference values can be defined in-place. Although SOAP 1.1 enabled this only at the top level, SOAP 1.2 specifications enable a declare-at-first-use concept, which is unique.

Summary

SOAP is a simple and elegant protocol that is an important constituent of First Generation Web Services technologies. This protocol is designed to exchange the data in an interoperable and extensible way. SOAP specifications define three main elements to encapsulate the message: <Envelope>, <Header>, and <Body>. Although the <Header> element entries help provide services to the payload, the <Body> element entries carry the textual payload. Binary information is carried as one or more MIME-encoded attachments. Along the SOAP message path, two or more applications can be involved in the message exchange types: an Initial Sender, an Ultimate Receiver, and zero or more Intermediaries. The Initial Sender creates the SOAP message, and the Ultimate Receiver receives and processes the <Body> part of the SOAP message. Intermediaries process the appropriate entries in the <Header> element to provide services. SOAP is designed to be independent of any transport protocol; however, HTTP is the preferred choice of a transport protocol for the majority of enterprises.

In the next chapter, we discuss the importance of the services description part of web services and describe in detail the vocabulary of Web Services Description Language (WSDL). Here, we explain how the anatomy of this element helps in enabling service orientation in the overall enterprise solution.

Endnotes

1. Dave Winer of Userland Software initiated the pioneering work that laid the foundation to the introduction of SOAP as a protocol. Dave's work on XML-RPC resulted in the simple and portable way of making remote procedure calls over HTTP. The RPC calls thus conceived were text-based, as against the conventional RPC calls. This work laid the foundation for SOAP.
2. The `encodingStyle` attribute is referred to as a *global attribute*. This attribute indicates the *serialization/deserialization* rules used on the data as part of the SOAP message. The value of this attribute would be a URL that identifies serialization/deserialization rules for the data. The most frequently used value for this attribute is `http://schemas.xmlsoap.org/soap/encoding/`.
3. The `actor` attribute is replaced by the `role` attribute in SOAP 1.2 specifications.
4. SOAP 1.2 specifications provide two predefined roles: None and Ultimate Receiver.
5. Although SOAP 1.2 is the latest of the specifications, we focus primarily on SOAP 1.1 with attachments specifications because this is compatible with Web Services—Interoperability, WS-I.
6. This example is inspired by the XMETHODS example available on the web SOAPClient.com site. There are many sample web services hosted by XMETHODS, and this example is based on the web service CATrafficService. Visit `http://www.soapclient.com/XmethodsServices.html` for further details.
7. The terms Sender and Receiver replace Client and Server, respectively, in SOAP 1.2 specifications.

5

Web Services and Web Services Description Language

Web Services Description Language (WSDL) *is considered one of the keys to the implementation of SOA. WSDL, an extension of the* Extensible Markup Language (XML), *provides an excellent combination of tags including a complete description of a service or a set of services. The description includes all related information required for any application, including service name, number and types of parameters required for invoking the service, return type, location of the server application, and, most important, details of the description of the service. Services described this way are discoverable and amenable for invocation by other services.*

WSDL (pronounced "Wisdel") is another XML vocabulary that forms one of the core building blocks of basic web services. WSDL is the description of one or more services through the use of a set of XML elements. WSDL provides a comprehensive definition and description of all the related web services information. The service description includes service name, parameters exchanged as part of the service, transport protocol binding information, data types used, and so on. This information is encoded into a special XML file called the WSDL file.[1] This chapter is designed to provide a comprehensive anatomical treatment of the WSDL language. It also discusses how WSDL helps in the process of service discovery and the service invocation component of web services.

WSDL—An XML Web Services Description Vocabulary

A web service, according to the *World Wide Web Consortium* (*W3C*), is essentially a software system offering a service that is designed to support machine-to-machine interaction over the network, such as the Internet/intranet. A service provider might offer just one such service or an aggregate of services that is discoverable and usable in an enterprise scenario. Although such services can exist anywhere on the intranet or Internet, they should be discoverable, understandable, and usable by systems or applications of one or more business partners/collaborators of the enterprise. The technology of WSDL essentially enables the automated discovery of the web service (or services) by using a systematic representation of all required services and related information using a predefined set of XML elements.

WSDL is an XML document that describes services in a systematic manner. Because the description is in XML format, applications can process this document to understand all the necessary details of the services. As you soon see, web services, in the WSDL parlance, can be defined[2] as communication between two systems. A more precise definition of web services can be represented as a set of communication endpoints capable of exchanging information. In the lexis of WSDL, these endpoints are called *ports*. For our purposes, the term *ports* refers to the applications offering services. Ports provide the abstract definition of web services through use of two other standard XML elements: *operations* and *messages*, and binding to a transfer protocol. These elements are arranged in a predefined manner inside the WSDL document.

The Web Services Triangle

Web services involve three important business participants. These are the *service provider*, the *service broker*, and the *service requester* (or *provider*, *broker*, and *requester*, respectively.) The requester is also referred to as the web services client. A provider could be a business, industry, or company providing services. A requester could be a business or a company in need of the service, whereas the broker is a company, business, or system that helps both the provider and requester to discover each other and carry out business transactions.

This section provides a top-level picture of how these categories of businesses interact with each other and help in effectuating web services. In Figure 5.1, these three participants are shown as the vertices of the web services triangle, presenting the interactions between providers, requesters, and brokers. The three types of interactions can be identified in Figure 5.1: *publish*, *find*, and *bind*. The interaction between the provider and the broker, publish, results in the publication of the service information. This is a unidirectional interaction, from provider to broker. Likewise, the interaction between the requester and the broker, find, is searching for a required service information. This is again a unidirectional interaction, from requester to broker. That said, the interaction between the provider and the requester, bind, results in bringing the provider and requester together. In this situation, the interaction is bidirectional, indicating a request-response interaction between them. The importance and role of WSDL is indicated in this figure.

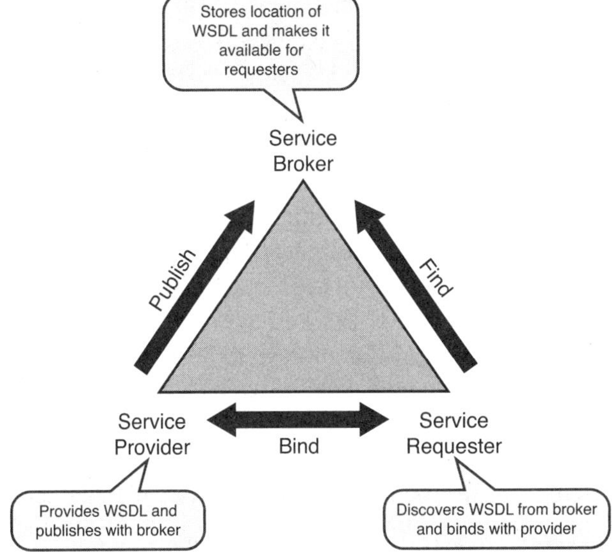

Figure 5.1 The web services triangle

The WSDL specification furnishes a set of seven unique XML elements for providing a comprehensive web service definition. A standardized arrangement of these seven elements provides a generic definition of a web service (or an aggregate of several web services), and this definition needs to be discovered for understanding the web services, including the parameters required for invoking the services, the return value, the transport protocol to be used for invoking the services, and so on.

Recall that, from the earlier definition of web services through WSDL parlance, the description is abstract in nature and decoupled from the transport protocol. The decoupling of the abstract definition of operation (service) and message from transport protocol has rendered the web services to be *protocol agnostic* in nature. This also enables the abstract definition of the service (or services) to be bound to multiple communication protocols.

The abstract definition of services through operations and messages is coded into a simple XML file. This file is represented by a `.wsdl` extension, indicating that it contains the description of web services. *Integrated Development Environments (IDEs)* and application development tools help generate this web services definition file and store it in a location accessible to (client or peer) applications interested in understanding and using the web services.

The WSDL file can be stored anywhere; however, such service description files are usually located on a suitable server. This server might or might not be hosting the service application. Normally, the WSDL files are placed on a server that is readily accessible to the client/peer applications. Application development tools and IDEs generate the WSDL file for a given service (or aggregate of services) during the services creation activity. The present-day application tools that can create a service using a specific programming language can also co-create the WSDL file describing the service. Although this is easy and understandable, generating the WSDL for the existing application can prove to be tricky. Why? Because the original service definition might be vague and might have changed over time. Moreover, some services might need to be rewritten for making future provisions for services delivery. Sophisticated development tools might use the source code for generating the web services description. More sophisticated tools can determine the available services of a deployed application in the run-time environment for generating the WSDL file. The client/peer application, upon accessing, reading, and understanding the WSDL file, comprehends the details of the available services definition. The process of generation of the WSDL file essentially *exposes* the service details to the clients/peers.

A client application can thus request a WSDL file, and the file can be downloaded on the client system. The client application then browses the WSDL file and understands all the details of the available web services. At last, the client can suitably invoke the exposed web service.

Service Invocation Fundamentals

Web services invocation can take place synchronously or asynchronously. Synchronous invocation, a two-way communication mechanism, means "invocation is happening at the same time." It essentially means that the service method or a function call is a blocking call. Blocking calls can be classified into two types:

- Request-Response
- Solicit-Response

In the *Request-Response* blocking call, the client initiates a request to an application on the server identified by a URL provided by the service provider. The client call would then be blocked until the server either sends the response or an error/exception occurs during the execution of the service. Client/server communication, distributed applications communications, and RPC type communications are examples of Request-Response blocking calls.

In the *Solicit-Response* blocking call, the server application solicits a response from a client. The server application initiates the call and looks for the response from the client in this mode of communication. Of the two, the Request-Response mechanism is the more popular mode of communication.

Other types of calls, essentially the nonblocking calls, are covered later in this chapter.

Synchronous Invocation and Fundamentals of RPC Mechanism

Recall that we introduced the basics of *remote procedure call* (*RPC*) in Chapter 2, "Evolution of IT Architectures." Before exploring the semantics of synchronous invocation of the web services, we review the fundamentals of the semantics of RPC, the basis of the synchronous web services invocation. The term remote procedure call is a successor to the term procedure call. The procedure call refers to the invocation of a procedure or method, or a function during the run-time environment in a local system. As against the normal procedure call, RPC is a term that describes invocation of a procedure or function/method on a remote system. RPC communication is neither a specification nor a standard; it is simply a technique or mechanism that makes remote applications communicate in an easy and elegant manner. The RPC mechanism helps in simplifying the call semantics of the remote functions by hiding all the transport and network communication issues. In the following section, we discuss the differences between the local (or procedure call) and the remote procedure call.

Local Call

During the run-time execution of a program, the application initiates a function call, and the call semantics take place in a predefined way as explained next. A typical client initiates a function/procedure call. Let's refer to this participant as the *caller* of the function. This procedure call involves the use of function/method name of another application. We refer to this as the server application or *callee*. The call invocation involves the passing of parameters that is required by the function of the server application. The call semantics explained here are shown in Figure 5.2. In a stand-alone system environment, both the caller and callee exist on the same system. The callee knows the exact memory address of the function that is invoked. The parameters required for the invocation of the procedure are also passed by their memory address locations. The semantics of such parameter passing are called *pass-by-reference*.

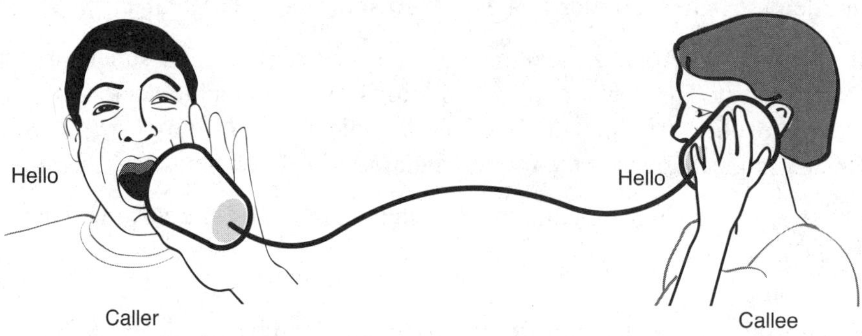

Figure 5.2 The local call semantics

Remote Procedure Call

Unlike the semantics of the local call, the Remote Procedure Call semantics take place somewhat differently. To begin with, the caller and callee applications reside on distributed/heterogeneous systems, and the two applications are connected on a LAN/WAN environment. The caller application must know the remote address of the callee application, the communication protocol, and such for invoking this procedure call. In addition, the call parameters that are being passed to the callee, and the response object that needs to be retrieved from the callee, need to be physically transported between the two systems, as shown in Figure 5.3.

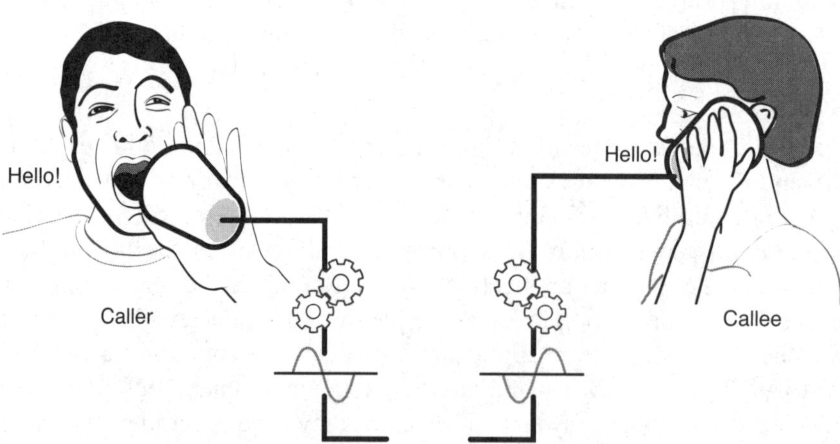

Figure 5.3 The remote call semantics

For this remote communication to succeed, both sides of the communication channel must use a standardized communication infrastructure. This communication infrastructure undertakes a full responsibility of ensuring the successful invocation of the procedure between caller and callee. The communication infrastructure on the callee side is called the *skeleton* or *tie*[3] and on the caller side, it is called the *stub* or *proxy*. Tools and IDEs that help in creating RPC applications generate the stub and skeleton files. Upon the deployment of the RPC application, the generated skeleton files are copied on to the callee or server system. The stub files needs to be copied at the caller or the client system, and these two applications communicate on the heterogeneous network. This is illustrated in Figure 5.3.

The stub is deployed on the client system, and it is accessible to the client application. Likewise, the skeleton is deployed on the server system and is accessible to the server application. Note that, in the local call semantics, the client and server systems communicate directly with each other. Moreover, the data exchanged between the two will be following the *pass-by-reference* model. There are four players in the RPC: client, stub, skeleton, and server. The client and server never communicate with each other directly. The client communicates with the stub and data exchange between client, and the stub is always *pass-by-value*. Similarly, the server communicates with the skeleton and the data exchange between server, and the skeleton is *pass-by-value*, too. The skeleton and the stub communicate directly, and the data exchange between them is *pass-by-value*.

When the invocation of a procedure involves the use of one or more parameters, unlike the situation in the stand-alone system, the parameters need to be passed by value. The RPC mode of invocation requires that the parameters are converted to the format understood by the communication infrastructure. This process is referred to as *marshalling*. Marshalling of the parameter objects is done at the caller side of communication. Likewise, generating the parameter object at the callee side is referred to as *unmarshalling*. Thus, any remote procedure invocation involves a pair of marshalling and unmarshalling on the caller and the callee side. On the caller side, when the caller passes any parameters to the remote procedure, the stub/proxy marshalls these parameters into the communication infrastructure. When the call reaches the remote side, the skeleton unmarshalls the parameters into the communication infrastructure of the remote side and passes it on to the procedure on the server application. Likewise, the results are marshalled by the skeleton on the remote side and sent across to the caller side. At the client side, the stub unmarshalls the result object back to its original values and then passes it on to the caller application.

The most striking part of the RPC communication mode is that it liberates the developer from coding the communication infrastructure part of the remote communication, including aspects such as marshalling and unmarshalling. Furthermore, this mode of communication simplifies the call semantics that are comparable to the semantics of just the local call. The caller makes a call to the callee application as if it were executing on a stand-alone system.

The RPC mode of communication now hinges on the stubs and skeleton communication infrastructure for achieving the necessary method/procedure invocation. Application tools and IDEs help the developer in generating the stubs and skeletons. Generation of stubs and skeleton is usually done at the compile time of the server application. Notice here that RPC communication mode is the tightly coupled synchronous mode of communication. A tight coupling mode indicates that the client and server applications should be aware of each other and should be executing in their respective systems when the invocation is initiated.

In Figure 5.4, we present detailed call semantics of the RPC between a client and the server in a heterogeneous environment. In this environment, the client makes a local call on the proxy/stub on the client system. The stub, in turn, assumes the remaining of the call completion responsibilities, including marshalling of the parameters and using the appropriate transport protocol. The communication infrastructure on the caller and the callee systems are shown as *layered* systems in this figure. They are *Remote Reference Layer (RRL)* and *Transport Layer (TL)*. When the caller initiates an invocation, the marshalling is initiated, and the call is first passed on to the RRL. The call is forwarded next to the TL and then reaches the remote system. On the remote system, the TL receives the call and then it is passed on to the RRL. Unmarshalling of the parameters would happen here, and the parameters are passed on to the executing server application. This completes the first half of the RPC invocation. When the server completes the execution of the method, the results are generated, and the result object is passed on to the RRL on the server side after marshalling. This layer forwards the call to the TL layer and then, eventually, the call reaches the client system. The TL at the client side intercepts the call and forwards it to the RRL, which unmarshalls the response object and passes it on to the client application.

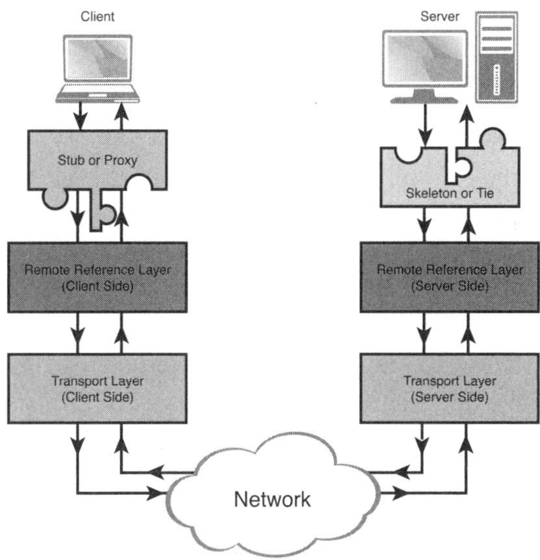

Figure 5.4 The detailed semantics of an RPC

Service Invocation and WSDL

Invocation of web services can happen between two or more applications that form a part or the whole of a process/workflow of the enterprise. It is critical that all participating applications understand the service invocation semantics and communication protocol for invocation. You need to understand how client applications can discover the web service, recognize invocation semantics, create the definition of the service proxy on its side, and eventually invoke the web service. The example we present here is essentially an RPC style invocation of the web service.

There are three important players involved in the whole process of web services invocation. The first is the web service provider or the server application, often referred to as the provider. Participation of this candidate in the process of the delivery of web services is mandatory. The second player is the client application or the service requester.[4] He is often referred to as the requester. Again, the participation of this player is mandatory. The third (an optional) player is called the service registry or the service broker. Interactions take place between the provider, requester, and broker in a specific and a definitive manner. Figure 5.5 presents the semantics of the interaction between all three participants. Although we termed the involvement of the broker as optional, we find it important to include here for the purpose of understanding the web services and service-oriented architecture. There are several steps/stages involved in the entire process. They are as follows:

1. Create the service.
2. Generate the web service description for the service.
3. Register the web service.
4. Publish the web service.
5. Discover the web service.
6. Understand the web service semantics.
7. Invocate the web service.

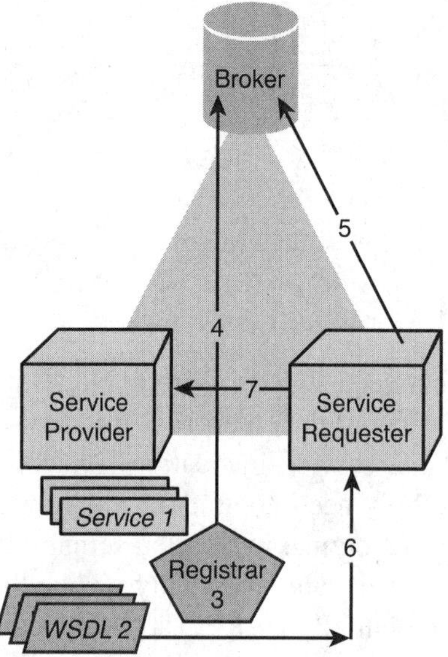

Figure 5.5 Web service invocation and WSDL

Creation of the Service

Clearly, a service provider creates a service. The service creation involves the creation of the application using a suitable programming language and tools on a typical platform. The application might have one or more services, and they can be the functions, methods, or subroutines of the application program. As is, these functions, methods, or subroutines can be termed *services*. Now the provider intends to offer these services as *web services*.

Generating the Web Service Description for the Service

Now that the provider intends to offer this service as a web service, application tools generate the WSDL document. Although an application can have one or more services, the provider might intend to generate the WSDL file that contains all or a few of the selected functions/methods as web services.

Registering the Web Service

The provider might find it convenient to publish the available services in a suitable electronic medium. The service publishing can be done in huge electronic registries. The service publication involves, among other things, the details of the provider, address, telephone number, fax number, details of the services, and so on. One important constituent of the details of the services is the URL location of the WSDL document.

Publication of the Web Service

This is essentially the publication of the location of WSDL document in the registry. This stage exposes the web services to the community of partners and collaborators of the enterprise. Registration and publication of the service information is done through a SOAP-RPC invocation. It essentially means that the electronic registry accepts the service registration and service publication through the use of SOAP.

Discovering the Web Service

A partner/client in need of a web service would typically search for the service information in the service registry. The client might use one or more key words to locate suitable services. Again, a client search should be a SOAP-RPC invocation on the service registry. In an actual enterprise scenario, searching for the services might yield multiple service providers and corresponding matching services. The client might need to choose a particular service provider based on other criteria such as price, quality, and so forth at this stage. Please note that this task of narrowing down the options and choosing a particular provider can happen manually and can take a significant amount of time.

Understanding the Web Services Semantics

After the client negotiates with a provider for a specific service, she would get the handle to the WSDL document that describes the required service for the client. The client now can download this document and examine the WSDL file to understand the entire web services and the semantics of the web services for service invocation. The client can also optionally generate the proxy[5] files at its side. The proxy files would be used by the client application for the web service invocation. Understanding the web services and service semantics might also happen offline over a time period.

Invocation of Web Service

The service invocation is involved in the initiation of a SOAP request over a transport protocol such as HTTP. The service invocation involved would be similar to the RPM method invocation over a distributed architecture of the enterprise network. The client application invokes the method call on the proxy, and the required parameters for the method call are passed on to the proxy as if the method call were on the same system. The completion of the invocation process is taken care of by the proxy libraries.

Although there are seven basic steps involved between three participants, four of them are considered important for the successful completion of the web services call. They are *service creation*, *generating the service description*, *registering the service*, and *service discovery*. In the following subsections, we describe these four essential steps in detail.

Service Creation

The service provider's first step is service creation. The provider might already have an existing service application or might intend to create a new service (or services) using a suitable platform choice IDE or application development tools. This is not yet referred to as the web service. Note the service application created can contain one or more services, and these services should be accessible in a distributed environment.

The types and nature of services required in an enterprise scenario are limited only by the organizational needs and the imagination of the service creator. Some of the most commonly required services in the enterprise scenario can be Purchase Order service, Invoice service, Courier service, Tax Calculator service, and so on. These services can be developed on any platform using the service creator's programming language and then deployed on any suitable system.

For some enterprises, service creation does not need to be the first step; it can instead be an optional step. But because businesses are dynamic in nature, even such enterprises might need to create newer services. In such cases, Service Creation would still remain as the first step in the process of implementing web services. Such enterprises might already have several service applications compatible with the workflow of the enterprise in a proprietary fashion. Enterprises moving toward implementing SOA, using web services as part of that strategy, will be interested in converting the existing service applications into web services-oriented applications.

Generating the Description for the Web Service

The next logical step is the generation of the WSDL document that presents the services defined in the service applications. Software tools and IDEs can generate the WSDL document for a given service or aggregate of services. Generating a web service description file using the contemporary programming languages using IDEs is a relatively easy option; however, generating the WSDL document for services on the legacy systems might not be as simple. Although there are software tools available on the market for generating WSDL documents for some of the popular legacy systems, hand coding of the WSDL document might not be ruled out for certain rare and unsupported services of the legacy systems.

After the WSDL document is generated, this file should be stored in a location that is accessible to the required client applications. Furthermore, the location of the WSDL document, in the form of a URL, needs to be published in a suitable service registry. The service provider might colocate the service application and the corresponding WSDL document in the same server. Although this is not mandatory, it is seen as the best practice. What is important in this situation is that the location of the WSDL document is accessible to the intended web service clients of the enterprise.

In a typical scenario, a client intending to use this web service gets a handle to this WSDL file from the service registry and proceeds to understand all the details of services and its semantics contained therein. The understanding of the WSDL document reveals three important information items to the client applications:

- Location of the web service
- Exposure of the web service (or services)
- Semantics of the web service invocation

Now that the document has been generated and understood, it is time to move to the next step.

Registering the Web Service

The next, although an optional,[6] step would be for the service provider to register with an electronic service registry. The provider might want to register in a public or a private registry, depending on the business requirements and preferences. As part of the registration, the provider needs to give detailed information about the business, including organization name, business address, telephone, fax, mobile numbers, types and nature of services, and so forth. As part of the service registration, the location information of the WSDL must also be provided because it needs to be published in this registry.

The provider should exercise caution when providing company details and the services in such registries. Irrelevant information might not attract clients, and nondisclosure of key information might not invoke interest among potential clients. Therefore, the provider needs to determine an optimal disclosure of the information, with an objective to attract prospective clients and further the business interests.

The process of new service registration is done only once for a given service (or services). However, because the business is dynamic in nature, changes in the products and services would obviously occur. It might be desirable to change and update the relevant service modifications in the registry. The provider should ensure that the information in the registry is up to date for the new and changed information regarding the business and services. Some of the changes in the services part directly affect the WSDL document in terms of its contents and the location. The clients must, therefore, pick up the new information from the service registry after the changes in the WSDL and its location are updated.

The registration of the new service (or services) and the updating of the existing services need to be done using the SOAP protocol. The provider might use standard web services applications/tools to carry out the process of registration.

Service Discovery

A client on the lookout for suitable services usually searches the service registry for services using suitable key words. The client might use a normal service registry browser or might use a standard application/tool designed to scan and grab the services information for appropriate business use. Scanning of the registry by applications/tools for services search can be done by initiating a SOAP request to the service registry. Although tools and standard search applications are available, you can use standardized programming languages for customized searches and drill-down searches. Standard APIs are available in many business-oriented programming languages that help with designing applications for customized search.

Presently, using an automated search to find the required service is still a distant task. Many of the searches and narrowing to the right service provider would essentially be manual exercises. Searching for services using a set of key words could result in the browsers/applications fetching multiple service providers that match the given key words. Further narrowing down to a suitable service provider would be done over a given period of time. After the requester decides on particular provider, both parties negotiate an agreement (termed a *Service Level Agreement* or *SLA*) on the terms and conditions of the use of the services. After both the parties forge an agreement toward the use of services, the provider will make available the WSDL document to the requester through a suitable means. One such means is to allow the client to use the WSDL document from the service registry.

After the client gets a handle to the WSDL file, suitable arrangements are made for creating/using web services applications that initiate using the services from the provider.

Invocation of Web Service

After the WSDL document is discovered, the client is ready to understand and invoke the web service. The WSDL document encodes all the required information about the services, such as location of the service, name of the web service, parameters required for service invocation, encoding type used, and so on. The requester and the provider next work on the agreement and strategies for the web service invocation. Two primary strategies for services invocation popularly used in the current scenario are:

- Using a low-level API to perform service invocation
- Generating the proxy locally to perform service invocation

Although both these strategies have advantages and disadvantages, using the generation of service proxy is considered an ideal strategy for services invocation. Notice here that the service proxy route is almost identical to that of the RPC route, in which stubs and skeletons are generated to help remote method invocation. Similar to RPC technology, application tools and IDEs can generate the proxy/stub for the client in the local system, and service invocation using this route is enabled simply and straightforwardly. Furthermore, if any changes in service definitions occur, the client needs to generate the proxy to be eligible for service invocation again.

Describing Web Services—The XML Way

The description of web services is accomplished through a set of seven XML elements. These elements are part of WSDL specifications governed by the XML Namespace convention as applied to WSDL specifications: `<types>`, `<messages>`, `<operations>`, `<portType>`,[7] `<binding>`, `<port>`,[8] and `<service>`. These elements are interrelated; therefore, their contents cannot be independently changed. Also, these elements are bound by a set of rules proposed by the WSDL specifications. The following section describes in detail each of the key elements and brings out the relationship between them.

WSDL Elements and Their Appearance Sequence

The `<definitions>` element is the root element of the WSDL document and hosts all seven elements that define one or more web services. One or more `<types>` elements appear at the top of the web services `<definition>` element. One or more `<message>` elements appear next. The next element in sequence is the `<portType>` element. Depending on the description of the web services, more than one `<portType>` element can appear one after the other. Notice that the `<portType>` element supports one or more `<operation>` elements. The next in the sequence is the `<binding>` element, and there can be one or more of them. Similarly, the `<portType>` element and the `<binding>` element support one or more `<operation>` elements. The `<service>` element appears at the end of the sequence. This element supports one or more `<port>` elements. These elements and their sequence are displayed in Figure 5.6.

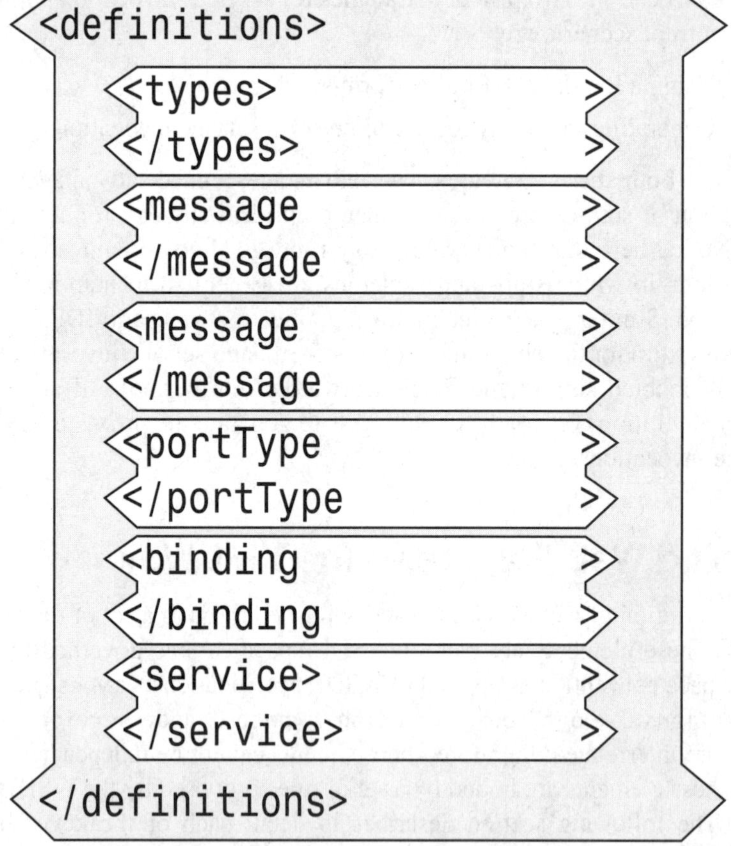

Figure 5.6 A sample WSDL document showing the top-level elements indicating the sequence of their appearance

Notice here that there are two occurrences of `<message>` elements, and `<port>` and `<operations>` elements do not occur here as top-level elements because they are obscured by `<binding>` and `<service>` elements. Although the sequence of the appearance of the seven elements is described here, note that the `<portType>` element is a crucial element around which the other three elements are spun into the realization of the definition of web services: `<operations>`, `<services>`, and `<binding>`. Two other elements, `<messages>` and `<types>`, take care of the parameter data types and the result data types. Finally, the `<port>` element provides the web services endpoint. Almost all the elements carry an attribute called `name`; the value of this attribute is different in different subelements. They identify different aspects of the web services and help in correlating different subelements of WSDL. Specific aspects of the `name` attribute are indicated in the respective elements discussed in the next section.

Anatomy of WSDL Document

Before we explore the details of the anatomy of the WDSL document, let's consider an example of a web service that reports the lowest hotel room rates for a given set of details. We call the web service *HotelServices* and the method name that fetches the best rate `getRates()`. The parameters passed to this web service would be data such as number of adults, room type, number of days, and so on, and the return value would be the best rate. Table 5.1 lists the type and nature of parameters used and the return value.

Table 5.1 Data Types Used in the Web Service HotelService

No.	Method Parameters	Description	Data Type
1	`noOfAdults`	Number of adults. Only two adults are allowed per room.	`int`
2	`noOfKids`	Number of children. One child per room. If there is more than one child, there is an option for additional room.	`int`
3	`noOfRooms`	Number of rooms required. If there are more than two adults and more than three kids, additional room requirement becomes necessary.	`int`
4	`startingDate`	Starting date.	`date`
5	`noOfDays`	Number of days of stay. For weekends and longer stays, special rates can be worked out.	`int`
6	`petsAllowed`	Some might require pets to be allowed inside the rooms, and some of the hotels might have a pet policy.	`boolean`
7	`rate`	Daily rate in USD.	`float`

The web services description for such a service would be available in the WSDL document. All the necessary information would be coded into the seven different types of WSDL elements. We will provide an anatomical description of each of these elements and show how the WSDL document can efficiently and effectively capture all the necessary description that is necessary for any web service.

The <types> Element

The details of a typical `<types>` element are shown in Figure 5.7. The element acts as a container for data type definitions using schema definitions such as XML Schema Definition. Schema definitions define the data type of the information using the `<message>` elements.

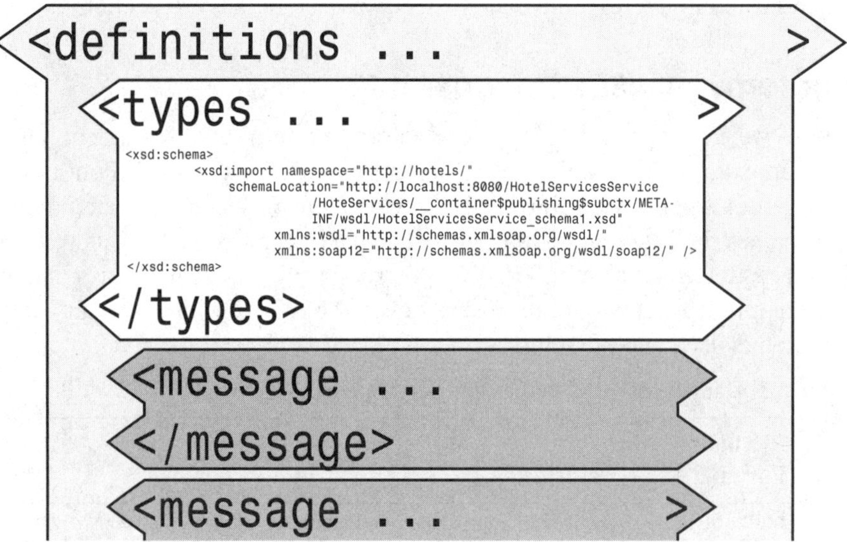

Figure 5.7 Details of `<types>` element

This element supports one or more `<schema>` elements as child elements. The `<schema>` elements define the data types that are used as part of web services. Using schema, both `<simpleType>` and `<complexType>` elements can be defined. Notice here that the schema is not inline, and the location of the file containing schema details is included as the content of the `<types>` element. The schema filename is `HotelServicesService_s-chema1.xsd`. The contents of this schema show several *derived* elements. For example, `noOfAdults`, `noOfKids`, and `noOfRooms` are of type `int`. The `petsAllowed` is of type `boolean`, and `startingDate` is of type `datetime`, and so on. The return data type is `float`. The contents of this file provide a full description of the data types used in web service. This is shown in Listing 5.1.

Listing 5.1 Data Types Encoded into the HotelServicesService_ schema1.xsd Schema File

```
<?xml version="1.0" encoding="UTF-8" standalone="yes" ?>
<xs:schema version="1.0" targetNamespace="http://hotels/"
xmlns:xs="http://www.w3.org/2001/XMLSchema">
   <xs:element name="getRates" type="ns1:getRates"
xmlns:ns1="http://hotels/" />
   <xs:complexType name="getRates">
      <xs:sequence>
    <xs:element name="noOfAdults" type="xs:int" />
    <xs:element name="noOfKids" type="xs:int" />
    <xs:element name="petsAllowed" type="xs:boolean" />
    <xs:element name="noOfRooms" type="xs:int" />
    <xs:element name="startingDate" type="xs:dateTime"
minOccurs="0" />
    <xs:element name="noOfDays" type="xs:int" />
      </xs:sequence>
    </xs:complexType>
    <xs:element name="getRatesResponse"
type="ns2:getRateResponse" xmlns:ns2="http://hotels/" />
    <xs:complexType name="getRatesResponse">
      <xs:sequence>
    <xs:element name="return" type="xs:float" />
      </xs:sequence>
    </xs:complexType>
</xs:schema>
```

The <message> Element

As shown in Figure 5.8, there are two `<message>` elements per web service description, which is an abstract, typed definition of the data being exchanged. This element references the data types defined within the `<types>` element. The message element contains a `<part>` element, and each `<message>` element contains an abstract element called `name`. The first occurrence of the message corresponds to the request, and the `name` attribute reflects it. In this case, it is `name = "getRates"`. The second occurrence reflects the response, and this is shown by the attribute value `name = "getRateResponse"`. As the attribute indicates, this corresponds to the web service response.

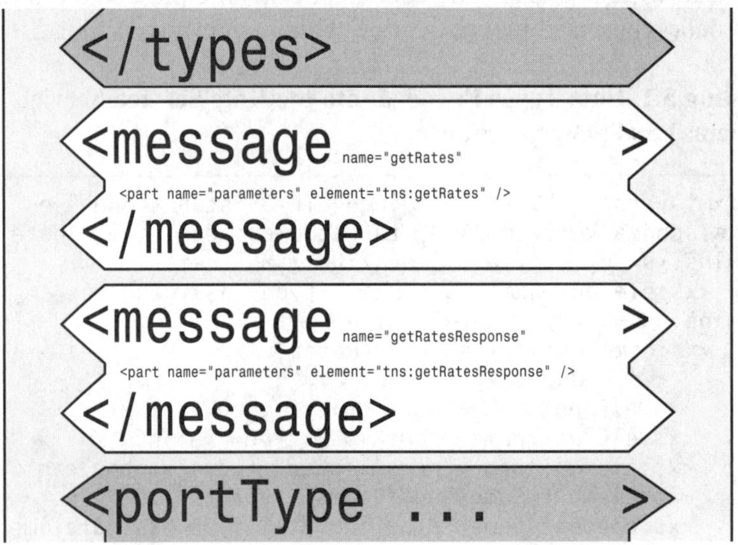

Figure 5.8 Message elements illustrated

The <portType> Element

The next in sequence is the <portType> element, found in Figure 5.9. Accordingly, this element describes one or more abstract set of operations supported by one or more endpoints. Because an <operation> element provides the definition of an abstract operation, more than one <operation> element appears inside the <portType> element depending on the number of web services offered by the service provider.

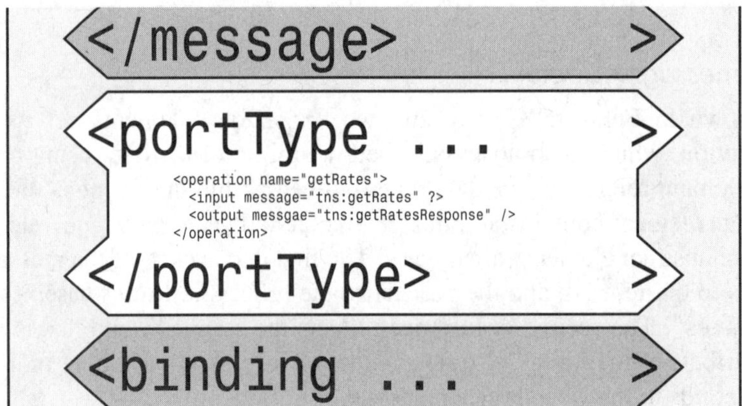

Figure 5.9 Details of <portType> element

The `name` attribute is an important constituent for both `<portType>` and `<operation>` elements, and note that they are different. The `name` attribute that appears inside the `<portType>` element corresponds to the web service name, and the `name` attribute that appears inside the `<operation>` elements corresponds to the method/function name that realizes a part or the whole of web service. Because one web service application might correspond to one or more operations, different values for the `name` attribute need to be used to distinguish between the operations within a `<portType>` element, and the value of this attribute should be unique. In our current example, there is only one operation, and it is identified by the `name` attribute as `name = "getRates"`.

Each `<operation>` element encodes `<input>` and `<output>` subelements. The `<input>` element is distinguished by its `name` attribute, and its value corresponds to the `name` attribute value of the `<message>` element that corresponds to the request part of the web service. Similarly, the `<output>` element is distinguished by its `name` attribute, and its value corresponds to the `name` attribute value of the `<message>` element that corresponds to the response part of the web service.

The <binding> Element

The `<binding>` element is next in the sequence. This element specifies a concrete protocol for transport binding and data format specification for a `<portType>` element. As exemplified in Figure 5.10, this element takes care of binding the web services to a suitable transport protocol.

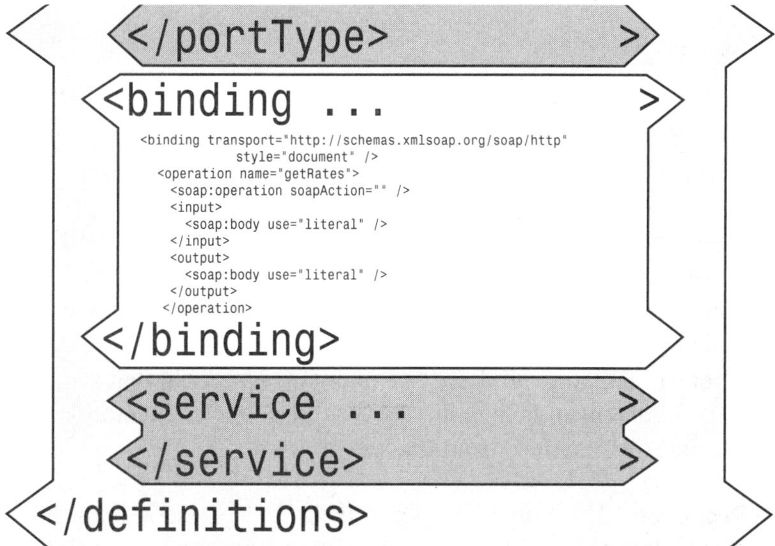

Figure 5.10 Details of the `<binding>` and `<operation>` elements

Depending on the type of the transport protocol chosen, the data format also varies accordingly. Although SOAP uses elements such as `<Header>` and `<Body>` inside `<Envelope>` to encode the information, HTTP supports header and body to encode the information. The binding element also defines input and output required for the action. In this case, the `<operation>` element corresponds to the action. An appropriate mapping on the `<operation>` element and its `<input>` and `<output>` in the `<binding>` element needs to be done. The transport protocol chosen is highlighted in Figure 5.10, and the transport is HTTP. Also notice that the binding element describes the `<input>` and `<output>` for the two services described.

The <operation> Element

As previously indicated, the `<operation>` elements are obscured by the `<binding>` element. This is also exemplified in Figure 5.10. Note that the `<operation>` and `<service>` elements are interrelated. The element `<operation>` is the abstract description of an action described by the `<service>` element. The `<operation>` element supports two standard elements, `<input>` and `<output>`. The `<input>` element corresponds to the action on the server-side application, and the `<output>` element corresponds to the action on the client-side application. Any `<operation>` element contains an `<input>` element and `<output>` elements for a given web service. The combination of these `<input>` and `<output>` elements within the `<operations>` element and the sequence of their appearance is based on the type of action or the type of the behavior. Four behavior types[9] can be identified under any business transaction circumstance:

- Request-Response
- Solicit Response
- One-Way
- Notification

Request-Response The Request-Response behavior corresponds to the synchronous mode of web services. The client requests and blocks the call until the response from the server is received. To indicate this behavior of web services exchange, both `<input>` and `<output>` elements are provided inside the `<operations>` element, and these two elements appear in that sequence. While the `<input>` element indicates the request from the client, the `<output>` element indicates the response from the server.

Solicit-Response The Solicit-Response behavior corresponds to the reverse of the Request-Response behavior. To indicate this, both the `<input>` and `<output>` elements appear, however, in the opposite order inside the `<operation>` element.

The server sends a Solicit and expects a Response from the client. Within the `<operation>` element, while the `<output>` element indicates the Solicit from the server, the `<input>` element indicates the Response from the client.

One-Way In this behavior, the client sends a request to the server but does not wait for a response. It never blocks the call to the server for a response. To indicate this behavior, the `<operation>` element carries only the `<input>` element. The `<input>` element indicates only the Request to the server application.

Notification The Notification behavior corresponds to the reverse of the One-Way behavior. The `<operation>` element therefore carries only the `<output>` element. The `<output>` element, therefore, indicates only the Response from the server to the clients. This behavior models the notification mechanism in a distributed environment.

The <service> Element

The last in the sequence is the `<service>` element. This element identifies the web service, as indicated by the value of the attribute name. Because a provider might host multiple web services, the `<service>` element models multiple services through a collection of `<port>` elements. Figure 5.11 shows the `<service>` element, hosting one `<port>` element indicating just one web service offered by the provider.

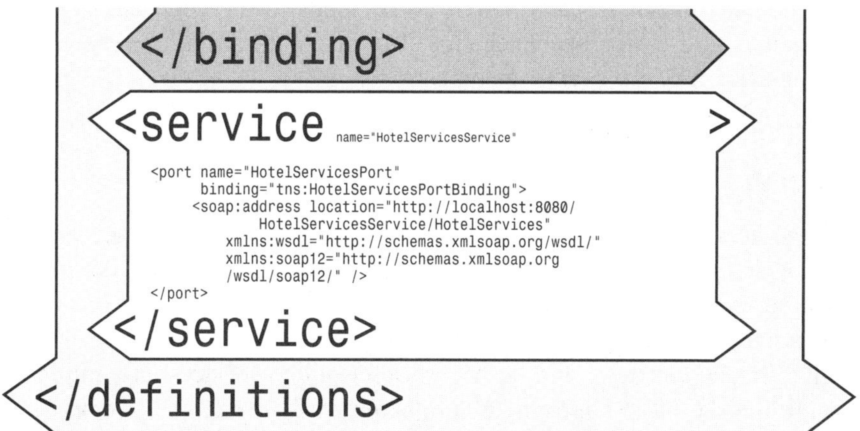

Figure 5.11 Details of `<service>` and `<port>` elements

The <port> Element

As shown in Figure 5.11, the element `<port>` indicates a single endpoint defined as a combination of a transport binding and a network address. In essence, the `<port>` is, therefore, the web service. The `<port>` element provides the name and the location of the system in which the web service is hosted. The `<port>` element models an individual web service. The location is the URL that includes the name of the web service application.

WSDL Version Differences and Dependencies

Most of the aspects of WSDL discussed in this document correspond to the WSDL 1.1 specification. The latest specification is WSDL 1.2, referred to as WSDL 2.0, as there are significant changes in the new specification. Some of the highlights of the new WSDL 2.0 specification are

- Additional semantics to the description language
- Replacing message constructs by XML Schema system in the `<types>` element
- Renaming of `<portType>` element to `<interfaces>` element
- Renaming of `<ports>` element to `<endpoint>` element

In line with the SOAP 1.2 specifications, the W3C has classified the new WSDL specifications into three parts. Part I corresponds to the core language, Part II corresponds to the Message Exchange Patterns, and Part III corresponds to the Binding aspects of the WSDL specifications.

Summary

Web services' definition is essentially a combination of two definitions: the abstract definition and the concrete definition. In the abstract definition, the WSDL document describes a web service implemented through the use of an appropriate combination of `<messages>`, `<operation>`, and `<interface>` elements. In the concrete web services description, services are implemented through the use of an appropriate combination of `<binding>`, `<service>`, and `<endpoint>` elements.

WSDL specifications provide an XML-based vocabulary for describing the web services. This description is effectuated with the help of seven elements. They are `<types>`, `<messages>`, `<operations>`, `<portType>` (or `<interface>` in the new specification), `<binding>`, `<port>` (or `<endpoint>` in the new specification), and `<service>`. These elements are inter-related, and not all of them appear as top-level elements in the WSDL document. Although the `<operation>` element appears within the <portType> element, the <port> element appears inside the <service> element. The <port> (or the <endpoint>) element carries all the information crucial to the web services—the name of the web service, the location of the web service, and the binding to the transport protocol. Because a WSDL file is said to expose the web services for the interested clients, any web service client application can read and understand the syntactic and semantic information of the web service by understanding the WSDL document. Seven steps can be identified to determine the different aspects of web services.

In the next chapter, we focus on the registries and UDDI aspects of web services. Registries are essentially service brokers who help in providing an online platform for the service providers and service requesters to *find* and *bind* each other for business transactions. UDDI is a specification designed to manage business and services-related information using the XML vocabulary.

Endnotes

1. The WSDL files use `.wsdl` as the file extension.
2. The new WSDL 2.0 specification describes web services as a combination of two definitions: abstract definition and concrete definition. More details regarding the new specifications are provided in the "WSDL Version Differences and Dependencies" section.
3. The skeleton or tie is the server-side communication infrastructure loaded on the server system. It constitutes several files of systems and libraries that handle file, network, and transport protocol, and so on. Of late, the skeleton part of the communication infrastructure is integrated with the application development and deployment environment, and no mention about the generation of skeleton or tie is made. Only stubs/proxies are generated, and they are made available to the client systems.
4. We have used the terminologies *client* and *service requester* (or requester) interchangeably in this chapter.
5. The term *proxy* used here is an important concept of the remote procedure call technology. A proxy is a client-side software library package that enables the client to get connected to remote service, without really worrying about details of the distributed nature of the remote application.
6. The provider and the requester can agree to eliminate the process and stage of the electronic registry altogether. The WSDL files reflecting the service can be transferred to the clients by a means that is mutually agreeable to both. For example, the location of the WSDL document could be sent to the client as an e-mail message.
7. In the new WSDL 2.0 specifications, the <portType> element has been replaced by the <interface> element.
8. In the new WSDL 2.0 specifications, the <port> element is replaced by the <endpoint> element.
9. In the latest WSDL specification, WSDL 2.0, the behaviors are termed Message Exchange Patterns. They are often referred to as MEPs. These four are essentially In-Out, Out-In, In-Only, and Out-Only. The behaviors discussed here as Request-Response, Solicit-Response, Notification, and One-Way respectively correspond to In-Out, Out-In, In-Only, and Out-Only behavior of the MEP. However, MEP provides additional and more robust behaviors of web services invocation models.

6

Registries and UDDI

Registries are the electronic databases that enable businesses to store and access business and services-related information in an Extensible Markup Language (XML) *format. Registries enable businesses to store this information as per popular taxonomies or industrial classification schema. These databases act as an electronic version of White, Yellow, or Green Pages. A Registry can be a public registry or a private registry. Although a public registry can be accessed by any individual or a company, private registries are accessible among a select few sections/groups of businesses.* Universal Description, Discovery and Integration *(*UDDI*) is a specification for such XML-based registries for businesses worldwide to list/find themselves on the World Wide Web. UDDI's goal is to promote online collaboration among the business in the world and streamline online transactions by enabling businesses to discover one another on the Internet and enable their systems interoperable for e-commerce.*

In the previous chapter, we provided an overview of the service broker (or broker). Recall, the service broker enables the service provider (or provider) and service requester (or requester) to interact in a common place, to identify each other for the purpose of furthering mutual business promotion in enterprise scenario. In the first place, the broker brings the provider and the requester on the same platform. Negotiation, discussions, and accessing of the services can take place as the next series of steps without the intervention of the broker.

The broker is now essentially an electronic registry service that enables publishing of the business-related information in an industry-desired format. The information published would be classified by each specific industry. Because this registry is an electronic service, both the provider and requester need to use an application to communicate with the registry. In fact, the registry application itself is a web service designed to cater to the needs of service providers and service requesters.

Prior to the computerization of the registry, the registries existed as *White Pages* and *Yellow Pages*—print books! Information on the business/service was printed in accordance with the popular industry classification schema in these books. These were published periodically and updated regularly for regular consumption for businesses, consumers, and other professionals. The printed version of the White Pages and Yellow Pages are popular even today and are actively used by the community.

UDDI is a specification that helps business and service providers in publishing online their business-related information and the service-related information in an XML format. UDDI specification also helps consumers to search and drill down for a specific business and service-related data. With UDDI in the picture, both the provider and requester would now be using software, IDE, or other tools to interact with the UDDI Registry services. The service provider uses tools to publish business/service-related information through a SOAP request. Similarly, the service requester would use tools to browse, drill down, and retrieve appropriate business/services-related information through a SOAP request.

Defining UDDI

UDDI is a set of specifications designed to publish/retrieve businesses and services-related information. Based on these specifications, organizations, businesses, and other enterprises can benefit from the services in a variety of ways, including publishing, modifying, updating, sharing, and using and exploiting key business and services information among appropriate business partners and collaborators. UDDI specifications essentially describe a way to store all the business and services-related information as XML data inside the Registry database. UDDI specifications also outline a set of XML Schema definitions that describe the data types to be used for representing business data. This format enables the businesses to query for services-related information using SOAP messages.

Taxonomy-Based Business Information

Recall that we discussed the publication of business/services-related data in White, Yellow, or Green Pages. Although White Pages can help in publishing and searching a very limited information band such as name, telephone, and contact address, Yellow Pages enable businesses to publish more detailed information on the business/service as per a popular industry classification schema. Yellow Pages also enable the consumers to search and narrow down to specific business/services based on such industry classification schema. Green Pages, on the other hand, enable companies to include technical data about the services, in addition to the White/Yellow Pages part of the business information for publication and retrieval.

Classification of business/services information is the key here. This classification helps in narrowing the search for getting across the required information quickly and easily. The science and technology of such classification is referred to as *taxonomy.*

Taxonomy or classification of business information has immensely benefited the business community. Several standard industry-based taxonomies are available that can help in categorizing the information. *North American Industry Classification System (NAICS)* and *Universal Standard Products and Code System (UNSPSC)* are some of the important standard taxonomies that are popularly used in the global business scenario.

UDDI Specifications and Services

Remember, UDDI is a set of specifications and services. The UDDI services are designed on the UDDI specifications. UDDI services help companies to publish and explore business opportunities, products, and services information. UDDI specifications help organizations to create applications that aid in storing, publishing, modifying, sharing, and exploring business information by the community and thus help companies' progress toward business automation.

The popularity of the UDDI as specifications and services has resulted in the creation of *UDDI Browser Registries (UBR).* The UBRs are large global, online public directories that offer services to businesses for storing the company information and the services-related data for public and global use. These UBRs are amenable to publishing business information, updating or modifying existing information, or searching for business information using a set of related key words. The UDDI specification is an industry-driven program. Major industry leaders such as Fujitsu, Ariba, IBM, Microsoft, Merrill Lynch, and so on are involved in establishing the UDDI specification.

Public Registries Versus Private Registries

The UDDI Registries can be public or private. The public registries are those that conform to the UDDI specifications set up by organizations such as IBM,

Microsoft, XMethods, and such. Private registries can be in full or partial conformance with the UDDI specifications. The private registries might be used within the intranet/extranet environment of a limited and closely collaborated businesses. A few have also set up test registries that enable professionals to gain valuable experience in working with such registries.

UDDI Nomenclature

The UDDI specifications use rich terminologies in defining the business and services-related information. You need to become familiar with some specific terminologies before exploring further, such as *Node API Sets*, *UDDI Node*, *UDDI Registry*, *Data Structure*, and *Information Model*.

Node API Sets

Node API sets are used for the implementation of inter-UDDI communication. The purpose of the Node API sets is to manipulate the data stored in different UDDI implementations. The Node API sets are available for implementing the most commonly called tasks such as Inquiry, Publication, Subscription, Security, and so forth.

UDDI Node

A UDDI Node is a system that hosts an application to support at least one of the Node API Sets. A UDDI Node is expected to

- Interact with the UDDI data using Node API Sets
- Access and manipulate data in the Registry database
- Possess membership with exactly one registry

UDDI Registries

A set of UDDI Nodes combine to form a UDDI Registry. The UDDI Nodes combining the UDDI Registry are designed to collectively manage the business data in the Registry database. Client systems are connected to the UDDI Registry to enable publication (*Add*, *Edit,* or *Update*) of business information in the registries. Clients also connect to the Registry to discover business/services-related information. The client could be doing a shallow search or drill-down search to find and gather business/service-related information. In Figure 6.1, we show a simplistic architectural representation of a UDDI Registry.

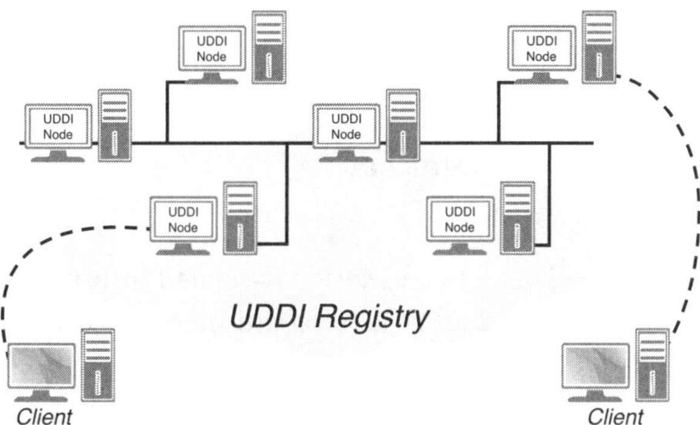

Figure 6.1 UDDI Registries and associated UDDI Nodes

Data Structure

The data structure forms one of the key parts of the UDDI specifications. Recall, the UDDI data structure is the XML representation of the persistent business data within the UDDI Nodes. The UDDI specification represents business and services-related data in six different types of data structures, known as entities. They are `<businessesEntity>` data structure representing Business Organization, `<businessService>` data structure representing Business Services, `<bindingTemplate>` data structure representing Binding Templates, `<tModel>` data structure representing Technical Model of the services description, `<publisherAssertion>` data structure representing Relationship, and `<subscription>` data structure. Together, these entities represent the core UDDI information model.

Information Model

The information model is another key component of the UDDI Registries and consists of the instances of persistent data structures (or entities). The UDDI specification defines an abstraction and representation of these entities, their properties, their attributes, and their inter-relation. The information model, in essence, represents business data, and the behavior of API sets that query and manages the data and transport.

Core UDDI

The six data structures, or entities, introduced earlier make up the largest portion of the information model:

- The <businessEntity> data structure
- The <businessService> data structure
- The <bindingTemplate> data structure
- The <tModel> data structure
- The <publisherAssertion> data structure
- The <subscription> data structure

These data structures make up the business and services-related information in a specific way. At the basic level, these data structures are merely the XML elements associated with UDDI-related namespaces. In the following subsections, we discuss the details of some of the important data structures.

The <businessEntity> Data Structure

This structure represents the top-level UDDI element in the UDDI Registry. This data structure captures the top-level business information of the organization. Information associated with this data structure includes the organization name, contact information, categorization information, identifiers, descriptions, and business relations. Any remaining data related to the rest of the business and service-related information is captured with the help of other data structures and forms a part of the business entity data structure.

This data structure defines an important attribute called businessKey. This unique key is provided either by the business at the time of initial registration or is generated by the Registry at the first time of publication of the service. Any information retrieval regarding the business or services from the UDDI Registry will contain this businessKey information. The graphical representation of the Business Entity data structure is shown in Figure 6.2.

UDDI specifications provide several XML elements that help capture a variety of business-related information. Nomenclatures used in naming these XML elements are intuitive about their contents and values. Some of the important elements that form a part of businessKey data structure are <name>, <description>, <contacts>, <businessServices>, <categoryBag>, and <identifierBag>. The <identifierBag> structure contains a list of identifiers, each valid in its own identification system. Likewise, the <categoryBag> structure contains the list of business categories that describe specific business aspects. Note that two elements, the <identifierBag> and the <categoryBag> data structures, also appear inside other data structures such as <businessService>, <businessTemplate>, and <tModel>.

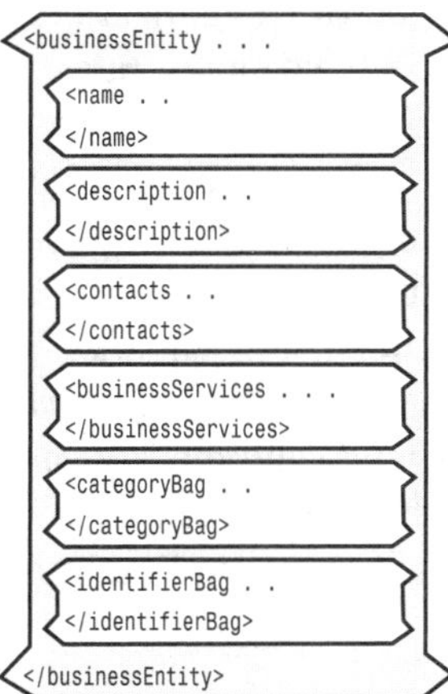

Figure 6.2 Details of the `<businessEntity>` data structure

The `<businessService>` Data Structure

This data structure helps in defining and describing one or more services-related information in the Registry. This data structure also provides a means to logically group a number of services describing a business process. An organization might be offering one or more sets of such services, and they should be represented using `<businessService>` data structures as a part of the `<businessEntity>` data structure. The structure of this element is shown in Figure 6.3.

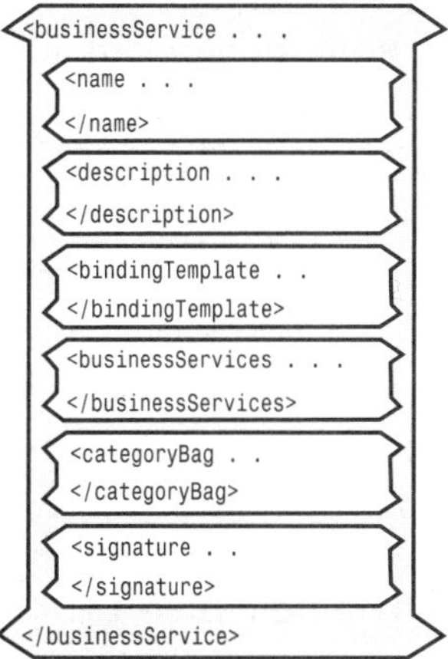

Figure 6.3 Details of the `<businessService>` data structure

The <businessService> data structure contains details such as name of the business service, description of services, classification or categorization, and so on. The <businessService> data structure defines two attributes: businessKey and serviceKey. The value of the businessKey attribute that appears in this element might be identical to or different from the value of businessKey defined in the <businessEntity> data structure. If the values of the businessKey attribute for the <businessEntity> data structure and that of <businessService> data structure are dissimilar, the service is being outsourced from another business organization or another service provider. This situation is termed *service projection*. The serviceKey attribute represents the service, and this key should be unique. The provider either provides the value for this key at the time of service publication, or the system will generate a unique serviceKey. The retrieval of service information returns the serviceKey.

The <bindingTemplate> Data Structure

This data structure represents the web service offered by the business organization. This data structure holds the list of services-related technical information needed by the applications to bind and invoke the web service. The <bindingTemplate> data structure defines two important elements: <accessPoint> and <tModelInstanceDetails>. Figure 6.4 shows the graphical representation of the <bindingTemplate> data structure. The <accessPoint> element represents a string that corresponds to an appropriate network address for invocation of the web service in question. The value could be a URL, e-mail address, or any other textual information. The <accessPoint> element supports an optional attribute called useType. There are four predefined useType attribute values: endpoint, bindingTemplate, hostingRedirector, and wsdlDocument. The attribute value wsdlDocument indicates that the accessPoint point to the WSDL document contains binding and service invocation information, including that of the actual service endpoint. Thus, the wsdlDocument attribute is important for the understanding of web services.

The <tModelInstanceDetails> and <tModelInstanceInfo> elements are important elements of the <bindingTemplate> data structure. Of the two, <tModelInstanceDetails> is the mandatory element. The <tModelInstanceInfo> element defines an attribute called tModelKey. This attribute is a mandatory attribute, and the value of this attribute represents a specification with which the web service is represented by the containing bindingTemplate compilation.

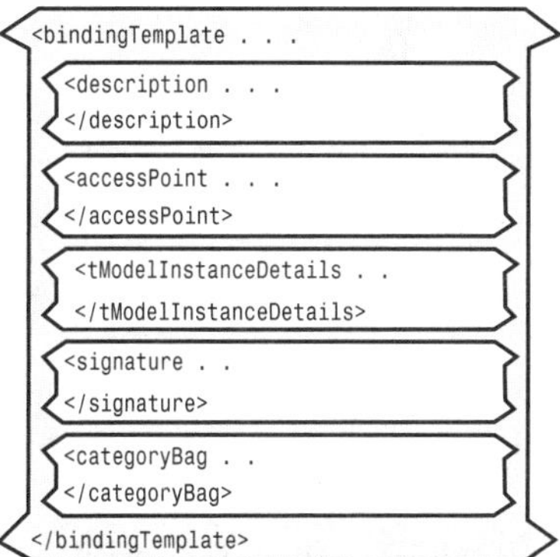
<bindingTemplate . . .
<description . . .
</description>
<accessPoint . . .
</accessPoint>
<tModelInstanceDetails . .
</tModelInstanceDetails>
<signature . .
</signature>
<categoryBag . .
</categoryBag>
</bindingTemplate>

Figure 6.4 Details of the `<bindingTemplate>` data structure

The `<tModel>` Data Structure

The `<tModel>` data structure is unique among all the other data structures we have presented. They represent the abstract description of a particular specification or behavior to which the web services adhere. The `<tModel>` (`tModel` stands for Technical Model) data structure is designed, keeping in mind, the requirement for both human-to-application interaction and application-to-application interaction, to represent the technical model information on services.

The `<tModel>` data structure consists of several XML elements, including `<name>`, `<description>`, and `<overviewDoc>`. The `<tModel>`data structure defines an attribute called `tModelKey`, which is an optional attribute. If present, a `tModelKey` uniquely identifies a `<tModel>` or the Technical Model. A `<tModel>` might be called the digital fingerprint for determining the specifics of interactions with web services. The UDDI information model previously described is presented graphically in Figure 6.5. This information model shows appropriate relationships among the various data structures described earlier and their relationships.

Two significant data structure relationships in the UDDI information model are *containment relation* and *reference relation*. The containment relationships are revealed in the `<businessEntity>`, `<businessService>`, and `<bindingTemplate>` set of data structures, whereas the reference relationships are revealed in the `<tModel>` data structures.

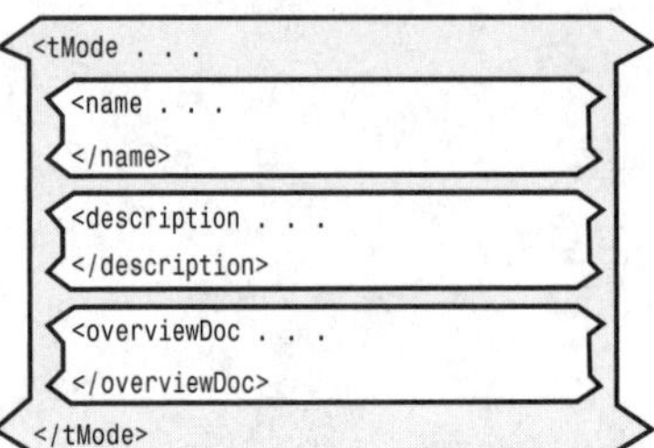

Figure 6.5 Details of the `<tModel>` data structure

The UDDI information model has been consciously designed with intent to reuse the `<tModel>` data structures. This is evident from the fact that the `instanceDetails` have pointers to the Industry consortium such as Rosetta Net, BASDA, and so on. Likewise, the `keyedReference` in the `identifierBag` or `categoryBag` also have pointers to Taxonomy Standards such as UNSPSC or DUNS numbers, and so on. These represent the `<tModels>`.

Publication of Business Information

With respect to UDDI specifications, there are several activities involved in service publication. They are creating, publishing, updating, and removing information related to a company, business, and services on the UDDI Business Registry.

The task of service publication is not a generic activity but is considered a secure and administration-oriented task. Normal users are unauthorized to carry out activities such as creation, publication, sharing, updating, and so on of business information. Specific individuals identified as administrators are granted access to such activities, through an appropriate authentication and authorization mechanism.

The task of service publication is completed using service-publishing tools. These tools are essentially web services-oriented applications that correspond with the registries using the SOAP message. This is imperative because registry services of UDDI are web services. Service-publishing applications can be created using appropriate UDDI APIs in popular languages that help generate applications that provide customized support to the UDDI Registry publication activities.

Creation and Modification of Business Information

Publication of business/service-related information in public registries is a serious business proposition. Any information published in such registries is revealed to anyone who is browsing/searching for information. It involves strategic decisions at the top level from the company management on what information and services are to be published. The disclosure on business and services should be optimum and should avoid any business-critical and confidential information. Publisher interfaces are used for creating, modifying, and deleting of business information in the UDDI Registry. As previously indicated, the publishing activities are authenticated operations. Four different kinds of *save operations* carry out/create/update each of the four important data structures in the UBRs:

- **Save business**—Represented by `<save_business>` element
- **Save service**—Represented by `<save_service>` element
- **Save binding**—Represented by `<save_binding>` element
- **Save tmodel**—Represented by `<save_tmodel>` element

Saving Business Information

This operation is carried out using the `<save_business>` element in the SOAP request. This operation saves business information within the `<businessEntity>` data structure within the UBR. A saving operation could be used either for the creation of the new business information for the first time or modifying (or updating) the existing business information. This is a top-level operation that does an information insertion or modification. This operation could affect a few or all the top-level data structures: `<businessEntity>`, `<businessService>`, `<bindingTemplate>`, and `<tModel>`.

When new business information is inserted into the UBR, the Registry generates a unique identification number. This number is referred to as the UUID. This is a very important number that uniquely identifies a specific registered business organization. UUID stands for Universal Unique Identifier. These unique numbers are essentially hexadecimal strings, and an algorithm defined by the ISO generates this unique number. The algorithm uses some specific entities such as time, hardware address, random number, and so on to generate the UUID number.

Saving Service Information

This operation is carried out using the `<save_service>` element in the SOAP message. This operation saves service information within the `<businessService>`

data structure part of the data in the UBR. A saving operation inserts a new service data or modifies the existing data inside the `<businessService>` data structures. This operation could also optionally affect the `<bindingTemplate>` and the `<tModel>` data structures.

Saving Binding Information

This operation is carried out using the `<save_binding>` element in the SOAP message. This operation results in the insertion of new binding information or modification of the information provided in the `<bindingTemplate>` data structure. This operation also optionally affects the contents of the `<tModel>` data structure.

Saving Technical Model Information

This operation is carried out using the `<save_tModel>` element in the SOAP message and results in the insertion or updating of the `<tModel>` data structure information. Because this is specific to the `<tModel>` data structure, other data structures are not affected during execution of this operation.

Deletion of Business Information

Service deletion operations on the UBRs might also have serious business implications. Decisions for deletion of the whole or part of services need to be addressed at the management level; therefore, this is essentially an authenticated operation. Deletion of business information can take place for four different data structures: delete business, delete service, delete binding, and delete technical model. There are four elements that take care of the deletion processing:

- Delete business (represented by `<delete_business>` element)
- Delete service (represented by `<delete_service>` element)
- Delete binding (represented by `<delete_binding>` element)
- Delete tModel (represented by `<delete_tmodel>` element)

Deleting Business Information

This operation is carried out using the `<delete_business>` element in the SOAP message. This operation results in the deletion of existing registered business information. This top-level deletion operation requires the UUID number of the organization. Delete business or any other operation that is involved in the process of deletion of information is an authentication operation. Deleting business information results in the deletion of all the related data structures: `<businessEntity>`, `<businessService>`, `<bindingTemplate>`, and `<tModel>`.

Deleting Service Information

This operation is carried out using the <delete_service> element in the SOAP message. This operation results in the deletion of existing registered service information. Again, this operation requires a valid UUID for deleting the business services data stored inside the <businessService> data structure. Deletion of the business service information results in removal of all the related binding template and technical model data structures.

Deleting Binding Information

This operation is carried out using the <delete_binding> element in the SOAP message. This operation results in the deletion of the information provided in the <bindingTemplate> data structure and could also affect the contents of the <tModel> data structure.

Deleting Technical Model Information

This operation is carried out using the <delete_tModel> element in the SOAP message and results in the insertion or updating of the <tModel> data structure information. Because this is specific to the <tModel> data structure, other data structures are not affected during the execution of this operation.

Discovering Web Services

After the business and services data is published in the UBR, this data is amenable for searching and browsing by the interested business community. Discovery of the services registry can enable clients to find out the details of a variety of information: the company, services, and other related information.

For the purpose of searching, the UBR provides an interface called the inquiry interface. The process of browsing or searching is a nondetrimental one, and potentially anyone has an access to the Registry browser application and can browse to discover suitable business information, including web services. Therefore, this is a nonauthenticated process, meaning any individual connected to the UBR can use the inquiry interface to obtain the details of the business and service information.

Browsing or searching a UBR can be carried out at two different levels: a shallow browse and a narrow drill-down search. Service-searching or services-querying applications help in the process of service discovery in the UBRs. These applications essentially use SOAP queries to communicate with the registries using SOAP. These queries include keywords used to look for suitable businesses and services. Again, using SOAP for quizzing and searching operations is imperative because Registry services of UDDI themselves are web services. Although standard browsers and IDEs provide tools that help in standardized browsing operations, custom browsing applications can be cultivated that use appropriate APIs to generate appropriate SOAP queries based on UDDI specifications. Discovering business information and web services information might need to be done at both the shallow browsing and narrow drill-down search levels.

Information Browsing and Retrieval

When we use terminology such as Finding/Searching/Browsing, we essentially indicate a shallow search of the UBR for top-level business/service data. Such superficial browsing can be carried out at four different levels of business data structures. They are Find Business, Find Service, Find Binding, and Find Technical Model. To carry out the browsing operations, we have four elements to browse at different levels of data structures:

- **Find Business**—Represented by `<find_business>` element
- **Find Service**—Represented by `<find_service>` element
- **Find Binding**—Represented by `<find_binding>` element
- **Find tModel**—Represented by `<find_tmodel>` element

Finding Business Information

This is a generic query operation carried out using the `<find_business>` element in the SOAP message. This operation results in fetching of one or more businesses in the UBR registered with business information. To narrow down to a required business partner, querying of the UBR can be done a multiple number of times before short-listing a few for an in-depth search.

Finding Binding Information

This operation is similar to the Find Business operation. Find Binding, once again, is a general query operation on the UBR, but with a more focused search on binding information. This operation is carried out using the `<find_binding>` element in the SOAP message to locate bindings within or across one or more registered Business Services.

Finding Service Information

Find Service is a general-purpose service query operation carried out using the `<find_service>` element in the SOAP message to locate specific services within the UBRs.

Finding Technical Model Information

This is a generic query operation on the technical model information on web services carried out using the <find_binding> element in the SOAP message to locate one or more <tModel> information structures.

Information Drill-Down

Drill-down/deep down searching refers to an in-depth search of the UBR for a detailed business/service data. A Drill-Down operation on a UBR can be conducted at four levels: Get Business Detail, Get Service Detail, Get Binding Detail, and Get Technical Model Detail. To carry out the deep dive operations, we have four elements that can take care of the drill down at different levels of data structures:

- **Get Business**—Represented by <get_BusinessDetail> element
- **Get Service**—Represented by <get_ServiceDetail> element
- **Get Binding**—Represented by <get_BindingDetail> element, and
- **Get tModel**—Represented by <get_tModelDetail> element

Drill-Down on Business Information

This operation retrieves the details of specific business information based on the UUID number and is carried out using the <get_BusinessDetail> element in the SOAP message.

Drill-Down on Service Information

This operation retrieves the detailed service information of a chosen organization. The UUID number is necessary for obtaining the details of specific information. This operation is carried out using the <get_ServiceDetail> element in the SOAP message.

Drill-Down on Binding Information

This operation retrieves the details of the binding information on services. This query requires the UUID number to retrieve the details of the binding information and is carried out using the <get_BindingDetail> element in the SOAP message.

Drill-Down on Technical Model Information

This operation retrieves the details of the technical model information on the services. This query requires the UUID number to retrieve the details of the technical model of the services. This operation is carried out using the <get_tModelDetail> element in the SOAP message.

Summary

Registries are the service brokers that help bring together the service providers and service requesters on a common platform. They also help them discover each other and thereby promote an engaging business association/partnership between them. UDDI is a specification, and the Registry service was created to help businesses imitate the service discovery and service invocation activities of the web services. UDDI Registries support two important tasks: service publication (create/update/remove) and service discovery. Although anyone can browse or drill down for specific information, only registered business administrators can create/update/delete information in the registries. Public and private UDDI Registries are available to business organizations and groups. Although public registries are designed as per the UDDI specifications, private registries can deviate from the specifications to suit the needs of a specific set of close business partners/collaborators.

In the next chapter, we cover the workflow/business process aspects of enterprise application and discuss in detail the related standardized XML vocabularies: Business Process Execution Language (BPEL) and Choreography Definition Language (CDL). We'll also highlight the importance and significance of these standards in managing the workflow in any enterprise.

7

Orchestration and Choreography

The pulse of any large enterprise is business process or work flow. As the enterprises grow and diversify, dependencies on the business process and work flow increase exponentially. Automating the business processes provides tremendous advantages to the enterprises; the need for such automation reflects the maturity of the enterprise and its capability to scale up and grow to the needs of the dynamic nature of business. In some instances, organizations automate the work flow to comply with business process standards. Emerging standards include WS-Business Process Execution Language *(*WS-BPEL*) for the process orchestration in the intranet scenarios and* WS-Choreography Definition Language *(*WS-CDL*), used in the collaborative scenarios over the Internet. This provides tremendous opportunity for these enterprises in implementation of SOA.*

Any large enterprise is composed of several divisions, departments, business units, and so on that interact with each other to complete various sets of activities (more commonly known as *business process* or *work flow*). Before the advent of web services, large enterprises' effort for application integration using middleware products helped a host of legacy applications interact with other applications to complete the sets of activities crucial to the enterprise. Applications (services) are invoked and communicate and interchange data with other services in a predefined manner.

The problem faced by most of the enterprises regarding the work flow of business process is that the processes are made up of multitudes of (typically coordinated) activities. These could occur in different divisions/departments. Moreover, these activities could be taking place on different computer systems and using a combination of synchronous and asynchronous processes. Furthermore, some of these activities could be chained, resulting in a chain of several processes in some specific order. Although some processes run sequentially, some other processes can run in parallel. Therefore, it is critical for the enterprises to successfully manage the coordinated activities in the order required to ultimately meet the enterprise business goals.

Importance of Business Process and Work Flow

A business process, as applied to the enterprises, might be defined as a recipe for achieving a specific commercial result. An enterprise has multiple business processes, and each business process has the following components: *inputs*, a *function* that acts on these inputs, and the resultant *outputs*. The inputs are prerequisites for the business process that must be in place before the function can be invoked on the inputs. When the function is applied to the inputs, certain outputs are generated as part of the business process.

As presented in Figure 7.1, a business process can be composed of several steps, and each step can be composed of an activity (or multiple activities). Any business process is bound by a definite life cycle, as are the activities. An activity can be one simple transaction or can be a combination of multiple transactions. Furthermore, the activities can be synchronous or asynchronous in nature. A simple business process can consist of a simple activity such as a withdrawal of cash from an ATM, and it can last for a few seconds to about one minute. Complex business process can consist of several simple (or complex) activities, carried over several steps, and can last for a long time. An example is a courier tracking service, which might be initiated when the shipment of a package begins from the production unit and can take several days to complete.

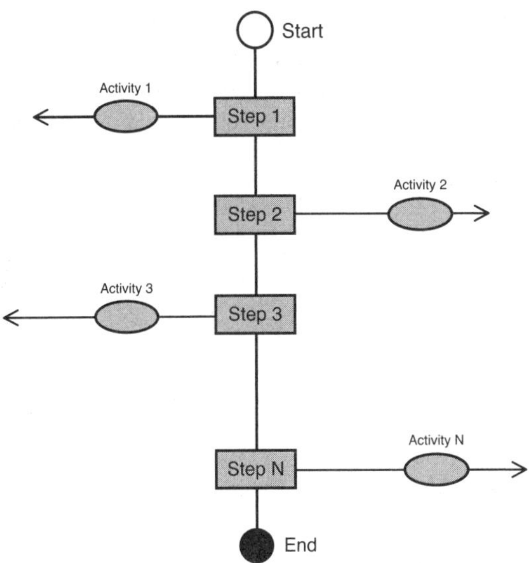

Figure 7.1 Schema of a typical business process or work flow

Orchestration

Orchestration is commonly used to indicate the business process or work flow of the enterprises. Orchestration is essentially a generic term, and it is not associated with any technology per se. Any technology or tools can be used to achieve the orchestration in the business process. Although the orchestration can be implemented by any technology, it is important that this technology helps in service orientation as well. Furthermore, this technology needs to be web services-oriented. *Business Process Execution Language* (*BPEL*) is one such second generation web services technology that helps in the implementation of work flow in the enterprise.

The technology for orchestration has contributions from two different schools: *Web Services Flow Language* (*WSFL*) from IBM and XLANG from Microsoft. BPEL is essentially a combination of these two orchestration languages. The early version was called *Business Process Execution Language for Web Services* (or *BPEL4WS*). The current specification is now known as WS-BPEL 2.0.

WS-Business Process Execution Language

Any business process can be broken down into several steps. Each step can be further broken down into a series of business activities. WS-BPEL specification provides an elegant means to express these activities with the help of a set of predefined XML elements. A logical construction using these elements results in a course-grained programming of a work flow that forms a part of the enterprise business process. There are a number of elements defined by BPEL to achieve this goal. These elements can be classified into four main categories: *declarations elements*, *basic elements*, *structured elements*, and *management elements*.

The Declarations Elements

These help in the declaration of process, variable, or partner-related information. For instance, the `<process>` element helps in the declaration of a business process. The `<process>` forms the root element in the business process definition document. The `<partnerLink>` element helps in declaration of the service collaboration that includes the role and target operations. This is the WSDL port type. The `<variable>` element, on the other hand, helps in the declaration of the data used for the particular business process in question.

The Basic Activity Elements

The basic elements of the BPEL language help in defining the basic aspects of the business process. These elements are also termed primitive activity elements. The elements belonging to this category can be further classified into two subcategories:[1] *process-related* and *service-related*. The elements belonging to the process-related category take care of the processing activities: namely, generation of the fault or suspending of a particular activity. The elements belonging to the service-related categories are involved in activities such as invoking a web service, sending a reply to the partner, and so on.

Process Related Some of the elements belonging to this category are `<assign>`, `<throw>`, `<wait>`, `<empty>`, and so on. The `<assign>` element, as the name indicates, helps in assigning the values to the variables. The `<throw>` element helps in generating a fault, when there is one, during the process execution. The `<wait>` element helps in suspending a particular operation for a specific period. The `<empty>` element, as the name indicates, does not have a role in the process.

Service Related Some of the elements belonging to this category are <invoke>, <reply>, and <receive>. The <invoke> element assists in the invocation of a partner web service. This invocation can be synchronous or asynchronous in nature. The <reply> element helps in replying to the partner's service request. The <receive> element, on the other hand, blocks a call and waits for the message from the partner.

The Structured Activity Elements

These elements help in the execution of programmed activities for the required business process. The programmed activities are essentially logical constructs sequencing and linking various activities that lead to a stateful business process. Some of the important elements that belong to this category are <while>, <switch>, <pick>, <flow>, <sequence>, and <eventHandlers>. Figure 7.2 exemplifies a few of the business and structured activities defined in the WS-BPEL specifications.

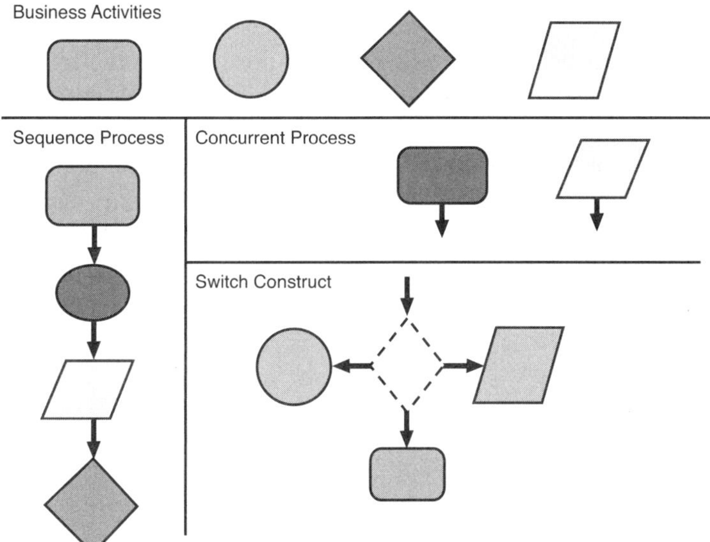

Figure 7.2 A few of the business and structural activities defined in WS-BPEL specifications

The <while> element, as the while construct of any programming language, enables the construction of a process instruction that requires looping activity. This is essentially similar to the "repeat while true" construct of the Java programming language. The <switch> element, as with Java, enables constructing a process instruction that requires a "switch based on case" kind of processing.

The `<sequence>` element executes a series of activities in a specific order. The business activities grouped under this structured activity need to execute the activities sequentially. It is also important that the previous activity is completed before the next activity is initiated. The `<pick>` element provides the ability to select one of several alternative paths. The `<flow>` element enables constructing the process execution in a concurrent manner. The business activities grouped with this structured activity do not need to wait for any sequence of activity to be completed before it initiates. The `<eventHandlers>` element helps in handling the events associated with the process. WS-BPEL provides an excellent programming-for-the-process environment to model the business process. After the basic activities are identified, the structural activities can be chosen to weave the process flow.

The Management Activities Elements

Some of the elements belonging to this category are `<compensate>`, `<correlate>`, `<faultHandlers>`, `<scope>`, and `<terminate>`. These elements help in managing the processes in a required manner. The use of the `<compensate>` element helps in implementing a compensating logic to reverse the previously completed business activity. Similarly, the use of `<correlate>` elements associate (or correlate) messages with specific process instances. The `<faultHandlers>` element provides exception handling capability for specific conditions. This is similar to the *try catch* of the Java programming language. The `<scope>` element defines the scope or bounds for the variables, fault handlers, compensation, and correlation elements. The `<terminate>` element, as the name indicates, helps in immediately ending a specific process.

Processing BPEL

As described earlier, the WS-BPEL specification provides an elegant algorithmic means to define a business process using XML elements. Unlike any other XML vocabulary, WS-BPEL provides a programmatic environment that relies on core web services vocabularies such as SOAP, UDDI, and WSDL. However, the specification does not support UML-like graphical support to express all the business process activities. Although this could be fairly exploited by a vendor, an integrated development environment, such as NetBeans,[2] provides intuitive graphical elements to design the business process visually. After the business process is described visually, the IDE generates the BPEL file, based on the process requirement. A typical IDE-generated BPEL process is shown in Figure 7.3.

The resulting BPEL file would be similar to the one shown in Listing 7.1. Notice here that the basic elements, structured elements, and management elements are interspread, providing an elegant process definition for the business process.

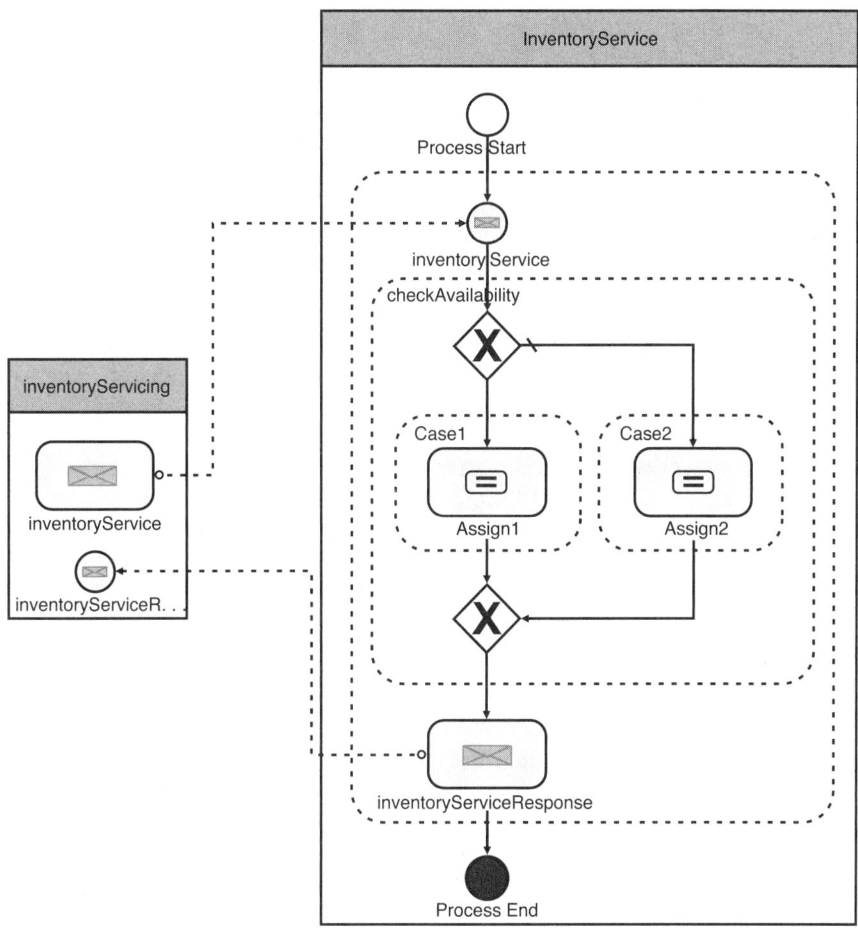

Figure 7.3 A typical business process definition implementation strategy using an IDE

Listing 7.1 Typical BPEL File Showing the Use of Different Process Elements

```
<process name="InventoryService"
         targetNamespace="http://manufacturing.org/wsdl/inventory/
bp2"
       xmlns:bpws="http://schemas.xmlsoap.org/ws/2004/03/business-
process/"
         xmlns="http://schemas.xmlsoap.org/ws/2004/03/business-
process/"
         xmlns:invs="http://manufacturing.org/wsdl/inventory/bp2">
```

```
   <import namespace="http://manufacturing.org/wsdl/inventory/
bp2" location="InventoryService.wsdl" importType=http://
schemas.xmlsoap.org/wsdl/">
   </import>
   <partnerLinks>
       <partnerLink name="inventoryServicing"
               partnerLinkType="invs:inventoryRequestingLT"
                  myRole="inventoryService"
                  partnerRole="inventoryServiceRequester"/>
   </partnerLinks>
   <variables>
       <variable name="inventoryServiceVar"
               messageType="invs:POMessage"></variable>
       <variable name="inventoryServiceResponseVar"
            messageType="invs:InventoryMessage"></variable>
   </variables>
   <sequence>
       <receive name="inventoryService"
              partnerLink="inventoryServicing"
              portType="invs:inventoryPortType"
              operation="inventoryService"
              variable="inventoryServiceVar"
              createInstance="yes"/>
       <if name="checkAvailability">
           <condition>starts-
with($inventoryServiceVar.purchaseOrder/orderDescription,
'OrderVal')</condition>
              <sequence name="Case1">
                  <assign name="Assign1">
                      <copy>
                   <from>$inventoryServiceVar.purchaseOrder/
orderId</from><to>$inventoryServiceResponseVar.inventoryPart/
orderId</to>
                      </copy>
                      <copy>
                         <from>true()</
from><to>$inventoryServiceResponseVar.inventoryPart/
inventoryStatus</to>
                      </copy>
                      <copy>
                         <from>'available'</
from><to>$inventoryServiceResponseVar.inventoryPart/
inventoryStatusMessage</to>
                      </copy>
                  </assign>
              </sequence>
           <else>
              <sequence name="Case2">
                  <assign name="Assign2">
```

```
                              <copy>
                           <from>$inventoryServiceVar.purchaseOrder/
orderId</from><to>$inventoryServiceResponseVar.inventoryPart/
orderId</to>
                              </copy>
                              <copy>
                                 <from>false()</
from><to>$inventoryServiceResponseVar.inventoryPart/
inventoryStatus</to>
                              </copy>
                              <copy>
                                 <from>'currently out of stock'</
from><to>$inventoryServiceResponseVar.inventoryPart/
inventoryStatusMessage</to>
                              </copy>
                           </assign>
                        </sequence>
                     </else>
                  </if>
                  <invoke name="inventoryServiceResponse"
                        partnerLink="inventoryServicing"
                      portType="invs:inventoryServiceCallbackPortType"
                        operation="inventoryServiceResponse"
                        inputVariable="inventoryServiceResponseVar"/>
      </sequence>
</process>
```

After this document is generated, it should be deployed in a BPEL execution environment. A BPEL execution environment contains a web services framework and a BPEL server for executing the process instances. The BPEL execution environment provides all the necessary life-cycle requirements, such as instantiation, correlation, transaction management, and so on as per the WS-BPEL specifications. Typically a BPEL execution environment works in combination with a web services environment such as Java Platform, Enterprise Edition and/or .NET environment. The BPEL execution environment is also accompanied by a process database and BPEL management console.

Choreography

Recall, we previously indicated that the interactions leading to information exchange between different applications leading to the business process or work flow occur between the different departments/divisions/practice units of the organization. With the Internet, extranet, and World Wide Web influencing the way business is being is conducted throughout the world, the requirement of information exchange between different organizations is on the rise. Many business and technology analysts predict business and technology alignment among multiple cooperating organizations would have a tremendous impact on the business process. A majority of the large enterprises would prefer web service-implemented SOA to effectuate the information interchange among these enterprises.

WS-CDL specification is the second-generation web services extension designed to promote the business interaction and information interchange among multiple cooperating business organizations. This group of industries and organizations interact as partners, collaborators, vendors, dealers, and so on and can opt to implement WS-CDL specifications. Before any such specifications are implemented, interested organizations must agree to collaborate, and the nature of the collaboration must be spelled out in complete detail. This collaboration must be public in nature for all the participants. Also, they must identify the services (preferably web services) that are shared commonly to implement the choreography. Furthermore, these organizations must identify the participants who complete specific business activities leading to the completion of the business process. Moreover, channels must be established between these organizations so that appropriate roles can exchange information. Ultimately, these organizations also need to decide on the specifics of the kinds of interactions that can take place through the channels. These interactions are termed the fundamental building blocks of choreography.

Because choreography is expected to take place among multiple organizations, it is important that the interactions and work units are designed carefully and in a reusable manner. Smaller choreography units must be constructed in such a way that larger choreography units can be assembled by two or more partners that use it as a part of the overall work flow among these organizations. Figure 7.4 presents channels, interaction, work units, and flow of work between different organizations.

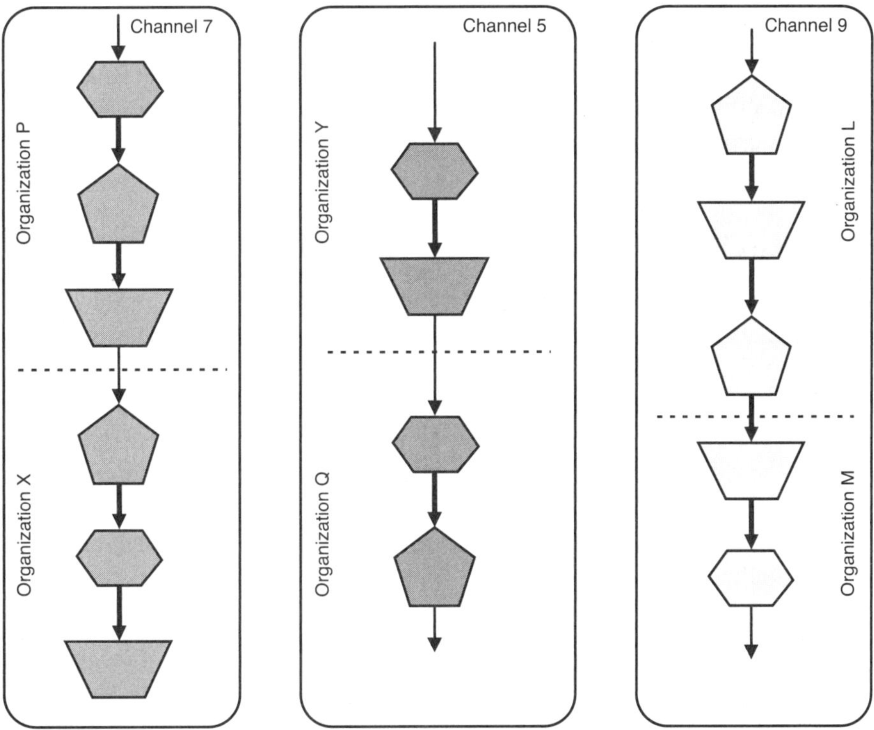

Figure 7.4 Choreography representing the channels, interactions, relationships, and roles

Orchestration and SOA

Large enterprises are typically spread over multiple geographical locations and often function as a congregate of several divisions, departments, and business units. Business processes that transpire through these divisions and departments were, at one point of time, manual in nature, slow, cumbersome, and even error-prone.

Although the first generation web services solutions can help these organizations implement applications as services by all the divisions, departments, and other practice units, it is important to recognize that process/work flow-oriented second generation web services, such as WS-BPEL, can establish these services as individual business units and enable them to execute as per the business rules defined by the organization. Business activities can now be defined, created, and sequenced as per a predefined order. They can also be grouped to form a complex activity and can be deployed as a dependent set of services. Thus, WS-BPEL specifications help business activities create meaningful services for the enterprise. Any changes in the process requirements are quickly addressed by these specifications. WS-BPEL forms a very important piece of technology that helps enterprises realize service-oriented architecture in a meaningful way.

Choreography and SOA

The essential difference between BPEL and choreography is the scope. The requirement is beyond the intranet boundaries of the organization's IT infrastructure firewall. As the demand for business automation between the partners and collaborators increases, the services of one organization should be used by the service of another organization, as part of their transaction. These services should be discoverable, sharable, and accountable. Under such circumstances, the business processes cannot be accomplished in isolation by any enterprise. The services and the processes need to be defined as per the agreement among all the trading partners.

Again, although First Generation Web Services help the individual organizations to define and expose their services, they can be shared as per the business agreement between participating collaborators. Second Generation Web Services specification such as WS-CDL can help to initiate interactions, define the channels, create roles, and assign responsibilities. Together with First Generation Web Services, WS-CDL specifications can help in achieving the interoperability, extensibility, discoverability, and so on desired by the organization.

Summary

Orchestration and choreography are the two important aspects of a business process; they are essentially key building blocks for the implementation of SOA. Business processes indicate the work flow or the orchestration of the enterprise. The WS-BPEL specification provides a set of XML elements. Along with the same help, the enterprise business process can be modeled as an algorithmic program and executed using a BPEL engine in a suitable web services environment such as Java Enterprise Edition.

The choreography part of the business process management attempts to manage a smooth interchange of information among multiple organizations that emphasizes a collective collaboration among those involved. This specification, often referred to as WS-CDL, is different from WS-BPEL in terms of its scope and application.

In the next chapter, we step into the realm of the Second Generation Web Services, namely WS-*. Here, we delve into some details of a few of the predominant Second Generation Web Services technologies such as WS-Addressing, WS-Security, WS-Reliable Messaging, and so forth.

Endnotes

1. This subcategorization is done by us for the purpose of convenience and understanding.
2. This aspect is covered in detail in Chapter 18, "Delivering SOA Using NetBeans SOA Pack: Case Study—Solution."

8

Advanced Web Services Infrastructure for Implementing SOA

The First Generation Web Services components, namely SOAP, WSDL, and UDDI, help create loosely coupled web services, whereas the Second Generation Web Services technologies, such as WS-BPEL and WS-CDL, help establish web services as a part of the business process among the agreeing collaborators. This is essential but not sufficient to cater to the needs of enterprise's ambitious requirement of SOA. Advanced supportive web services technologies such as addressing, security, reliability, quality of service, collaboration, and such are essential for the enterprise's needs of satisfactory SOA. To that end, WS-Addressing, WS-Security, WS-Reliability, and WS-Collaboration, collectively referred to as WS-, are some important advanced web services vocabularies that can help provide support in building SOA.*

The First Generation Web Services SOAP, WSDL, and UDDI provided a sound basis for the enterprises to initiate thinking in terms of services and interoperability. Although SOAP provided a firm basis for message exchange as part of the process, WSDL documents helped in describing the services in an interoperable way. UDDI specifications and services provide an arena for the service provider and service requester to discover each other and partner for enabling business automation. Furthermore, orchestration and choreography technologies, namely WS-BPEL and WS-CDL, provide a means to organize the business process to transpire in a smooth and elegant manner. Not all the technologies mentioned are necessary for successful service orientation. Recall, in Chapter 1, "Introduction," we indicated that not all three constituents of First Generation Web Services—SOAP, WSDL, and UDDI—are required for building web services. Likewise, WS-BPEL and WS-CDL are not essential to build the business process. Whether WS-BPEL and WS-CDL are required depends on the ultimate goal of the business process needs of the enterprise: Are the enterprises attempting to bring about the integration within the firewalls of the intranet or attempting to bring about collaborative business integration with business partners and collaborators over the Internet?

Although the core web services are essential, they are only building blocks in creating services for SOA implementation. For large and sprawling enterprises, implementation of robust and elegant service-oriented architecture requires much more than the basic building blocks. Robust and elegant infrastructure frameworks, tools, technologies, and specifications are necessary to design and deploy solutions. The First Generation Web Services have evolved to meet the functional requirements. Similarly, the Second Generation Web Services have evolved to meet the nonfunctional requirements of the enterprises. The Second Generation Web Services are essentially a set of advanced web services specifications driven by several groups of consortium of industries and vendors. Some of the specifications have already been consolidated to different extents and have been endorsed by leading industry consortia. Together, these specifications are referred to as WS-* (pronounced "WS star"). There are several specifications; some of the more crucial ones are

- WS-Collaboration
- WS-Addressing
- WS-Reliability and WS-Reliable Messaging[1]
- WS-Security

It is imperative that you note this Second Generation[2] Web Services specifications listed here are only indicative in nature, and more advanced web services specifications can emerge in the future. Also, for any particular enterprise, not all the advanced specifications are necessary. Depending on the requirement, an enterprise might choose to implement a subset of the WS-*, along with the core specifications and the orchestration and choreography technologies for implementing the SOA. These advanced specifications are termed the Second Generation Web Services specifications in this book. They are also referred to as contemporary web services extension specifications or Second Generation Web Services extension specifications.

Message Exchange Patterns

Although core web services specifications of the first generation are building blocks, all the advanced web services extensions invariably use SOAP for a variety of process or work-flow requirements of the enterprises. SOAP message exchange can be used in synchronous and asynchronous communications[3] of the enterprise processes. Collectively, such varieties of message exchanges could be termed *Message Exchange Patterns* (*MEP*s). Many MEPs can be identified in the broad field of services-oriented architecture, and we address some of the important ones in this chapter.

First, it is important that we revisit the pattern of the message exchanges before the arrival of the Second Generation Web Services specifications and the associated MEPs. These message exchanges are

- Request-Response
- Solicit-Response
- One-Way
- Notification

These varieties of message exchanges as part of the web services invocation principles, as applicable in the First Generation Web Services, were presented in Chapter 5, "Web Services and WSDL." WSDL Specification version 1.1 supports all the preceding varieties of message exchanges. It is worth noting that, out of these four varieties, only Request-Response and One-Way are recommended by the WS-I Basic Profile. The newer version of the WSDL specification, version 2.0,[4] however, supports eight different varieties, referred to as MEPs.

- **In-Out Pattern**—Equivalent to the Request-Response of the traditional MEP.
- **Out-In Pattern**—Equivalent to the Solicit-Response of the traditional MEP.
- **In-Only Pattern**—Equivalent to the One-Way or the Push technology of the traditional MEP.
- **Out-Only Patterns**—Equivalent to the Notification of the traditional MEP.
- **Robust In-Only Pattern**—An improvement over the In-Only MEP, in which the system provisions generating the error/fault response, when one is encountered during the transmission of the message.

- **Robust Out-Only Pattern**—An improvement over the Out-Only MEP, in which the system provisions generating the error/fault response when one is encountered during the transmission of the message.
- **In-Optional-Out Pattern**—An improved version of In-Out MEP. Notice that the name of the MEP itself indicates that the response part of the MEP is optional. Furthermore, this MEP supports fault/error generation when a transmission error occurs during the process of message exchange.
- **Out-Optional-In Pattern**—An improvised version of Out-In MEP. Notice that the name of the MEP itself indicates that the request part of the MEP is optional. Furthermore, this MEP supports fault/error generation when there is a transmission error during the process of message exchange.

One important note is that there are strong dependencies between the messages, their exchange patterns, and the new generation web services extensions. Also, there are several levels of interdependencies among the new generation web services, and these advanced specifications heavily use the first-generation building blocks, particularly SOAP and WSDL.

WS-*—The New Generation

Although the First Generation Web Services specifications acted as the building blocks of web services, they essentially focused on the functional aspects of services. The nonfunctional requirements such as security, reliability, quality of service, work flow, business process, and so on were not addressed by the core specifications.[5] The Second Generation Web Services have emerged to address these nonfunctional requirements of the enterprises. For any enterprise, there will be a number of nonfunctional requirements to be met, and there are a number of advanced web services technologies available to meet such demands. The following is an alphabetical list of some of the important infrastructure specifications and frameworks:

- WS-Addressing
- WS-Atomic Transaction
- WS-Coordination
- WS-Eventing
- WS-Metadata Exchange
- WS-Notification
- WS-Policy Framework
- WS-Reliability or WS-Reliable Messaging
- WS-Security

The importance of their requirement is essentially enterprise requirement-dependent. The specification definitions and the areas they address are covered briefly in the following subsections.

WS-Addressing

WS-Addressing is a specification authored originally by IBM, Microsoft, BEA, Sun, and SAP. The specification was submitted to W3C for standardization. This specification enables the web services to communicate addressing information. It essentially consists of two parts: a structure for communicating a reference to a Web service endpoint, and a set of Message Addressing Properties. These properties associate addressing information with a specific message.

WS-Atomic Transaction

WS-Atomic Transaction is a specification that defines protocols for distributed transaction processes to be used as part of WS-Coordination. Atomic transactions are essentially the ACID transactions—atomicity, consistency, isolation, and durability, and the specifications address and confirm that protocols meet the requirements of the enterprises.

WS-Coordination

The *WS-Coordination* specification describes an extensible framework that facilitates the protocols used in the enterprises that coordinate the *actions* of applications in a distributed environment. This framework includes other related specifications such as WS-Atomic Transaction, WS-Business Activity, and WS-BPEL. Developed jointly by IBM, BEA, and Microsoft, this specification helps multiple distributed applications to function correctly so that the result of the distributed transactions behaves as expected.

WS-Eventing

The *WS-Eventing* specification, initiated by Microsoft, focuses on addressing the requirements of the *Publish/Subscribe* (or *Pub/Sub*) web services messaging infrastructure of the organization. Eventing helps in notification of the subscribers of specific web services consumers when a particular web services is initialized/completed.

WS-Metadata Exchange

The term *Metadata* in the WS-Metadata Exchange specification refers to the data on the web services. The participants in the web services exchange (particularly the requester) might need additional data regarding the web service being a consumer. This specification enables the requester to send a standardized message requesting some or all information regarding the web service being consumed.

WS-Notification

The *WS-Notification* specification, initiated by IBM, addresses the requirements of the Publish/Subscribe web services messaging infrastructure of the organization.

WS-Policy Framework

The *WS-Policy Framework* is composed of three different policy-related specifications. They are WS-Policy, WS-Policy Attachments, and WS-Policy Assertions. WS-Policy is a specification that enables web services to advertise their policies (on nonfunctional requirements such as security,[6] quality of service, and so on) and enables web service consumers to specify their policy requirements.

WS-Reliability/WS-Reliable Messaging

WS-Reliability or *WS-Reliable Messaging* is a SOAP[7]-based specification that enables fulfilling the reliable messaging requirements critical to a part of the whole specific web service. These specifications attempts to define reliability in the context of present day web services implementations.

WS-Security

WS-Security is a broad-ranging framework composed of several other specifications and frameworks. Many consortia have contributed to the development of these supplementary and complementary frameworks and specifications.

In the next section, we provide some working definitions of a few of the important Second Generation Web Services specifications. We also present their scope and application scenarios and utility value proposition for the enterprises, highlighting their importance in the principles of SOA. The definitions are presented in alphabetical order; note that their order of preference for any enterprise is purely requirement-driven.

WS-*—A Working Definition

We provide here the working definitions of the most frequently used Second Generation Web Services technologies by the enterprises: addressing, security, and reliability.

Addressing

Communication between two applications needs to take place in a trusted, reliable, and secure environment. When such communications occur in the extranet or Internet environment, and these communications are associated with transactions, it is important that each of the applications know about the address of the application, whereabouts, and other necessary details. The WS-Addressing specification attempts to impart the whereabouts or address features to the communicating applications. The address features include the following:

- Source of the message
- Destination of the message
- Routing details of the message
- Instructions for what needs to be done in case of faults and nondelivery, and so on

WS-Addressing specifications implement these features within the scope of the SOAP header feature of the SOAP specification. This is presented in Figure 8.1. The WS-Addressing specification defines two types of SOAP headers: *Message Addressing Properties* and *Endpoint References*[8] (EPR).

Message Addressing Properties

In this type of SOAP header, addressing information can be included using the following standardized header entries: *destination*, *source endpoint*, *reply endpoint*, *fault endpoint*, *message ID*, *relationship*, and *action*. The message ID is a very special and important header entry that is specifically used in WS-Reliable Messaging specification.

Endpoint References

An Endpoint references type of SOAP header encapsulates the information useful for addressing a message to a web service, using the following header entries: *address*, *reference properties*, *reference parameters*, *service port, port type*, and *policy.*

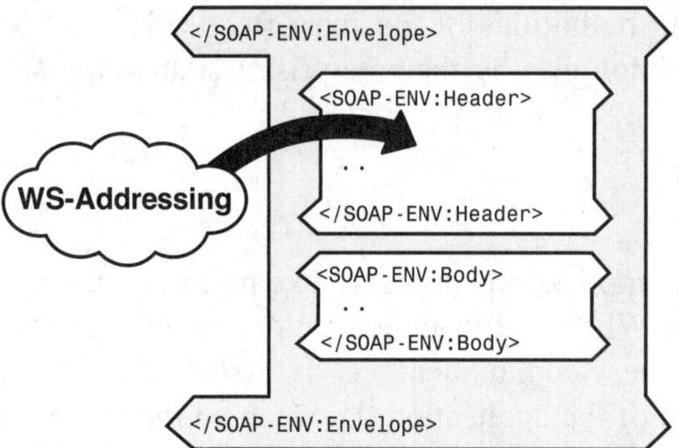

Figure 8.1 WS-Addressing and its relationship with SOAP message structure

Reliability and Reliable Messaging

One of the concerns of asynchronous-oriented communication is the reliability of the message delivery. There could be several issues including

- Delivery of the message to the target system
- Detecting whether there is a failure of delivery of the message
- Sequencing and prioritizing a series of messages that must be delivered

WS-Reliable Messaging specifications are designed to help in effectively managing various message delivery requirements for the enterprises. These specifications also help in tackling issues related to message sequencing, delivering, notification, and so on. If the message cannot be delivered, a suitable fault message is generated so that redelivery of the lost message is ensured. Reliability in message delivery can be ensured by building suitable rules by the WS-Reliable Messaging specifications. These reliability rules are implemented as SOAP header entries. This concept is illustrated in Figure 8.2.

Reliable Messaging specification identifies four participants involved in the delivery of messages: *Message Source*, *Reliable Message Source* (or *RM Source*), *Reliable Message Destination* (or *RM Destination*), and *Message Destination*. Any message delivery between the Message Source and Message Destination cannot transpire without the involvement of the RM Source and RM Destination. The Message Source always transmits the message (or a sequence of messages) to the RM Source, and the rest of the message transmission task is taken over by the latter. When the transmission of the message (or sequence of messages) is completed, the RM Destination takes care of delivering the same to the Message Destination.

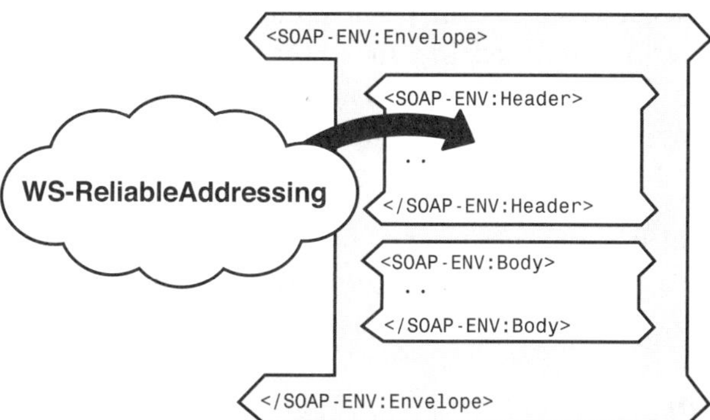

Figure 8.2 WS-Reliable Messaging and its relationship with SOAP message structure

Acknowledgment of the message delivery is one of the important features of reliable messaging. WS-Reliability enables a variety of acknowledgment scenarios. *Acknowledgment* of the receipt of the messages, *Sequence Acknowledgment* of the delivery of a set of messages, *Request Acknowledgment* by the RM Source and *Negative Acknowledgment* by RM Destination enable a robust quality of service for delivering the messages reliably. The entire process—from the initiation of the message to the delivery of the message in a reliable scenario—is illustrated in Figure 8.3.

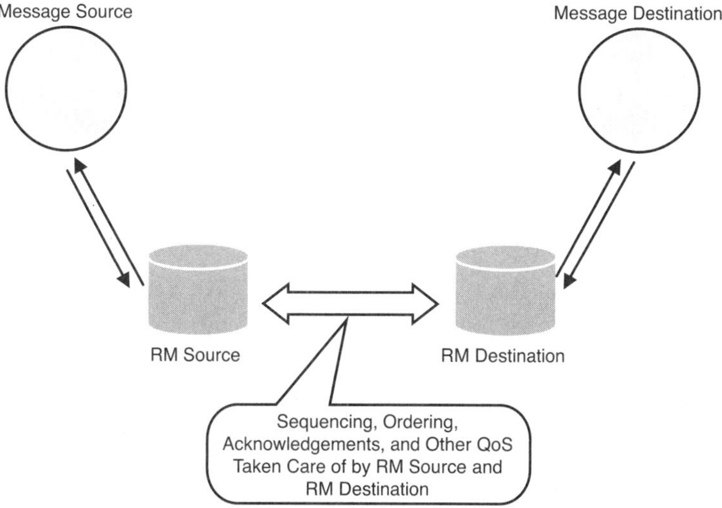

Figure 8.3 Participants of the Reliable Message Delivery System

The acknowledgment of the receipt of the message enables the RM Source to understand the message has been successfully delivered. Similarly, the Sequence Acknowledgment of the receipt indicates that the ordering of the delivered message is appropriately done. Similarly, RM Destination can be allowed to send the Negative Acknowledgment indicating that the delivery of the message to the RM Source is unsuccessful.

WS-Reliable Messaging also allows defining of four different patterns of delivery sequences. These delivery sequences are referred to as Delivery Assurances. They are *AtMostOnce*, *AtLeastOnce*, *ExactlyOnce*, and *InOrder*.

The AtMostOnce Pattern

In this pattern of delivery assurance, one or zero message delivery is ensured. An error condition results if more than one identical message is delivered in the system.

The AtLeastOnce Pattern

In this pattern, one or more delivery assurances are promised. However, if there is no delivery of the message, this results in an error condition.

The ExactlyOnce Pattern

This pattern ensures just one delivery of the message. An error condition results if zero or more than one identical message is delivered.

The InOrder Pattern

This pattern of delivery assurance is useful to ensure the order of the delivery of a set of messages. If the set of messages is not delivered as per the predefined sequence, an error condition results. This pattern can also be clubbed with that of the other delivery assurance patterns previously discussed.

Security

Security is, perhaps, one of the most important and most widely required nonfunctional requirements for any enterprise. There are wide varieties of technologies, rules, and practices used to provide security cover to the enterprise applications. In the world of web services and SOA, security might be provided through a set of frameworks and specifications called WS-Security. There are many security-related frameworks, supplementary frameworks, and specifications that constitute WS-Security specifications. Some of the important ones are

- WS-Security Policy
- WS-Federation

- XML-Signature
- XML-Encryption
- Secure Socket Layer

Provisioning of security to an enterprise application can be conceptually divided into three different levels:

- The User/Requester-Level Security
- The Transport-Level Security
- The Message-Level Security

Requester-Level Security

For ensuring the security in the enterprise application, it is important that some checks are implemented as a security blanket. They are *Identification*, *Authentication*, and *Authorization*.

Identification *Identification* is essentially the property of identity of a person. The employee ID of an employee or *Social Security number* (*SSN*) of a citizen of a country are examples of identification.

Authentication *Authentication* is the process of verification of a requester trying to use a service that is secured. Authentication confirms the identification of the requester trying to access the service or information. The process of authentication could involve passwords, *Personal Identification Number* (*PIN*), *Trading Partner Identification Number* (*TPIN*), and so on.

Authorization *Authorization* is the process of permitting the requester to access a service (or set of services) in an appropriate way. Authorization to use a service (or a part of it) could be based on the *Access Control List (ACL).*

Single Sign-On

An enterprise solution that has been architected using the principles of SOA and implemented using web services could encounter some unique challenges. Different services and service-oriented applications might require security checks such as Identification Authentication, Authorization, and so on. Such security checks, although desirable, can prove expensive and might turn nasty when human users are prompted to authenticate (and be authorized) while related and interconnected services are being sought.

Such situations can be avoided if a blanket security clearance, such as *Single Sign-On (SSO)*, is implemented. The technology of SSO enables the service requester to identify and authenticate for the first time during a particular session. After this is done, the security context generated during the SSO is shared among different services. There are several technologies of SSOs available that are implemented and used by large enterprises. Some of the popular ones are Kerberos and Federation.

Kerberos This popular SSO technology is available on a variety of platforms such as Microsoft Windows, different flavors of UNIX systems, and the mainframe systems. In this technology, the process of authentication is entirely externalized. When the requester signs into the Kerberos server, a ticket is issued. This ticket is produced by the client applications when they attempt to access the other servers for accessing the services.

Federation The technologies of Federation use standards-based protocols to enable an application to assert the identification of a service requester to another application. This process eliminates the redundant authentication. *Security Assertion Markup Language* (*SAML*) and WS-Federation employ this SSO technology.

Liberty Alliance or *Project Liberty* is a broad-based industry standard consortium involved in defining a federated identification management for web services communication protocols. Industry leaders such as IBM, Sun Microsystems, Novell, Intel, Oracle, VeriSign, RSA Security, Hewlett-Packard, and so on are involved in the development efforts of the SSO based on the concepts of federated identity management. This federated SSO is based on SAML and is suitable for intranet and Internet environments.

Transport-Level Security

Protecting the message at the transport level is essentially providing protection to the message itself while it is transported from one system to the other. In the context of enterprises implementing the SOA through web services, the message needs to be protected along the SOAP message path, and this level of security can be achieved by using *Secure Socket Layers (SSL)*. It is important to note that synchronous operations between the requester and provider can be effectively implemented providing transport level security because there are no intermediaries. However, when asynchronous communications are involved and intermediaries are required, it is important that the intermediaries do not view or modify the message in any way. Such scenarios require transport-level security.

Message-Level Security

Confidentiality is important for any enterprise. When information is exchanged, the confidentiality and integrity of the information contained in the message is not viewed or altered any way by the intermediaries or inappropriate persons. The confidentiality of the message is said to be maintained when the content of the message is not viewed unauthorized. Likewise, the integrity of the message is said to be maintained when the message is not altered any way by the intermediaries or any other unauthorized persons.

Enterprises that are involved in frequently exchanging confidential information need to implement message-level security. Message-level security provides not only the transport-level security, but also maintains the confidentiality and integrity of the message. Technologies such as encryption and digital signature help protect the message. Under the WS-Security frameworks, there are many ways of providing the confidentiality and integrity; however, for our purposes, we focus on two WS-Security extensions: XML Encryption and XML Signature. These extensions can provide secure and robust message level security.

XML Encryption *XML Encryption* is an encryption technology specifically designed for encrypting the data represented by XML. The advantage of using XML Encryption is that the encryption can be applied to either the entire message or to specific parts of a specific message. For example, when credit card information is sent, it is possible that just the card number and the expiration date can be encrypted and sent rather than sending the complete details of the credit card information.

XML Signature This technology helps provide authenticity to the accompanying message. The XML document containing the data is accompanied by a code generated by a special algorithm, based on the content of the message. This code is called the *digital signature*. The XML document with the digital signature will together be delivered to the recipient of the message. The recipient needs to verify the digital signature, and the verification of the signature will succeed if and only if the contents of the message accompanying the digital signature have not been altered in any way.

XML Encryption and XML Signature are included as part of the SOAP message. Although the digital signature can be sent as a part of the `<Header>` elements, encrypted messages are encoded into the `<Body>` elements, as represented in Figure 8.4.

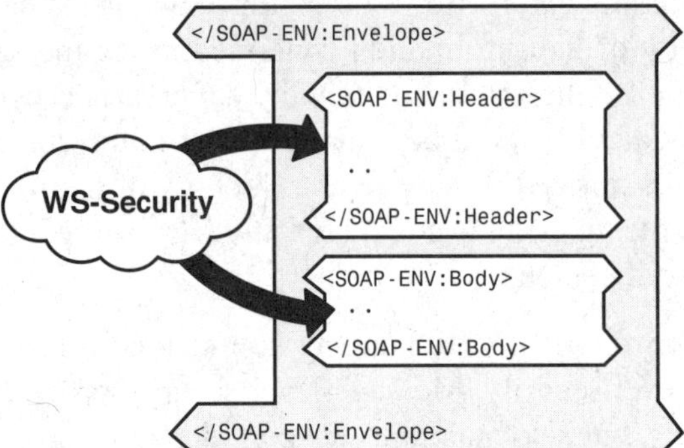

Figure 8.4 WS-Security and its relationship with SOAP message structure

WS-* and SOA

The First Generation Web Services—SOAP, WSDL, and UDDI—provided the foundation for interoperability and message interchange using XML. SOAP specification played a key role in message interchange through the synchronous and asynchronous route. As the enterprises and organizations realized the power of web services and realized the possibility of achieving business automation, the requirements of the nonfunctional requirements for business integration through web services loomed large. Several industrial consortia started building/contributing toward achieving the same. This resulted in the second generation of web services. They are also termed *web services extensions* because many of them are inherently the extensions in SOAP and other advanced XML vocabularies. These extensions are particularly needed by the industry consortia because they help the organizations to architect (or re-architect) the enterprise solutions to extract the maximum benefit for service orientation. Service orientation helps achieve the following goals:

- Reliability
- Interoperability
- Extensibility
- Loose coupling
- Security
- Quality of service

You've now read, in detail, how specifically each of the WS-* specifications is designed and how it helps in achieving different nonfunctional requirements. In the next section, we cover how some of these new generation specifications help in promoting SOA.

WS-Reliable Messaging and SOA

Reliability is inherently induced by the WS-Reliable Messaging through the use of SOAP header entries. This Second Generation Web Services extension helps the SOAP messages to appropriately define and use the quality of service as per the business rules and requirements. It also helps to define different kinds of acknowledgments and fault handling systems. Overall, WS-Reliable Messaging helps implement a robust *quality of service* (*QoS*), as a part of SOA, for the services that transpire within the organization.

WS-Security and SOA

Security is of utmost importance to any enterprise and is therefore rendered as a service by the web services technologies. Recall that WS-Security is a collection of frameworks and specifications. Each of the specifications/frameworks deals with different aspects of the security as required by the policies and requirements defined by the organization. Clearly, security helps to improve the QoS in the enterprise.

WS-I Basic Profile

The creation of *Web Services Interoperability (WS-I)* was one of the significant milestones in the history of web services and SOA. The birth of WS-I signaled the beginning of one of the most important aspect of web services and SOA—the agreement among several different consortia that interoperability is the key issue.

One of the first significant steps initiated by WS-I was the introduction of a set of specifications called the WS-I Basic Profile. This is an important step for assembling a set of mature core web services specifications composed of a commonly supported web services platform.

The WS-I Basic Profile is standardized on the following core specifications:

- XML 1.0
- XML Schema 1.0
- SOAP 1.1
- WSDL 1.1
- UDDI 2.0

This Basic Profile specification also provides a set of design standards and recommends how a specific feature needs to be implemented. It also covers information regarding do's and don'ts on the web services implementation.

Summary

Although the First Generation Web Services technologies addressed the functional requirements, the Second Generation Web Services technologies gradually evolved addressing the nonfunctional requirements. As a result, a number of advanced web services extensions have emerged, and the specifications and frameworks toward this have been contributed by competing industry consortia. For example, WS-Reliability and WS-Reliable Messaging specifications have a common agenda, and the specifications have duplicating and overlapping proposals. Nevertheless, some of the important extensions that are commonly accepted by most of the industry consortia are WS-Addressing, WS-Security, WS-Reliability, and so on. Each of these specifications helps include nonfunctional requirements such as reliability, security, loose-coupling, interoperability, composability, QOS, and more. The fact that industry consortia are coming together to create organizations such as web services interoperability signals a promising future for the technology of web services and SOA.

In the next part, we devote our attention toward the Java platform, the Enterprise Edition technology, its structure and architecture, and its evolution as the most potent and important solution to enterprise application requirements. The concepts of components and containers, the tiered structure of the Java EE platform, web technologies, the new persistence model for the Enterprise JavaBeans, and support for web services are discussed in this part.

Endnotes

1. WS-Reliability and WS-Reliable Messaging are the competing Web Services standards developed and supported by different sets of industry consortia. Both these specifications have a common agenda, and the specifications overlap in many aspects. There are differences as well. In this book, we bring in appropriate aspects of either of the specifications when highlighting the reliability requirement of the services delivery.
2. Many authors and books do consider WS-BPEL and WS-CDL as the Second Generation Web Services. In this book, we are not in disagreement with that. However, we have attempted to group the orchestration and choreography elements as the essential building blocks of the SOA.
3. Asynchronous patterns are not discussed in this chapter. They are separately covered in Chapter 16, "Advanced Service Oriented Architecture."
4. In this chapter, we continue to focus on WSDL Specification version 1.1 because this specification is part of the WS-I Basic Profile.
5. We have coined the term New Generation here to indicate that the specifications indicated here are essentially to take care of the nonfunctional requirements of the SOA.
6. The WS-Policy Framework is part of the WS-Security Framework.
7. For some enterprises, SOAP over HTTP might not sufficiently guarantee the nonfunctional requirements such as reliability, security, and so on.
8. Message Addressing Properties are also known as Message Information headers (or MI headers).

Part III

Java Platform, Enterprise Edition and ESB

9

Java Platform, Enterprise Edition Overview

The latest version of Java Platform, Enterprise Edition *(*Java EE*) evolved from the industry's need for a secure, reliable, highly available, and scalable platform to develop enterprise applications. The new Enterprise Edition platform enables developers to focus on the presentation or business logic instead of dealing with complex system-level issues such as performance and scalability. The main focus of the new Java EE is ease of development to increase developer productivity. The end goals are to attract even more developers to the platform and broaden the use of technologies within the platform. The core technology concepts that achieve these goals include extensive use of Java annotations, dependency injection, and* Plain-Old Java Object *(*POJO*) model. These concepts are leveraged in multiple APIs within the Java Platform, Enterprise Edition.*

The first version of Java 2 Platform, Enterprise Edition (J2EE) was announced by Sun Microsystems in late 1999. The corresponding *Reference Implementation (RI)* along with the *Blueprints* and Java Pet Store prototype example was released in December 1999. This signaled the arrival of a new technology, which can be defined as the standard for building portable, robust, scalable, and multi-tiered server-side applications. This technology simplifies enterprise application development to a great extent by providing a collection of *application programming interfaces* (*API*s) and services that applications can rely upon. Since then, this technology has improved and morphed to meet the ever-changing demands of the enterprise solution requirements. Recently, Sun Microsystems rechristened this technology as *Java Platform, Enterprise Edition* (*Java Enterprise Edition* or *Java EE*), indicating that new technology is a significant improvement over its predecessors.[1] The new name is Java Platform, Enterprise Edition, and the current version is 5.[2]

Java EE technology has gained a broad adoption from middleware vendors and enterprise developers. By developing applications that adhere to the standard, customers can avoid middleware vendor lock-in because their applications can run on Java EE products developed by other vendors with no or minimal porting. Currently, about 25 vendors have released a Java EE-compatible product.[3] The large number of the Java and Java EE developer base makes it easier, and in most cases affordable, for companies to locate resources required to implement a solution based on Java EE than a vendor-specific, proprietary solution. Java EE technology has created new business opportunities for tools, training, consulting, and support services, all of which lower the cost and risk of a Java EE-based solution.

The Java EE standard is defined through the *Java Community Process (JCP)*. The Java EE platform is specified by a collection of specifications. Each API within Java EE is defined in a separate specification, and an umbrella Java EE specification ties all API specifications together and defines additional requirements and services for the overall platform. Each specification is driven by an Expert Group, which consists of relevant experts in the industry for the particular technology. In additional to the specification, delivery of the RI and the *Technology Compatibility Kit (TCK)* is required before a specification can be declared final. The RI is a functional implementation that conforms to the requirements of the specification. The TCK is a set of tests that verify whether an implementation is compatible with the specification. By definition, the RI always passes 100% of the tests specified in the TCK. The Java EE standard JCP deliverable includes the Java EE platform umbrella specification and a set of API specifications, the Java EE Reference Implementation, and the Java EE Compatibility Test Suite, which includes the TCKs of all required APIs plus additional platform-level tests.

In addition to the Java Community Process, Sun Microsystems has created the Java EE licensee and branding program, which requires any Java EE vendor's product implementation to pass every test prescribed in the Java EE Compatibility Test Suite before the final, deployable version of product becomes available. This program has achieved a high level of compatibility between Java EE products from different vendors. Given that compatibility is the key foundation on which the entire Java EE ecosystem is built, companies that implement Java EE-based solutions would, therefore, insist on using Java EE-compatible implementations and adhere to Java EE standards when building Java EE applications to ensure portability, interoperability, and so on.

Java EE Technology Categories

The Java EE technology can be loosely grouped into four different categories: web application technologies, web services technologies, enterprise application technologies, and common platform technologies. The categories of Java platform Enterprise Edition technologies are presented in Figure 9.1. More details on some of these technologies are covered in subsequent chapters.

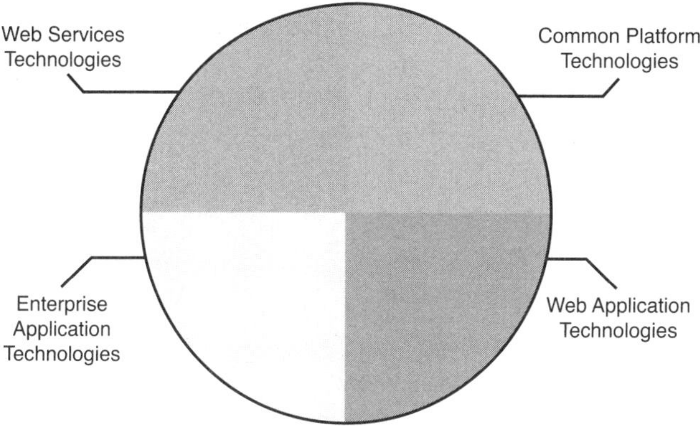

Figure 9.1 Java EE technology categories

Because Java EE is layered on top of *Java Standard Edition* (*Java SE*) technology, Java EE applications can use all the APIs defined in Java SE as well. In fact, several APIs were initially defined in earlier versions of Java EE and have been moved into the Java SE platform, such as *Java Database Connectivity (JDBC)* and *Java Name and Directory Interface (JNDI)*.

Web Application Technologies

The web application technologies in Java EE are categorized into four different web technologies: *Java Servlets*, *JavaServer Pages (JSP)*, *JavaServer Pages Standard Tag Library (JSTL)*, and *JavaServer Faces (JSF)* technology. These technologies work together as a unified stack to simplify the building of a web-based application, as illustrated in Figure 9.2.

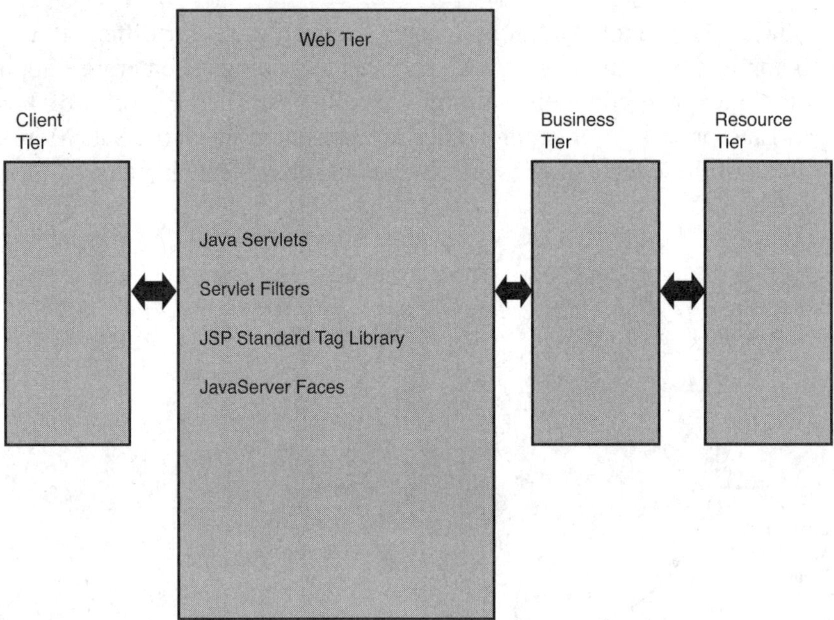

Figure 9.2 Overview of the role of web application technologies in the Java EE architecture

Java Servlet

Java Servlet is the foundation for all the web tier technologies in Java EE. Java Servlet technology provides web application developers with a simple mechanism for defining the logic in the Java programming language to handle the request/response-oriented web-based HTTP communication protocol.

JSP

JSP technology provides a quick and simplified way to create dynamic web content. JSP technology enables rapid development of web-based applications that are platform-independent. JSP is written in a markup language format familiar to web page developers and designers. In fact, developers can use JSP technology without learning Java. JSP enables a clear separation between the user interface and layout from the logic responsible for dynamic content generation, such as database queries. This enables separation of roles. For example, a web designer can focus on user interface implementation, whereas the Java developers can focus on backend business/database access logic and integration.

JSP supports tag libraries, which define a set of reusable markup tags for use inside a JSP page. Tag libraries reduce the need to embed Java code in a JSP page and provide a construct that is much friendlier to the web page designers. Another feature supported by JSP is *Expression Language* (*EL*), which provides a simple way for web page authors to access external data objects written in Java from a JSP page.

JSTL

The JSTL encapsulates, as simple tags, the core functionality common to many web applications. JSTL has support for common structural tasks such as iteration (iteration tag), condition (conditional tags), and so on for manipulating XML documents, providing internationalization functionality, SQL tags for database access, and such. It also provides a framework for integrating existing custom tags with JSTL tags.

JSF

JSF technology simplifies the building of user interfaces for web-based applications through its well-defined component, state, and event framework. A typical application based on JSF can be broken down into three parts:

- A set of reusable JSF components
- A set of JSP pages that make use of the JSF components
- A configuration XML file that enables the users to specify page navigation and other parameters needed for the application

JSF has a flexible and extensible architecture. In JSF, render kits present the user interface in a markup language such as HTML. JSF comes with the HTML render kit, but it is possible to plug in multiple render kits. For example, a render kit can be plugged in to display components such as *Wireless Markup Language (WML)*, which is optimized for display on mobile phones.

JSF also provides support for converters and validators. Although converters translate user input to a format that can be consumed by the components and vice versa, validators check the correctness of the user input.

Web Services Technologies

The web services technologies form the foundation for SOA support in the Java EE platform. As illustrated in Figure 9.3, the key technologies that provide a variety of web services-related features are Java API for XML Web Services, Java Architecture for XML Binding, and Java API for XML Registries.

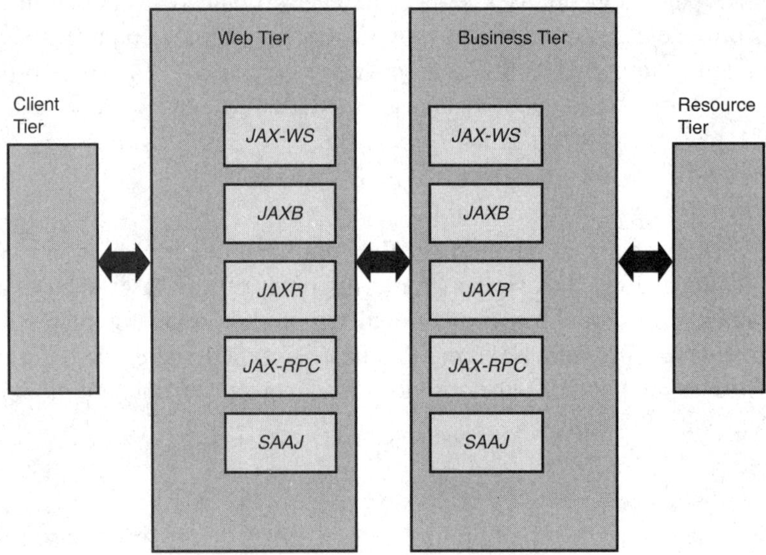

Figure 9.3 Overview of the web services technologies in the Java EE architecture

Java API for XML Web Services

Java API for XML Web Services (JAX-WS) is the next generation web services API to consume or implement XML-based web services. JAX-WS technology is the successor to JAX-RPC. It is also the foundation for the Second Generation Web Services technologies such as WS-Addressing, WS-Security, and WS-Reliability or WS-Reliable Messaging. Using JAX-WS technology, a developer can define a web service by simply creating a POJO Java class with appropriate annotations. JAX-WS tools then generate the corresponding *Web Services Description Language* (*WSDL*) file. A developer can also start from an existing WSDL and use JAX-WS tools to generate annotated Java classes and interfaces. Data binding in JAX-WS is handled by Java Architecture for XML Binding, which is covered in the next section.

JAX-WS technology is compliant with important web service standards, including SOAP, WSDL, and WS-I Basic Profile. The latter standard, in particular, ensures interoperability between web services implemented using a different product or platform.

JAX-WS technology is extensible to new encodings, transports, and protocols. By default, SOAP 1.1 over HTTP is used as the binding. However, it is possible to specify other bindings, such as SOAP 1.2 over HTTP or Representational State Transfer (REST)-style binding. JAX-WS also supports asynchronous interactions between client and server.

Java Architecture for XML Binding

Java Architecture for XML Binding (JAXB) provides a convenient way to bind an XML schema to a representation in Java and vice versa. This enables Java developers to process XML data in their applications without requiring an in-depth knowledge of XML. JAXB technology is also used as the data-binding mechanism for JAX-WS technology. JAXB provides full XML schema support, including schema evolution. With schema evolution, it is possible to bind a Java class to a particular version of schema and use the same Java class to work with an update version, provided there is sufficient compatibility between the versions.

JAXB technology heavily uses the annotation feature of the new Java language to reduce the size and increase the portability of the generated Java code. Consequently, the Java classes generated by JAXB technology can be used in any JAXB-compatible environment. JAXB also supports validation. When an XML document is converted to a Java object, validation against the XML schema can be performed automatically.

SOAP with Attachments API for Java

SOAP with Attachments API for Java (SAAJ) provides a low-level API to produce and consume messages that conform to SOAP 1.1, SOAP 1.2, and SOAP with Attachments specifications. Most enterprise application developers do not need to use SAAJ directly because the low-level SOAP message processing is addressed by the JAX-WS technology-based tools. Nevertheless, the SAAJ API is useful in advanced scenarios, such as intercepting and modifying a SOAP message as part of a JAX-WS handler.

Java API for XML Registries

In a service-oriented architecture scenario, services are often published to a centralized Registry to facilitate discovery of these services. The *Java API for XML Registries* (*JAXR*) technology provides a protocol-independent interface to access these types of registries and repositories. The JAXR technology currently supports both of the major standards for XML Registry: *UDDI registry* standard and *ebXML Registry and Repository* standard. JAXR also defines a uniform information model for classification and association of different services and provides rich query capabilities.

Web Services Metadata

The web services metadata specification defines the syntax of the Java annotations used to implement a particular web service. Some examples of annotations defined in the specification are

- `@WebService`—Indicates that a Java class or interface defines a web service
- `@WebMethod`—Indicates that a Java method is exposed as a web service operation
- `@WebParam`—Specifies mapping of a Java method parameter to a parameter name defined in WSDL

Java API for XML-Based RPC

Java API for XML-Based RPC (JAX-RPC) was introduced in J2EE 1.4 to provide RPC-like functionality to define and access SOAP 1.1-based web services. In the latest version of Java EE, this technology has been replaced by the next generation web service technology, JAX-WS. The new technology offers better ease of development and provides more functionality. JAX-RPC still remains in the Java EE platform for maintaining the backward compatibility.

Enterprise Application Technologies

The enterprise application technologies include APIs typically used for implementing server-side business logic and resource integrations. These technologies, as shown in Figure 9.4, include the *Enterprise JavaBeans (EJB)*, *Java Persistence API (JPA)*, and *Java Message Service (JMS).*

EJB

EJB technology is the server-side component architecture for Java EE. EJB technology enables rapid and simplified development of components that are distributed, transactional, secure, and portable in nature. These components handle the business logic part of the enterprise solution. EJB components typically are executed inside a managed environment called a *container*. The container interposes to provide additional services such as concurrency, scalability, transactions, security, and distribution.

In EJB 3.0 specification, Java annotations simplify development of EJB components. It is no longer necessary to write unneeded container interfaces, and requirement of a deployment descriptor for the EJBs is optional. This new feature has rendered the *stateless session EJB*, *stateful session EJB*, and *message-driven EJB*s to just ordinary Java classes or POJOs.

Interceptor is a new and powerful feature supported in EJB 3.0 specification. It enables user-defined logic to be interposed before and after business method invocations. It enables flexible business logic customization without modifying the source code of an EJB component.

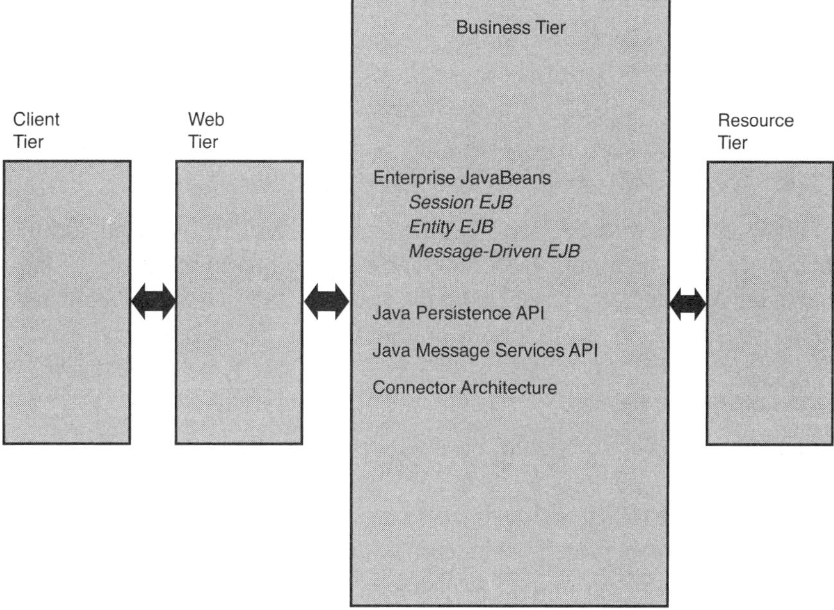

Figure 9.4 Overview of Enterprise application technology in Java EE architecture

JPA

JPA supports *object-relational mapping* (*OR Mapping* or *ORM*) and enables developers to access and update relational databases without an in-depth knowledge of SQL. Data in relational databases is represented as POJO Java objects known as entities. For example, in a simple mapping case, a database table is mapped to an entity class wherein each column of the table is mapped to a field in the entity class. Relationships between entities are supported, and so is inheritance.

A query language, called the Java Persistence Query Language, is defined as part of the API. This SQL-like query language can operate over an abstract persistence schema of entities. In addition to entity retrieval, predicate-based bulk updates and deletes are supported.

One of the key benefits of using the JPA and the corresponding Java Persistence Query Language is database portability. The application server is responsible for handling the differences between different databases. The JPA also defines a Service Provider Interface (SPI) to support plugability of persistence providers into an application server.

JMS API

JMS API is a messaging standard that enables application components to create, send, receive, and process messages. It enables distributed communication that is loosely coupled, reliable, and asynchronous. Distributed transactions are supported such that the sending or receiving of a JMS message can be combined with a database access in the same global transaction.

JMS is integrated with EJB through message-driven EJB, invoked automatically when there is an incoming JMS message delivered to an application server. The Connector Architecture, described next, specifies the plugability between a JMS provider and an application server through the use of a resource adapter.

Connector Architecture

Connector Architecture enables Java EE applications to access data from external *Enterprise Information Systems (EIS)*, such as *Enterprise Resource Planning (ERP)*, *Customer Relationship Management (CRM)*, legacy mainframe systems, and JMS implementations. Connector is the key technology to support *Enterprise Application Integration (EAI)* between Java EE systems and heterogeneous EIS. Connector defines a contract between an application server and a resource adapter, which is a software module capable of connecting and communicating with a specific EIS. Among other things, the contract focuses on three specific areas: connection, security, and transaction management. The connection management contract enables resource adapters to leverage the connection pooling capability of an application server. The security contract defines how an application server should authenticate with the EIS through the resource adapter.

The transaction management contract enables data access and updates to the EIS to be part of a global transaction managed by the application server.

Common Platform Technologies

As the name indicates, Common Platform technologies are those technologies commonly required and used as part of any Java EE application. Some of the technologies commonly used across any enterprise application would be annotations, transactions, e-mail, messaging, and so on.

Common Annotations

The common annotations specification defines annotations that can be reused across different specifications within the Java EE platform, including resource dependencies, security roles, and references.

Java Transaction API

The *Java Transaction API (JTA)* specifies standard Java interfaces between a Transaction Manager and the parties involved in a distributed transaction system: the *Resource Manager*, the *Application Server*, and the *Transactional Applications*. In any Java EE platform, the Resource Manager can be a relational database, a JMS provider, or an Enterprise Information System connected through a resource adapter. A Java EE application server is required to support the "two-phase commit" protocol, which ensures access to multiple Resource Managers to be grouped in the same global transaction.

Streaming API for XML

Streaming API for XML (StAX) is a streaming, pull-parsing API for reading and writing XML documents. In a pull-parsing API model, an application invokes the parser to request the next element in an XML document as needed. This contrasts with the push-parsing API, such as *Simple API for XML (SAX)*, in which the parser would invoke the application-defined handlers as parsing progresses. StAX technology enables developers to process XML documents in a fast and simple way while maintaining a light memory footprint. StAX is used internally by JAXB technology to perform a low-level processing of XML documents.

JavaMail and JavaBeans Activation Framework

Enterprise applications often use e-mails to communicate with end users in an asynchronous manner. For example, a confirmation is normally sent to the user via e-mail soon after the user has completed a particular transaction. The *JavaMail* API provides a protocol-independent interface for applications to send and receive e-mail messages. It can work with standard protocols such as *Simple Mail Transfer Protocol (SMTP)*, *Post Office Protocol (POP3)*, and *Internet Message Access Protocol (IMAP)*. JavaMail uses *JavaBeans Activation Framework (JAF)* to handle data in different MIME types and formats.

Java EE Application Deployment

Java EE Application Deployment defines a standard API for deploying Java EE applications and components to an application server. It also defines a standard data model to represent vendor-specific deployment information that might be required by different application servers. The standard data model enables Java

EE development tools to support deployment to multiple application servers in a standard fashion.

Java EE Management

Java EE Management describes how a Java EE platform application server can be managed and monitored in a standard way. The management model defined in the specification provides information on deployed applications and information on related technologies such as JDBC, JMS, and connector resources configured in the application server. Java EE Management is based on the *Java Management Extensions (JMX)* specification. Standard mappings to *Common Information Model (CIM)* and SNMP *Management Information Base (MIB)* are included as part of the specification. Remote access to the management information can be done via the standard *Management EJB (MEJB)* and through the remote JMX connectors.

Java Authorization Contract for Containers

Java Authorization Contract for Containers (*JACC*) is a plugability interface that supports the installation and configuration of authorization providers into an application server. Authorization enables an administrator to specify access rights to methods and functions of Java EE components' individual users and groups. Although an application server must include a default authorization provider, a custom authorization provider would enable an enterprise to implement security policies suitable for the particular needs of an enterprise.

What's New in Java EE 5

Java EE is a powerful and comprehensive platform that has adopted the simplicity and elegance of the Java programming language. Although programming and development in Java is relatively easy, development of the enterprise application using the Java EE platform can be, at times, challenging and demanding. To address this challenge, Sun Microsystems has introduced several new features and improvements in the new platform. The main focus of Java EE 5, however, is ease of development and increased developer productivity. The goal of the platform is to essentially attract even more developers to the platform and to broaden the use of technologies within the platform. The core technology concepts used to achieve these goals include extensive use of Java annotations,[4] dependency injection, and the use of the POJO model. These concepts are leveraged in multiple APIs within the Java EE 5 platform.

Java Annotations

Java annotation is a metadata construct to mark up elements of Java code. A Java annotation begins with the @ symbol and can be associated with a Java class, interface, method, or field declaration. An optional parameter list of name-value pairs can follow an annotation for further customization. In the Java EE platform, annotations provide additional information to the application server so that it can handle and process the application in a specific way. In J2EE 1.4 or earlier versions, most of this information was stored in the XML-based deployment descriptors that accompany any J2EE application. In the new platform, deployment descriptors are optional, and the same information can be specified using the Java annotations feature.[5] The Java EE 5 platform provides a good number of default values so that, in most cases, annotations can be omitted altogether and the default behavior would be suitable for most applications.[6]

The following is an example of a code snippet on annotation use in a Java EE-based application:

```
@Stateless
public class AccountBean implements Account {
    ...
    public void reflectAccountInformation(String s) {
        System.out.println(''The account details are : '' + s);
    }
    ....
}
```

In the preceding example, the annotation `@Stateless` is associated with the class declaration and indicates the class is defining a stateless session bean. The application server interprets this annotation and automatically exposes the business logic defined as an EJB. Annotations in the Java EE platform help the developer community in many ways in defining the enterprise application. Some of the scenarios in which the annotations are leveraged in Java EE include

- Defining and using web services applications
- Defining and using Enterprise JavaBeans
- Mapping Java classes to XML
- Mapping Java classes to relational databases
- Specifying external dependencies
- Making XML deployment descriptors optional
- Dependency injection

Dependency injection is essentially a design pattern that resolves dependencies required by a software component. This is also referred to as *Inversion of Control*. A dependency in the Java EE context can be a value for a configuration parameter, a resource manager such as a JDBC data source, or a reference to another software component. The basic idea of this pattern is that the preceding dependencies are transparently injected or initialized in the component by the runtime environment, instead of an explicit method call by the component to obtain each dependency.

The following is an example of a code snippet showing dependency injection:

```
@Stateless
public TravelReservationBean implements TravelReservation {
    ...
    @Resource private DataSource bookingDB;
    ...
    public findReservation(int confirmationNumber) {
        ...
        Connection dbcon = bookingDB.getConnection();
        ...
    }
}
```

In the preceding example, the `bookingDB` field in the `TravelReservationBean` class is annotated with the `@Resource` annotation. Whenever the application server creates an instance of `TravelReservationBean` Stateless Session EJB, it automatically assigns the appropriate JDBC data source to the `bookingDB` field. Subsequently, the business logic of the bean can use the field directly to obtain a database connection.

There are a number of advantages of using dependency injection. For example, it results in less, but more precise, code because the boilerplate code needed to obtain each dependency is replaced by annotations that are more concise and intuitive. In the preceding example, if resource injection is not used, the code snippet would look like this:

```
@Stateless
public TravelReservationBean implements TravelReservation {

    public findReservation(int confirmationNumber) {
        ...
        Context ctx = new InitialContext();
        DataSource bookingDB =
            (DataSource)ctx.lookup("jdbc/bookingDB");
        Connection dbcon = bookingDB.getConnection();
        ...
    }
}
```

With dependency injection, the same component can be run in a different runtime environment without modification. For example, it is possible to run the preceding component outside of an application server in a unit testing scenario as long as some basic dependency injection support is available in the unit testing environment. Dependency injection helps in decoupling the source code from the actual dependency values and thus enables different dependency values to be bound later without changing the code. The use of injection for declaring component dependencies also improves component-level modularization and reduces tight coupling between multiple components.

The Java EE platform enables a variety of dependencies to the injected into the enterprise application. Some of the dependencies that can be injected into a Java EE application are

- Environment variables
- EJB references
- Resource factory references (JDBC, JMS, Connector, and so forth)
- Java EE runtime services such as transaction manager and *object request broker* (*ORB*)
- Persistence unit and context in support of object-relational mapping

POJO Model

Java developers use Java classes and objects to encapsulate their business logic. The idea of the POJO model is to stay as close as possible to the regular Java object model even if the object might not behave like a regular Java object. According to the POJO model, there should be minimal difference between the source code of a regular Java object as compared to the source code that defines an Enterprise JavaBean (or a web service, for that matter). Examples include a definition of an RMI object and an EJB or a web service definition. Let's consider a simple web service definition in the Java EE 5 platform:

```
@WebService
public class WeatherServiceBean {
    ...
    public String getWeatherReport(int zipcode) {
        ...
    }
    ...
}
```

The only difference between the preceding web service and a regular Java class would be the addition of the `@WebService` annotation. No extra Java interfaces or methods need to be defined to implement a web service. The benefits of using the POJO model should be obvious. Minimal extra source code is required when defining Java EE components. In addition, Java developers are already familiar with the POJO model, so it will be a much easier transition to adopt the new Java EE platform.

Developer Productivity

Enterprise businesses are dynamic in nature and changing at an ever-increasing rate. Architecting and developing solutions for such enterprise requirements is always a challenge. Other challenges to consider are that both time-to-market and developer productivity are of utmost importance in the life cycle of the enterprise solution development. Although the J2EE technology helped many enterprises to tackle the problem, the newer Java EE technologies hold much more promise in that direction. Table 9.1 highlights the advantages of the new technology over the old and brings out a few of the quantitative differences.

The announcement of the new technology encouraged many curious J2EE developers to test-drive the new technology. The migration exercises for test driving such technologies are always a better yardstick in judging several aspects of the technology. It is interesting to review some of the anecdotal studies conducted by the developer community in the recent past. Debu Panda, a product manager at Oracle, successfully migrated the Adventure Builder application from the Java Blueprints, from J2EE 1.4 to Java EE 5.[7] The migrated application was leaner by 36% of the number of Java classes. Similarly, Raghu Kodali, a product manager at Oracle, migrated an application named RosterApp in the J2EE 1.4 tutorial to Java EE 5.[8] The migrated application had about 60% fewer Java classes and about 80% fewer deployment descriptor files. Arun Gupta, an engineer at Sun Microsystems, migrated a sample application defined by the *Web Services Interoperability (WS-I)* organization from JAX-RPC 1.1 to JAX- WS 2.0, the new web service API in Java EE 5.[9] The experiment was highly successful, and the new application had approximately half the number of Java classes. Ryan Lubke, an engineer at Sun Microsystems, examined a web application called Duke's Bank that was updated from using JavaServer Pages to JavaServer Faces, a new web-tier technology added to the Java EE 5 platform.[10] Table 9.1 provides a summary of the savings in the amount of code between J2EE 1.4 and Java EE 5.

Table 9.1 Highlighting the Advantages of the New Java EE Technology over J2EE Technology

Application	Property Evaluated	J2EE 1.4	Java EE 5	Savings
Adventure Builder	Number of classes	67	43	36% fewer classes
	Lines of code	3284	2722	15% fewer lines
RosterApp	Number of classes	17	7	59% fewer classes
	Lines of code	987	716	27% fewer lines
	Number of XML DD	9	2	78% fewer files
	Number of lines in DD	792	26	97% fewer lines
WI-Sample	Number of source files	128	61	52% fewer files
	Total file size	364.8KB	83.4KB	77% smaller file size
Duke Bank's Sample	Lines of code	2674	2395	10% fewer lines

These experiences clearly support the argument that new Java EE technology helps in achieving better developer productivity and a better time-to-market for realizing the enterprise solution. The new technology helps in many aspects of enterprise solution development—reducing the number of Java classes, reducing (or eliminating) boiler-plate code, reducing the file size, and reducing the number of deployment descriptors and other files.

Java EE Component Model

A Java Enterprise Edition application consists of many Java EE components, organized and packaged within a Java EE application in a standard fashion. These components might be classified into one of four different types: *application client*, *web component*, *EJB components*, and *resource adapters*. These components, along with their containers and communication patterns, are shown in Figure 9.5. In Java EE technology, there is no separate component type for web services. Instead, a web service is either mapped to a web component or an EJB component.

Application Client

An application client typically runs on a client desktop, providing a rich GUI or command-line front-end to services running on the server-side. An application client is similar to an ordinary Java program, with additional Java EE services supported, such as resource injection and various Java EE APIs.

Web Components

A Java EE web component can be a Servlet, JSP, or JSF component. Web components are typically used to implement the web-based presentation tier of a Java EE application. A Servlet component can also be used to expose a web service.

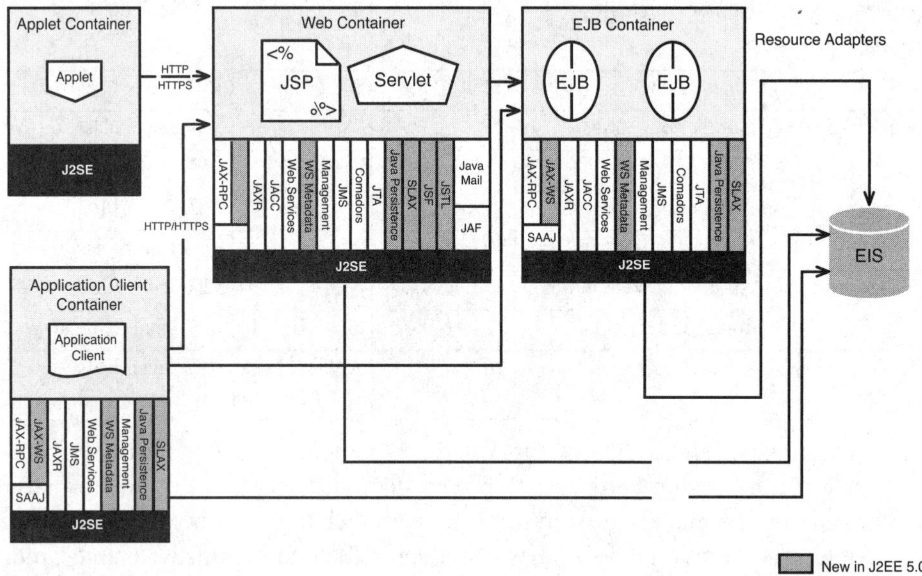

Figure 9.5 The end-to-end architecture view of the new Java EE technology

EJB Components

An EJB component can be a Session Bean, an Entity Bean, or a Message-driven Bean. These EJB components are typically used to encapsulate business logic that needs to be exposed in a distributed, secure, and transactional manner.

Resource Adapter

A resource adapter is a component responsible for connectivity to an EIS as defined in the Connector architecture. Typically, a resource adapter is EIS-specific because most EISs use a proprietary protocol to communicate with their clients. A resource adapter can be shared across multiple Java EE applications and can be accessed from web or EJB components.

Java EE Quality of Services

By providing *quality of services (QoS)* needed by enterprise applications, Java EE enables developers to focus on the presentation or business logic instead of dealing with complex system-level issues such as performance and scalability. Although some aspects of the QoS are exposed through various APIs, a majority of the QoS are made available to the applications transparently by the runtime environment in which the components are running. For example, the performance and scalability of an EJB component is provided transparently by the application server without using special APIs.

Distribution

One of the significant features of Java EE technology is that the services deployed on this platform are automatically exposed for access from remote clients. A web application can be accessed via *Hypertext Transfer Protocol Secure* (*HTTPS*) or *HTTP over Secure Socket Layer* (*SSL*). A session EJB, on the other hand, can be accessed via *Internet Inter-ORB Protocol (IIOP)*, IIOP over SSL, or even a vendor-specific distributed protocol. Likewise, a message-driven EJB can be triggered through a delivery of a JMS message. Furthermore, a web service deployed using Java EE technology can be invoked through *Simple Object Access Protocol* (*SOAP*) over HTTP or SOAP over HTTPS.

Data Integrity

Data integrity is of utmost importance for any enterprise. The Java EE platform provides a first-class support for distributed transactions to ensure the transaction, even if it spans across multiple machines and multiple resource managers. The transaction either takes place fully or is nullified in its entirety. Transaction management in Java EE frees developers from dealing with complex data integrity issues such as atomicity, consistency, concurrent updates, and failure recovery.

Security

Java EE provides mechanisms to support various aspects of the security requirement. The standard security requirements include *authentication*, *authorization*, *integrity*, and *confidentiality*.

The new technology provides an elegant mechanism for both authentication and authorization aspects of the security requirement. Although authentication establishes or confirms a client's identity based on supplied security credentials such as username/password pair or security certificate, authorization determines whether a client (both authenticated or unauthenticated) has the permission to access protected resources in the system. Java EE resources that can be protected include web components, EJB, and web services. Web components are protected by restricting access to specific URL patterns. EJB and web services protection can be specified on a per business method basis. Message integrity ensures that messages transmitted between clients and servers are not maliciously or accidentally altered by unintended users. Message confidentiality ensures that the message content is readable only by its intended recipients.

Performance and Scalability

Performance in distributed systems such as Java EE is typically characterized by response time and scalability. In the Java EE context, *response time* is the length of time required for a client request (such as an HTTP or SOAP request) to be fulfilled from the initiation of the transaction to the end of transaction. Scalability is often measured in terms of the number of concurrent requests an application server can service without significantly degrading the response time of each request. Due to the portability nature of the Java EE platform, it is possible to compare different products by running an industry-standard benchmark across different vendor implementations. One such benchmark is SPECjAppServer,[11] which was specifically developed to measure the performance of Java EE-compatible application servers. According to the latest results, SPECjAppServer 2004 measures workload in multiple areas of Java EE and includes access to web tier, EJB, JMS, and databases. Publications of the benchmark results from vendors are available for evaluation purposes.

Availability

The availability QoS essentially refers to the availability of the enterprise application to the users accessing the system. Typically, the availability component of the nonfunctional requirement of the enterprise solution is achieved through the use of multiple instances of application server process, clusters, and load balancers (or a combination thereof) to distribute the requests to these instances. Any high-end Java EE application server typically supports two variations of the enterprise application availability: *service availability* and *data availability*. Service availability means the services deployed in an application server remain accessible and functional even if there is a process or system failure. If a particular instance fails, requests to this instance will be redirected to and serviced by a different instance. Data availability means that the application states specific to user sessions, such as login sessions, will survive a failure. In Java EE, data availability is supported for HTTP sessions in web components and stateful

EJBs in application components. In most cases, support for availability is transparent to the applications and does not require code-level modifications.

Interoperability

Most enterprises deploy and support heterogeneous systems in their data centers. Interoperability among such heterogeneous systems would be a crucial requirement for most of the enterprises. Interoperability among different Java EE vendor products is achieved through the strict Java EE compatibility requirements. The Java EE compatibility Test Suite includes test cases that check whether a vendor implementation can communicate with the standard Java EE reference implementation. Interoperability between Java EE systems and non-Java EE systems is achieved through open standards, including HTTP, HTTP over SSL, SOAP, WS-I Basic Profile, and WSDL. This enables different web browsers or non-Java clients, such as C++ clients, to access web and web services hosted by Java EE application servers. It also enables Java EE components to access web services that might be hosted by a non-Java EE environment, such as the Microsoft .NET platform.

Concurrency

Java EE provides the power of concurrency without requiring knowledge of multithreading. For example, the business logic of an enterprise bean is always executed in a single-threaded fashion. This means developers do not need to worry about threads and related concurrency issues such as synchronization, deadlocks, and so on. The application server interposes and supports multithreading by creating new instances of Enterprise JavaBeans running under different threads as needed to satisfy simultaneous requests. This greatly reduces the complexity and potential multithreading-related defects in Java EE applications.

Summary

The new Java Enterprise Edition technologies provide radically improved features for enterprise solution developers. This technology enables developers to focus on the presentation and business logic instead of dealing with complex system-level issues such as performance, scalability, and availability. The emergence of the component-container paradigm has resulted in the evolution of web components and business components. Furthermore, this technology has enormously influenced the way enterprise applications are developed, deployed, and used. Separations of concerns are elegantly handled by letting different components on the web tier, and application tiers are responsible for appropriate enterprise application functions.

The main focus of the new version of the Java Enterprise Edition platform is ease of development and increased developer productivity. The essential goal of Java EE technology is to attract even more developers to the platform and broaden the use of technologies within the platform. The core technologies used to achieve these goals include extensive use of Java annotations, dependency injection, Plain Old Java Object model, and more.

In the next chapter, we focus on the web presentation layer of Java EE. Here, we explore web component technologies such as Servlet and JavaServer Pages, and framework-oriented technologies such as JavaServer Faces. We also deliberate on a variety of clients that communicate with these web components via the Internet/intranet environment. These web components, in turn, perform specific tasks as per the requirement of the enterprise process.

Endnotes

1. In the latest release, the number "2" was dropped from the name of the platform.
2. The version number in the current version of the technology is referred to as Java EE 5.
3. The adoption of this technology by vendors is increasing at an increasing rate.
4. This book touches upon some of these Java features, as applicable to the Java platform Enterprise Edition. For a more detailed treatment of such Java features, we recommend *The Java Programming Language*, Fourth Edition by Ken Arnold, James Gosling, and David Holmes, published by Prentice Hall PTR.
5. Note that this does not mean the information is simply moved from XML to annotations.
6. Use of annotations is considered a good practice by the developer community. With the current version of the Java EE platform, the developer can opt for the annotation route or the XML-based deployment descriptor route. This is ensured for a smooth transition from the J2EE technologies platform.
7. More details can be found at `www.theserverside.com/news/thread.tss?thread_id=35777`.
8. More details can be found at `http://java.sys-con.com/read/117755_1.htm`.
9. More details can be found at `http://weblogs.java.net/blog/arungupta/archive/javaone/BOF-9162.pdf`.
10. More details can be found at `http://blogs.sun.com/roller/page/rlubke?entry=does_jsf_simplify_web_application`.
11. More information on the SPEC jAppServer benchmark can be found at `www.spec.org/jAppServer/`.

10

Web Technologies in Java EE

T*he core building blocks of the web presentation layer of* Java Platform, Enterprise Edition *(*Java EE*) are Servlets,* JavaServer Pages *(*JSP*), and* JavaServer Faces *(*JSF*). A variety of clients can communicate with these web components via the Internet/intranet environment. These web components, in turn, can perform specific tasks at the back-end as per the requirements of the enterprise processes. Together, these components help in making the enterprise application building a simple process.*

Web technologies essentially address the presentation or *user interface* (*UI*) aspects of the enterprise application, delivering whole or part of the enterprise solution. Services can be created and composed, as per the principles of SOA, using Java EE technologies. The Java EE includes a number of web technologies that can implement the presentation layer of an Enterprise application. The Java Servlets, JSP, and Servlet Filters represent the core components of Java EE web technology. The most basic aspect of all Java EE-based web technologies is the Java Servlet API. This technology provides a simple mechanism for users to implement a Java Servlet class to handle *Hypertext Transfer Protocol* (*HTTP*) requests and generate dynamic web content. JSP simplifies the experience by enabling users to build their dynamic web pages in HTML-style tag format in a text file directly, without the need to learn Java. Two new web technologies have been added to the latest Java EE 5: *JavaServer Pages Standard Tag Library* (*JSTL*) and JSF. JSTL provides a set of standard, common tags useful in web applications written in JSP. The JSF technology, on the other hand, is a comprehensive, standard Java web framework for developing user interfaces of web applications. One key feature of JSF is support for creating and assembling multiple UI components into a web page. With the addition of JSF into the new platform, JSF has become the preferred framework for building web technology-based Java EE applications. In this chapter, we provide a brief description of each of the web technologies in Java EE; however, the focus is on JSF. This is the recommended framework for building Enterprise web applications.

Java Servlet

The Java Servlet API was the first Java-based API, introduced by Sun Microsystems in early 1997. A servlet defines one or more methods that correspond to the standard HTTP methods, such as `doGet()` for the HTTP `GET` method, `doPost()` for the HTTP `POST` method, and so on. These methods accept two parameters: `HttpServletRequest` and `HttpServletResponse`. The `HttpServletRequest` object carries information about the incoming HTTP request from a client. The `HttpServletResponse` is used by the servlet to provide a response, after appropriately processing the request. The reply is returned to the client as the response to its HTTP request. This communication mechanism is illustrated in Figure 10.1. The following code provides an example of a simple servlet:

```
public class MyServlet extends HttpServlet {
    public doGet(HttpServletRequest request,
HttpServletResponse response)
        throws ServletException, IOException {
        PrintWriter out = response.getWriter() {
        out.println("<html>");
        out.println("<head>");
        out.println("<title>Confirm Stock Sale</title>");
        out.println("</head>");
        out.println("<body>");
        ....
        // Read and process HttpServletRequest object
        ....
        // Process for business and/or presentation logic
        ....
       // Start writing output into HttpServletResponse object
        ....
        out.println("</body>");
        out.println("</html>");
    }
    ...
    // Other support and utility methods
    ...
}
```

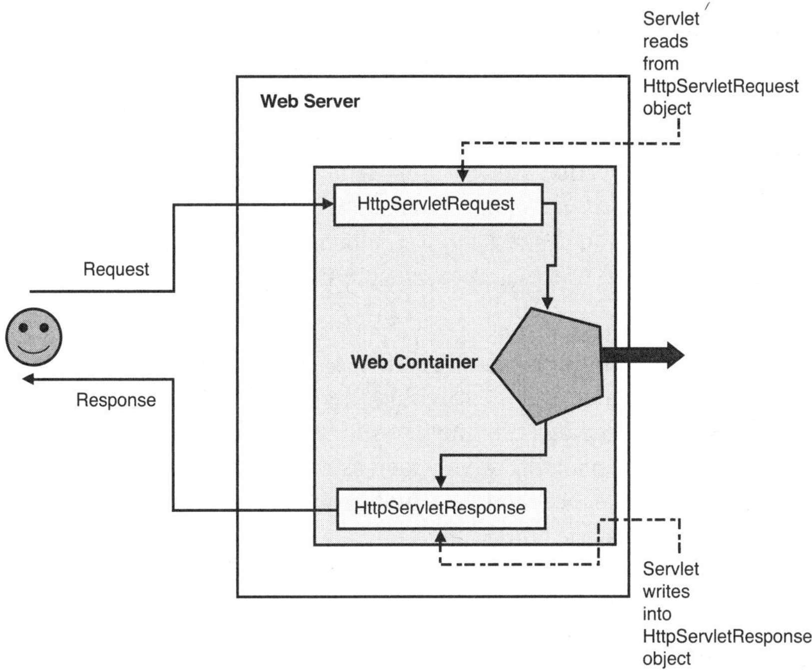

Figure 10.1 Servlet communication mechanism

This example shows implementation of a servlet that supports the HTTP `GET` operation. The servlet prints an appropriate response into the HTML page. Note that the servlet is not restricted to writing the response in HTML format that will be displayed in browsers. Servlets can also be used to write output in other formats such as XML or binary as a response to an HTTP request. For example, a servlet can implement a web service that can be accessed through HTTP.

Although the Java Servlet API is powerful and flexible, it is sometimes too low level and tedious to use to generate HTML. Designing a servlet for HTML output requires a sufficient number of boilerplate codes such as `out.println(" ... ");`. In addition, it is difficult for a web designer to edit the web content because the business logic and UI elements are intermixed in Java code. With the introduction of newer web technologies, the usage of Servlet is typically limited to implementation of services that provide non-UI contents, such as a web service or a remote service to support Ajax-based JavasScript invocations. Technologies such as JSP or JSF are more suitable for implementation of web UI and are presented in the following subsections.

JSP

JSP is a dynamic, page-oriented web technology that provides tag syntax similar to HTML tags. Web page designers find JSP attractive because an understanding of programming languages such as Java is not required. Instead, they can use a syntax they are familiar with for constructing the HTML pages. With this technology, a web application can be created using a number of inter-related JSP pages. Within each JSP page, one can suitably mix the standard HTML tags and JSP tags to provide the desired service. When the JSP runtime encounters a JSP tag, it applies special processing to execute the logic specified by the tag in the web server.

To execute a programming language such as Java within a JSP page, the user would provide the code fragment within the begin tag `<%` and end tag `%>`. In addition, the individual can provide a scripting language expression; the result is converted to a string and will be included as part of the page content. To enclose a scripting language expression, use the begin tag `<%=` and end tag `%>`. The following example illustrates this:

```
<%@ page contentType="text/html; charset =UTF-8" %>
<html>
  <head>
    <title>Account Information</title>
  </head>
  <body>
    ....
    // other processed output code
    ....
    Date: <%= new java.util.Date() %>
    ....
    // other processed output code
    ....
  </body>
</html>
```

In the preceding example, the `<%@page ... %>` directive declares information that applies to the entire JSP page. In this case it specifies the content type and the encoding character set. The `<%= new java.util.Date() %>` is a Java language expression. It will be evaluated at runtime, and the current date will be displayed as part of the web page.

One downside of using programming language in the JSP is the possibility of intermixing business logic and presentation elements in the JSP page. If not managed carefully, this can become difficult to maintain; however, techniques can minimize the intermixing and provide sufficient separation of the UI elements for editing by web designers.

Besides programming language fragments, custom JSP tags can be used within a JSP page to execute custom logic. The advantage of using custom JSP tags is that they use the same kind of syntax as HTML tags, making the process familiar to web designer and web editing tools.

JSP Standard Tag Library

Java EE technology provides a standard tag library called JSTL, which includes a set of tags for common business logic, functions, formatting, and database access within a web application. Developers and designers of dynamic web pages can easily and intuitively design the web pages using the JSTL in JSP page construction.

In the following example, the `<sql:setDataSource>` tag specifies the database information. The `<sql:query>` tag executes a SQL query on a database. The `<c:forEach>` tag is an iteration that is used to iterate through every row of the query result set. Notice here that the usage of the tag `<c:forEach>` is similar to the *for loop* of any typical programming language. Finally, the `<c:out>` tag outputs the value of the row number, in the present case, of the database table column to the web page.

```
<%@ taglib prefix="c" uri="http://java.sun.com/jsp/jstl/core"
%>
<%@ taglib prefix="sql" uri="http://java.sun.com/jsp/jstl/sql"
%>
...
<sql:setDataSource dataSource="jdbc/EmployeeDB"/>

<sql:query var="dbresult">
  select id from Employees
</sql:query>

<c:forEach var="row" items="#{dbresult.rows}">
  <c:out value="#{row['id']}"/>
</c:forEach>
...
```

JSF

JSF is a comprehensive framework used for building web applications. It supports a *Model-View-Controller (MVC)* paradigm, as exemplified in Figure 10.2, providing a well-defined demarcation between presentation and business logic. It also has a clearly stated component model, which enables rapid assembly of UI components to form a web page.

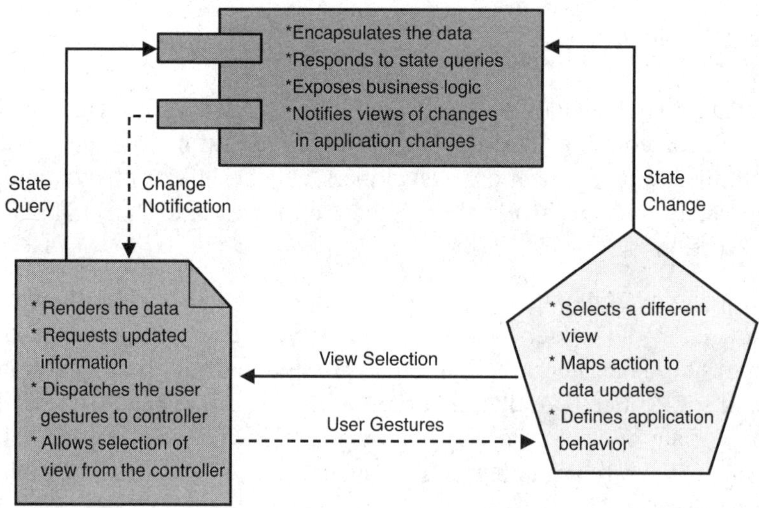

Figure 10.2 Conceptual view of the MVC architecture

MVC Paradigm in JSF

The MVC paradigm is a popular approach used to decouple the user interface from the application states and business logic. The Model in JSF is a collection of Managed Beans. The Managed Beans are regular JavaBeans managed by the JSF runtime and are used to store application or UI component states, such as the value of an input field. The View in JSF consists of a set of JSF pages used to define the presentation logic of a web application. Typically HTML, JSP, and JSF tags can be used in a JSF page. The Controller in JSF is implemented using the Faces Servlet, which processes incoming web HTTP requests and directs them to the appropriate view page based on the navigation rules stored in an XML configuration file.

User Interface Component Framework

The presentation view of a JSF application is composed using a standard set of JSF UI components. A UI component represents a widget such as a text field or pull-down menu displayed as part of a web page. Conceptually, it is similar to a component in the Swing in Java Standard Edition[1] used on client-side Java. And although the JSF technology provides a standard set of components, a web application is free to use other JSF-based component libraries as well. It is also possible for a developer to write a custom component that can be used in any JSF application.

A component in JSF consists of three entities: *component class*, *JSP tag*, and optional *renderer*. The component class implements the processing logic of the component. The JSP tag is used in a JSF page to reference the component. The renderer is used to generate the actual UI representation of the component.

The following is an example of a simple JSF page that includes two input fields and a Submit button:

```
<%@ page contentType="text/html"%>
<%@ taglib uri="http://java.sun.com/jsf/core" prefix="f"%>
<%@ taglib uri="http://java.sun.com/jsf/html" prefix="h"%>
<f:view>
  <html>
    <head>
      <title>Simple JSF page</title>
    </head>
    <body>
      <h:form>
        <table>
          <tr>
            <td>Login:</td>
            <td><h:inputText id="login"
                             value="#{ManagedBean.login}">
          </tr>
          <tr>
            <td>Password:</td>
            <td><h:inputSecret id="password"
                              value="#{ManagedBean.password}">
          </tr>
        </table>
        <p><h:commandButton value="Submit"
                            action="authenticate" /></p>
      </h:form>
    </body>
  </html>
</f:view>
```

The preceding page includes both HTML tags and JSF tags. The first JSF tag is `<f:view>`, which serves as a container for all JSF components used within a page. The next tag is `<h:form>`, which specifies an input form component and contains a number of input components. In this case, there are two input field components. The `<h:inputText>` tag specifies a user input field. The input field is bound to the property login of the Java class `ManagedBean`. This represents the linkage between the *View* and the *Model* in the MVC paradigm. The JSF runtime synchronizes the data between the input fields in the browser with the property of the Java object. The `<h:inputSecret>` tag specifies a password input field, in which the text entered is masked. It is also bound to a managed bean. Finally, the `<h:commandButton>` tag specifies a Submit button. When the user clicks on the button, the information in the two input fields will be submitted to the web application. The Submit button then generates an action "authenticate," which determines the navigation to the next page based on the specified navigation rule in JSF.

Navigation Model

JSF defines a complete navigation model that enables a developer to define the complete page flow of the web application in a single XML configuration file. During the development of a web application, views in the form of JSP pages are frequently added or removed and existing views are modified. It would be a maintenance nightmare if the navigation logic were hard-coded and spread across many places.

Consider a typical security-related operation that forms a part of the enterprise application. This part of the application consists of three JSP pages: `Login.jsp`, `Accepted.jsp`, and `Rejected.jsp`. The `Login.jsp` page, as illustrated in Figure 10.3, provides a view for the users to enter their username and password. When the user submits the credentials, the `Accepted.jsp` page displays if the user has entered the correct username and password combination. Otherwise, the `Rejected.jsp` page displays.

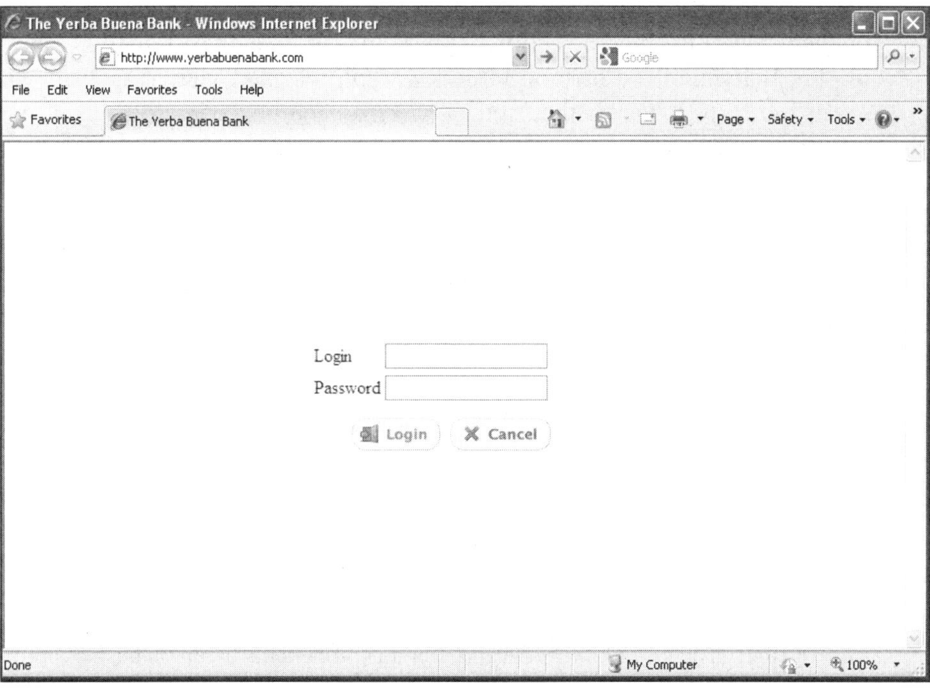

Figure 10.3 Example showing two input text fields with Login and Cancel buttons

The following example characterizes just how the preceding navigation can be represented in the JSF configuration file:

```
<navigation-rule>
  <from-view-id>/Login.jsp</from-view-id>
  <navigation-case>
    <from-action>#{LoginBean.action}</from-action>
    <from-outcome>accept</form-outcome>
    <to-view-id>/Accepted.jsp</to-view-id>
  </navigation-case>
  <navigation-case>
    <from-action>#{LoginBean.action}</from-action>
    <from-outcome>decline</form-outcome>
    <to-view-id>/Rejected.jsp</to-view-id>
  </navigation-case>
</navigation-rule>
```

The preceding XML snippet, as exemplified in Figure 10.4, specifies the view `Login.jsp` will navigate to either `Accepted.jsp` or `Rejected.jsp` depending on the result of the method action of the Managed Bean, which in this example is the `LoginBean`. If the method returns *accept*, the next view displayed will be `Accepted.jsp`. If the method returns *decline*, the next view displayed will be `Rejected.jsp`.

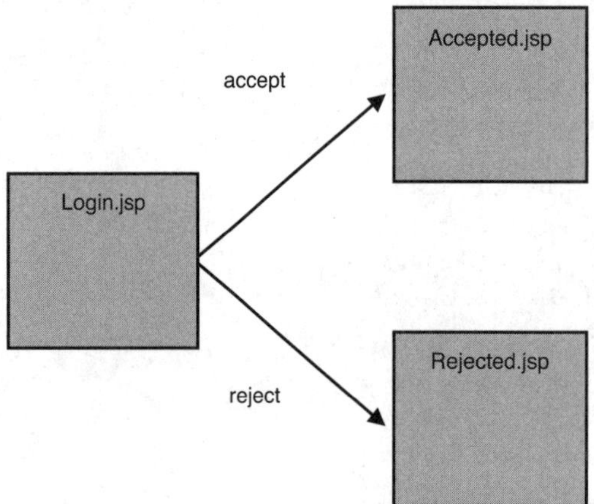

Figure 10.4 The navigation between different components based on business process requirement

Managed Beans

JSF Managed Beans are regular Java objects whose life cycle is managed by the JSF runtime. They are used to maintain application states and to define business logic that will be executed when certain events happen in the web application. The events could be something as simple as a user clicking on a Submit button or pressing a Return key. Managed Beans are registered with the runtime using an XML configuration file.

User interface components in JSF typically use one or more Managed Beans to maintain the actual state of the component. For example, a text field component might use a Java property of a Managed Bean to store the content of the text field. When a web form is submitted, the JSF runtime updates the associated Managed Bean properties with the updated values on the web form.

Two commonly used measures to define the scope or lifetime of Managed Beans are *request* and *session*. A Managed Bean with request scope is created and remains available within a single HTTP request. Likewise, a Managed Bean with session scope is created and remains available within a single HTTP session.

This is useful when it is necessary to store information across multiple HTTP requests, such as when managing the content of a shopping cart.

Dependency injection is supported in Managed Beans. For example, `@Resource` annotation can be used in Managed Beans to inject dependencies like resource factory references (JDBC, JMS, Connector, and so on) and environment variables into a field when an Enterprise bean is constructed. The `@EJB` annotation can be used to inject EJB references, which makes the process of invoking another Enterprise bean just like calling a Java method of a regular Java object.

When Managed Beans consist of properties that are UI components, such Managed Beans are referred to as *Backing Beans*. In such beans, instead of bean properties bound to the UI component values, they are bound to the UI component themselves.

Unified Expression Language

The Java language is powerful, although it can be a bit awkward and difficult for some web page designers to use directly on JSP or JSF pages. Instead, JSP, JSTL, and JSF now support the unified expression language, which provides an easy and compact way to access Managed Bean properties and methods. A unified expression is surrounded by delimiters `#{` and `}`. It can be integrated in a straightforward way into XML or JSP tag attributes so that the actual values of the attributes can be dynamically evaluated at runtime. A typical usage of the Unified Expression Language is provided here:

```
<h:outputText value="#{managedBean.address}"/>
```

The preceding expression would retrieve the text by invoking `managedBean.getAddress()` and display it in the web page.

The expression language can also be used to update the Managed Beans properties when a web form is submitted, as illustrated in the following example:

```
<h:inputText value="#{managedBean.address}"/>
```

In the preceding example, the JSF runtime invokes `ManagedBean.setAddress()` with the updated value of the input field upon web form submission.

Furthermore, the expression language supports common operators to combine or manipulate the expression value. The following is an example of usage of arithmetic operators:

```
<h:outputText value="Payment include 10% late fee is:
#{managedBean.fee * 1.1}"/>
```

The conditional operator in the form of `#{A ? B : C}` is also supported, which means if A is evaluated to `true`, B is returned. Otherwise C is returned. Here is an example:

```
<h:outputText value="Total price is:
#{managedBean.premiumCustomer ? managedBean.fee * 0.9 :
managedBean.fee}"/>
```

In the preceding example, a premium customer as determined by method `managedBean.getPremiumCustomer()` receives a 10% discount.

Data Conversion and Validation

Strings are the primary data representation used in web forms and requests. Although the application logic can choose to treat all data as strings, in many cases it will be less error-prone if the data can be converted to a suitable Java primitive or object type, such as `Integer`, `Float`, and `Date`. JSF has built-in support for most common numeric and date types. The data conversion happens transparently when data is retrieved from or stored in Managed Bean properties. It is also possible to define custom converters and associate them with JSF components.

Let's consider the following Managed Bean:

```
public class MyManagedBean {
    private Date date;
    public Date getDate() {
        return date;
    }
    public void setDate(Date date) {
        this.date = date;
    }
    ...
}
```

and the following snippet on the JSF page:

```
<h:inputText value="#{managedBean.date}"/>
```

When the user submits the form, the JSF runtime implicitly converts the string representation entered by the user in the input text field to `java.util.Date` object based on the property type in the Managed Bean. It is also possible to have more explicit control on the conversion:

```
<h:inputText value="#{managedBean.date}">
    <f:convertDateTime dateStyle="short"/>
</h:inputText>
```

In addition to data conversion, JSF technology provides a data validation mechanism to deal with format errors in user input. JSF provides only basic validations, such as the length of a string or the range of a number. But it is possible to define custom validators, which can validate more complex data types, such as telephone numbers, addresses, and so on. When the JSF runtime detects an invalid value, it displays a default or user-specified error message. An example follows:

```
<h:inputText value="#{managedBean.number}" id="num1to5">
    <f:validateLongRange minimum="1" maximum="5"/>
</h:inputText>
<h:message for="num1to5"/>
```

In this example, if the user enters a number that is not between 1 and 5, the JSF runtime returns an error message in the location specified by the `<h:message>` tag.

JSF Events

The JSF event mechanism decouples the component generating the event and the Managed Bean listener that processes the event. JSF supports three types of events: *action events*, *value change events*, and *phase events*. An action event is generated when a web form is submitted. A value change event is generated when the value of a UI component is changed. A phase event, used in more advanced scenarios, is generated as JSF runtime processes proceed through various steps of the request processing life cycle.

To handle a JSF event, the user can write a listener class that implements the appropriate listener interface. For the sake of simplicity, it is also possible to write only a listener method instead of implementing the listener interface. The following is an example of action event handling in JSF using a listener method:

```
<h:commandButton value="Submit" actionListener="#{Managed-
Bean.handleSubmitAction}"/>

public class ManagedBean {
    ...
    public void handleSubmitAction(ActionEvent e) {
        // ... handle submit action
    }
}
```

The Managed Bean here enables to appropriately configure the action event using the `handleSubmitAction()` method.

Backing Bean Approach

The use of Backing Beans is a recommended approach for JSF applications. In this approach, the user would define and register a Managed Bean, or Backing Bean, for each JSF page. The Backing Bean includes properties that correspond to the input fields on the page. In addition, the Backing Bean defines action or action listener methods that are bound to components that would generate action events (for example, `commandButton`). The action methods can return a string result that is used, together with the navigation rules specified in the XML configuration file, to determine the next page in the sequence of JSF page navigation.

Using the login page, presented in the "User Interface Component Framework" section, as an example, the Backing Bean would look like this:

```
public class LoginBackingBean {
    // properties corresponding to the input fields
    private String username;
    private String password;
    public String getUsername() {return username; }
    public void setUsername(String username) {this.username =
username; }
    ...
    // action method
    public String loginAction() {
        boolean result = authenticate(username, password);
        if (result) {
           return "success";
        } else {
           return "failure";
        }
    }

    private boolean authenticate(String username,
                                 String password) {
       // method to validate username and password
       ...
    }
}
```

The Backing Bean approach provides an elegant separation opportunity between View, Model, and Controller logic at a page-level granularity. This model also makes it easy for tools to automatically generate the Backing Bean skeleton code based on the JSF tags in a page.

Summary

Servlets, JSP, and so on coupled with frameworks such as JSF form the core building blocks for the web presentation layer in the Java Platform, Enterprise Edition. Together, these web components can perform specific tasks as per the requirement of the process/workflow of the Enterprise. They also can interact with the EJB on the business tier for accessing business logic and data. Ultimately, they can help to simplify the Enterprise application building process as per the requirement of SOA.

In the next chapter, we delve into the details of the persistence aspects of the Enterprise information. Here, we provide you with a detailed presentation on the new Java Persistence API that provides a standardized mechanism for implementing the Object-Relational mapping of the persistent data. We also describe in detail the new simplified Enterprise JavaBeans model and specification called EJB 3.0.

Endnote

1. Earlier referred to as Java 2 Standard Edition (or J2SE).

11

Enterprise JavaBeans and Persistence

A key requirement of Enterprise components is to persist or access data stored in relational databases. The new Java Persistence API *(JPA) provides a powerful, standard object-relational mapping facility usable by any component in the Java Platform, Enterprise Edition. Entity objects are plain Java objects that can be used in detached modes as well, obviating the need for patterns such as Data Transfer Objects. Many object-oriented language features, such as inheritance and polymorphism, are supported by the mapping, resulting in more readable and maintainable domain object models. The JPA includes support for several advanced features that are particularly appropriate in an Enterprise setting, such as named queries and optimistic locking. In addition to Java Persistence, the latest Enterprise JavaBeans specification defines a much simpler model for writing session beans and message-driven beans.*

Services created and composed, as per the SOA principles (or otherwise) frequently need to manage data persistence activities. The data accessing services are essentially back-end activities, whereas business components such as EJB 3.0 and the new JPA technology enable for an elegant data persistence mechanism.

The goal of the new Enterprise JavaBeans specification (EJB 3.0) is to simplify the building of transactional, secure Enterprise applications. The specification can be divided into two main parts: the *core EJB API* and the *new JPA*. Although the previous versions of EJB technology (EJB 2.1 and its predecessors) were powerful, they were difficult to use. The new EJB 3.0 specification simplifies the

API using the new Java concepts of *Annotations* and *Dependency Injection* while retaining the same power and flexibility. The objective of the newly introduced JPA is to provide a standard, simple API and model to support object-relational mapping between relational databases and Java objects. The JPA aims to unify the diverse set of persistence technologies currently available, such as *Java Data Objects* (*JDO*), Hibernate, and so on. Unlike the core EJB technology, JPA is designed to support both Java Standard Edition (SE) and Java EE environments.

Core EJB 3.0 API

Core EJB 3.0 API makes the development of Session EJBs and Message-Driven EJB easier. The new core beans enable fewer required classes and interfaces, whereas support for dependency injection and the Deployment Descriptors is optional. The entity beans, on the other hand, are replaced with the new persistence model defined in the JPA. All existing EJB applications and components continue to work in an EJB 3.0 container to maintain backward compatibility. Furthermore, the older EJB components can be incrementally upgraded to EJB 3.0 without affecting existing clients.

Here is an example of how a stateless session EJB is created:

```
@Stateless
@Remote
public class VacationManagementBean {
    @Resource DataSource vacationDB;

    public void recordVacation(String empId,
                               Date   start,
                               int    length) {
        ...
        Connection con = vacationDB.getConnection();
        ...
    }
}
```

In the preceding example, annotation `@Stateless` marks the class as stateless session EJB. `@Remote` declares the business methods as remote and thus can be invoked by clients outside of the EJB container. An instance of the data source is injected transparently into the field `vacationDB`. Unlike EJB 2.1, no extra methods, interfaces, or XML Deployment Descriptor is required.

The following annotations can be used to declare a Java class or interface as an Enterprise bean:

- `@Stateless`—Declares a stateless session bean.
- `@Stateful`—Declares a stateful session bean.
- `@MessageDriven`—Declares a message-driven bean.
- `@Entity`—Declares an entity class.
- `@Local`—Declares local business interfaces for a session bean. A local interface can be invoked only by clients within the same EJB container. This is the default if no `@Local` or `@Remote` annotation is explicitly used.
- `@Remote`—Declares remote business interfaces for a session bean.

Dependency Injection

As described in Chapter 9, "Java Platform, Enterprise Edition Overview," `@Resource` annotation can be used in Enterprise beans to inject dependencies like resource factory references (JDBC, JMS, Connector, and such) and environment variables into a field when an Enterprise bean is constructed. Likewise, the `@EJB` annotation can be used to inject EJB references, which makes invoking another Enterprise bean just like calling a Java method of a regular Java object. The following is an example of EJB reference injection usage as applicable to an application client:

```
public class MyClient {
    @EJB VacationManagementBean vacationBean;
    public void myMethod() {
        ...
        vacationBean.recordVacation("123",
DateFormat.parse("12/24/2006"), 10));
        ...
    }
    ...
}
```

Container Services

Container services enable handling transactions, managing security, and handling other life cycle-related callback events. These services can be invoked using appropriate Java annotations. Some of the key annotations that invoke container services are `@TransactionAttribute`, `@RolesAllowed`, `@PermitAll`, `@DenyAll`, `@PostConstruct`, `@PostActivate`, `@PreDestroy`, `@PrePassivate`, and so on. These container-related services can be classified into broad categories, including transaction, security, and life cycle.

Transaction

@TransactionAttribute—By default, all business methods in Enterprise beans use container-managed transactions, with the transaction attribute value of REQUIRED. However, the @TransactionAttribute annotation can change the default behavior. Parameters accepted for this annotation include MANDATORY, NEVER, NOT_SUPPORTED, REQUIRED, REQUIRES_NEW, and SUPPORTS. This annotation can be applied at either the class or the method level. If the class level is used, all methods within the class are affected. In the following example, we provide the code snippet used for changing the transaction attribute to MANDATORY:

```
@Stateless
public class VacationManagementBean {
    ...
    // Transaction must have been started before calling method
    @TransactionAttribute(MANDATORY)
    ...
    public void recordVacation(String empId,
                                Date start,
                                int length) {
        ...
    }
}
```

Security

@RolesAllowed, @PermitAll, @DenyAll—By default, business methods can be invoked by all security roles. Several security-related attributes can fix and fine-tune the requirements as per the application requirement. For example, the @RolesAllowed annotation can restrict business method invocation to specific roles, such as administrators. Likewise, the @DenyAll annotation means that no security roles are allowed to invoke the specified methods. These annotations can be applied at either the class or the method level. If used at the class level, it affects all methods within the class. The following is an example that illustrates that only the employees and administrator users of the application can invoke the recordVacation() method of a specific application:

```
@Stateless
public class VacationManagementBean {
    ...
    // restrict method to employees and administrators only
    @RolesAllowed({"Employee", "Administrator"})
    public void recordVacation(String empId, Date start, int
length) {
        ...
    }
}
```

Life Cycle

`@PostConstruct`, `@PostActivate`, `@PreDestroy`, `@PrePassivate`—These annotations signify the EJB-specific life-cycle callback events. If a method is annotated with one of these life-cycle callback events, the method will be called by the container after bean construction and activation and before bean destruction and passivation, respectively. These annotations are typically used to invoke appropriate initialization and clean-up logic. In addition to being associated with a bean method, these annotations can be specified on interceptors.

Interceptors

Interceptors are a new feature in EJB 3.0 that permits interception of invocations of business methods, message listener methods, and life-cycle events. They are useful for applying similar logic across multiple operations of an Enterprise bean. For example, the interceptor mechanism can be used to implement a simple audit feature that would record all invocations of business methods of an Enterprise bean. Multiple interceptors can form a chain, and they will be invoked in a specific order.

The following is an example of the use of interceptors:

```
@Interceptors({
    com.example.LoggingInterceptor.class,
    com.example.AnotherInterceptor.class
})
@Stateless
public class VacationManagementBean {
    ...
}
public class LoggingInterceptor {
    @AroundInvoke
    public Object log(InvocationContext ctx) throws Exception {
        System.out.println(ctx.getMethod().toString());
        return ctx.proceed();
    }
}
```

New JPA

In new JPA, an entity is defined as a Java object that can be suitably persisted in the database. When compared to the entity beans defined in previous versions of the EJB specification, the new entities are lightweight, intuitive, and require less coding. For example, there are no required interfaces or EJB life-cycle methods that need to be implemented in the new entity EJBs. For the most part, an entity can be used just like any regular Java objects with the usual support for object-oriented features such as inheritance and polymorphism. It can even be serialized across different processes or machines. This is useful when sending an entity to the presentation tier of a Java EE application.

The following is an example of an entity that represents a student:

```
@Entity
public class Student {
    @Id private int id;
    private String firstName;
    private String lastName;
    @ManyToOne private Department dept;
    @ManyToMany private Set<Course> courses = new HashSet();
    public int getId() {
       return id;
    }
    public void setId(int id) {
       this.id = id;
    }
    ...
}
```

In the preceding code snippet, the `@Entity` annotation declares this class as an entity. The `@Id` annotation marks the field as the persistent identity for the class, which uniquely identifies any entity of this class. Typically the identity field will be mapped to the *primary key* of a relational table. The `@ManyToOne` annotation specifies a many-to-one relationship between the Student and Department entity classes. This relation basically indicates that a student can belong to exactly one department, and a department can include multiple students. The `@ManyToMany` annotation, on the other hand, specifies a many-to-many relationship between the Student and Course entity classes. For example, a student can enroll in multiple courses, and a course roster can include multiple students.

Entity Class

An entity class is annotated using the `@Entity` annotation. An entity can also extend another *entity* or a *regular* (nonentity) class. Moreover, an entity might have both *persistent* and *nonpersistent* (or transient) states. Only persistent states will be stored in the database. Optionally, an entity can be declared as *serializable*.

Every entity must have a persistent identity, which maps to a primary key in the database. Multiple forms of primary key are supported using the following annotations:

- `@Id`—Single field primary key.
- `@GeneratedValue`—Single field primary key value is generated automatically.
- `@EmbeddedId`—Primary key is represented as an embedded entity class.
- `@IdClass`—Composite primary key that maps to multiple fields of the entity.

The following is an example of a composite primary key:

```
@IdClass(PersonPK.class)
@Entity
public Person {
    @Id String lastName;
    @Id Date birthDate;
    ...
}
```

Relationships

The new JPA supports *one-to-one*, *one-to-many*, *many-to-many*, and *many-to-one* relationships among entities. Relationships are represented as instance variables in the new entities, so it is straightforward to navigate or update relationships between entities using the JPA. To represent the many sides of a relationship, a Java collection type such as *Collection*, *Set*, *List*, and *Map* can be used.

Relationships can be *unidirectional* or *bidirectional*. In a unidirectional relationship between two entities A and B, one can navigate directly from entity A to B but not vice versa. In a bidirectional relationship, navigation can happen between A and B in both directions. A bidirectional relationship consists of an owning side and an inverse side. The owning side typically corresponds to a *foreign key.* To tie the owning side and inverse side together, the inverse side of the relationship is required to specify the name of the instance variable of the owning-side relationship. Note, however, that when updating a bidirectional relationship, the application, not the container or application server, is responsible for modifying both sides of the relationship.

The following annotations are used to specify relationships in entities:

- `@OneToOne`—Specifies one-to-one relationship
- `@OneToMany`—Specifies one-to-many relationship
- `@ManyToOne`—Specifies many-to-one relationship
- `@ManyToMany`—Specifies many-to-many-relationship

The following is an example of a *bidirectional* relationship:

```
@Entity
public class Student {
    ...
    // owning side of bidirectional relationship
    @ManyToOne private Department dept;
    ...
}

@Entity
public class Department {
    ...
    // Inverse side of bidirectional relationship
    // note the use of mappedBy
    @OneToMany(mappedBy="dept")
    private Set<Student> students = new HashSet();
    ...
}
```

Inheritance

An entity can extend other entities, mapped superclasses, or other ordinary Java classes. When an entity A extends another entity B, all persistent (and nonpersistent) fields in B will be inherited by A. When an entity extends an ordinary Java class, the entire inherited field remains nonpersistent. A mapped superclass is a regular Java class associated with annotation `@MappedSuperclass`. It is not an entity and thus cannot be persisted directly in the database. However, it provides common persistent states to subclass entities. JPA supports *polymorphism* as well. This means that if a relationship field or result of a query is expected to hold a particular entity type, it can hold any entity subclasses as well. The following is an example of the use of inheritance in the new JPA:

```
@MappedSuperclass public class Person {
    @Id protected int id;
    protected String firstName;
    protected String lastName;
    ...
}

@Entity public class Student extends Person {
    @ManyToMany private Set<Course> courses =
        new HashSet();
    ...
```

```
}

@Entity public class Faculty extends Person {
    protected float salary;
    @OneToMany private Set<Course> teaching =
        new HashSet();
    ...
}
```

Entity Manager

The entity manager API is an important interface in JPA and is used to manage the life cycle of entities and persistent context. It includes operations to persist and destroy entities, to locate an existing entity using its *primary key*, and to create Java Persistence Query objects. There are two ways to obtain a reference to an entity manager instance. In the new Java EE environment, the annotation `@PersistenceContext` can be used to inject an entity manager into a field using the following syntax:

```
@PersistenceContext EntityManager em;
```

In the Java Platform, Standard Edition environment, the entity manager can be instantiated explicitly using the entity manager factory, for example

```
...
EntityManagerFactory emf =
      Persistence.createEntityManagerFactory("UnversitySys-
tem");
EntityManager em = emf.createEntityManager();
...
```

In the Java Platform, Standard Edition environment, the application is responsible for managing the life cycle of the entity manager and its factory. An explicit `close()` method needs to be invoked when the application finishes the use of the entity manager and its factory.

Entity Life-Cycle Operations

An entity life cycle consists of four states: *new state*, *managed state*, *detached state*, and *Removed state*. These states and the relationship between them are illustrated in Figure 11.1.

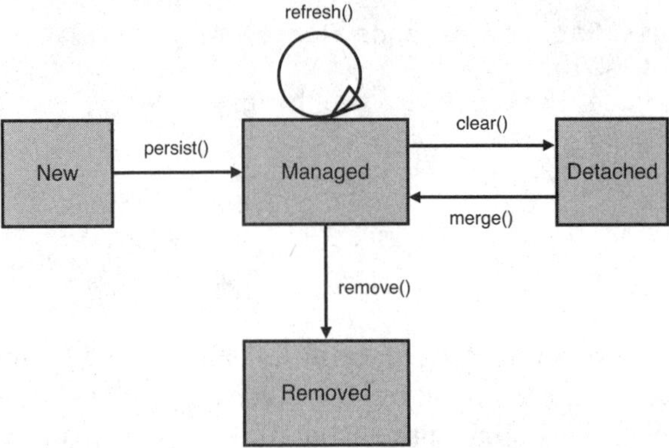

Figure 11.1 Entity life-cycle operations illustrated

The New State

A new entity can be instantiated just like any other regular Java object. When an entity is created, it is not managed by the Entity Manager and it is not persistent. At this point, an entity is basically the same as a regular Java object.

The Managed State

An entity becomes managed when it is under the control of the entity manager. This is achieved using the persist method of the entity manager. The entity is now persistent and will be persisted in the database upon transaction completion. The following example demonstrates how to persist a new student:

```
...
EntityManager em = ...  // obtain entity manager reference
Student student  = new Student(...);
em.persist(student);
...
```

After an entity is persisted, it is possible to reload its state from the database using the `refresh()` method of the Entity Manager.

The Detached State

An entity is said to be in a detached state when it is removed from the control of the entity manager. This typically happens when an entity object is serialized and transported across the network to a different tier such as the presentation tier. A user can also explicitly detach all the objects managed by an entity manager using the `EntityManager.clear()` method. A detached entity includes content from the database but is no longer linked to the database. Updates to a detached entity will not affect the database content. Detached entities are primarily used as Data Transfer Objects (DTO), which can be used to encapsulate persistent business data and to exchange data between different tiers of an enterprise application.

Consider the scenario in which an entity is serialized across to a different tier, meaning it is not in a detached state. The application updates the detached entity and sends it back to the original tier. To synchronize the updates with the database, it would be necessary to reattach or merge the entity using the `EntityManager.merge()` method. After merging, the entity is managed by the entity manager again, and the changes to the entity will be written back to the database upon the completion of transaction. The following is an example of an entity being sent to a remote EJB for updates:

```
...
EntityManager em = ...  // obtain entity manager reference
MyEJB ejb = ... // obtain reference to remote EJB
Student student = em.find(Student.class, "123");
Student updatedStudent = ejb.updateStudent(student);
// student will become detached upon
// serialization to remote EJB  em.merge(updatedStudent);
// merge updated student so it can be written to database
...
```

The Removed State

The `EntityManager.remove()` method can delete an entity from the database upon transaction completion, as shown in the following example:

```
...
EntityManager em = ...  // obtain entity manager reference
Student student = em.find(Student.class, "123");
em.remove(student);
...
```

Cascading is supported for operations `persist()`, `remove()`, and `merge()`. Suppose cascading is specified on a particular relationship. This means when an operation is applied to an entity, the same operation will be applied in a transitive manner on all associated entities that are part of the relationship. The following is an example:

```
@Entity public class Order {
    @Id protected int id;
    @OneToMany(cascade={PERSIST, REMOTE, MERGE})
    protected Set<LineItem> lineItems = new HashSet();
    ...
}
```

In the preceding example, if an `Order` entity is removed; all associated `lineItems` will also be removed automatically.

Java Persistence Query Language

JPA includes support for a query language that can be used to locate entities and to perform bulk update or delete operations. The query language has syntax similar to SQL but operates on the entity abstract schema instead of the actual relational schema. It also supports additional operations not available in standard SQL.

The following is an example of a simple query in the Persistence query language:

```
SELECT s FROM Student s WHERE s.firstName = 'John'
```

As expected, the preceding query would return all students with the first name John.

Using Relationships in Query Language

Java Persistence query language supports the use of relationship through path expressions and the `JOIN` clause. The syntax for a path expression is the same as the Java field navigation using the dot symbol, as in `student.dept`. This navigation works only for the single side of the relationship. For example, it is not possible to use a path expression to navigate from a student to the set of enrolled courses. In addition to relationship, the same expression syntax can be used to access field variables in the entity, like `student.firstName`. Here is an example of a query using path expression:

```
SELECT s FROM Student s WHERE s.dept.name = 'Computer Science'
```

The preceding query returns all the students that belong to the department of computer science. The path expression can also be used in the `SELECT` clause:

```
SELECT s.dept.name FROM Student s WHERE s.firstName = 'John'
```

The preceding query returns the names of all departments that include a student with the first name John.

The `JOIN` clause is used to select data from two or more types of entities that are related to one another. The last query previously described can be written using a `JOIN` clause:

```
SELECT d.name FROM Student s JOIN Department d WHERE s.firstName
= 'John'
```

The JOIN clause is particularly useful for entities with many-to-many relationships, where path expression cannot be used to navigate many-to-many relationships, as shown in the following example:

```
SELECT c.name FROM Student s JOIN Course c WHERE s.id = '453'
```

The preceding query returns all the classes enrolled by the student with id equal to 453.

Query Creation

JPA supports both static and dynamic queries. A static query is defined using annotations @NamedQuery and @NamedNativeQuery. A dynamic query is specified at runtime with a query string using the entity manager interface. Either static or dynamic queries can be parameterized with concrete parameter values provided at runtime. The following is an example of a parameterized dynamic query:

```
@PersistenceContext EntityManager em;

public List findByLastName(String lastName) {
    return em.createQuery("SELECT s FROM Student s WHERE
s.lastName = :lastname").setParameter("lastname", last-
Name).getResultList();
}
```

In the preceding example, lastname is a parameter for the query, which is substituted with the value of the local variable lastName at runtime. Here is the same example using the static query:

```
@NamedQuery(name="FindStudentByLastName",

   query="SELECT s FROM Student s WHERE s.lastName = :lastname")
@Entity public class Student {
    ...
    public List findByLastName(String lastName) {
        return em.createNamedQuery("FindStudentByLastName")
          .setParameter("lastname", lastName).getResultList();
    ...
    }
}
```

Bulk Update and Delete

In addition to retrieving entities from the database, the query mechanism can be used to perform bulk updates and deletes. The following example demonstrates how to increase the salary of all faculty members by 5%:

```
...
@PersistenceContext EntityManager em;
Query q = em.createQuery("UPDATE Faculty f SET f.salary
                        = f.salary *1.05");
int numRows = q.executeUpdate();
...
```

In this next example, a query is used to delete courses that existed before the year 1995:

```
...
Query q = em.createQuery( "DELETE from Course c WHERE c.year <
1995");
int numRows = q.executeUpdate();
...
```

Database Portability

The key benefit of using the new JPA is portability across different databases. Most databases support a variant of native SQL language, and an application using native SQL is often tied to a particular database. Queries written in the Java Persistence query are portable across all databases supported by a Java Persistence provider. The provider is responsible for mapping the queries to the appropriate native SQL of the target database. For example, Java Persistence query supports the string function `locate`, which returns the location of a substring in a string. If the target database is Oracle, the provider would map the function to the Oracle `INSTR` function. When the target database is Sybase, on the other hand, the `locate` function will be mapped to the Sybase `CHARINDEX` function. All the database-specific translation is transparent to the developers.

Java Persistence does support the direct use of native SQL when Java Persistence Query Language is not sufficient. Obviously, the use of this feature would mean the application is not portable across different databases. Under such circumstances, Native query can be created statically using `@NameNativeQuery` annotation or dynamically using the `EntityManager.createNativeQuery()` method. The following is an example of using native SQL:

```
...
PersistenceContext EntityManager em;
String nativeQueryStr = "select ... ; // database-specific SQL
Query q = em.createNativeQuery(nativeQueryStr, Student.class);
List students = q.getResultList();
...
```

Object-Relational Mapping

JPA defines how the persistent entity states and relationships are mapped to relational database tables. In a simple mapping scenario, an entity class is mapped to a relational table, and persistent fields within an entity are mapped to table columns. Appropriate table names, column names, and types will be derived automatically based on the entity class. When the defaults are not sufficient, the object-relational mapping can be customized using annotations. The following annotations are supported for basic mapping:

- `@Table`—Specifies the primary table for an entity. This can be used to specify the table name.
- `@SecondaryTable`—Specifies the secondary tables for an entity. This is used if an entity is stored across multiple tables.
- `@Column`—Specifies the mapped column for a persistent field. This can be used to specify the column name, type, and constraints such as nullability.

The following is an example of a simple mapping:

```
@Entity
public class Student {
    @Id int id;
    @Column(length="50") String name;
    @Column(name="ADDR") String address;
}
```

The preceding entity will be mapped to the following relational schema:

```
...
create table STUDENT (
    ID   INTEGER   not null,
    NAME VARCHAR(50),
    ADDR VARCHAR(255),
    CONTRAINT STUDENT_PK PRIMARY KEY (ID)
);
...
```

Relationship Mapping

There are two strategies to map a relationship: *foreign key* and *join table*. As usual, default mapping is automatically derived by the runtime, and if necessary, customization can be applied through the use of annotations. The foreign key approach can be used to map all relationships except many-to-many relationships. To map a relationship between two entities, a foreign key column is defined in the mapped table of the entity on the "many" side of the relationship.

In the join table approach, a separate join table is used to store the relationships between two entity types. This mapping is typically used in the case of many-to-many relationships, where a foreign key column is not sufficient because it can store only a single value. The following annotations can be used to customize the mapping of a relationship:

- `@JoinTable`—Specifies a join table for mapping of relationships. This can be used to specify the name of the table and the join columns.
- `@JoinColumn`—Specifies a mapped foreign key column. This can be used to specify the name, type, and constraints of the column.
- `@PrimaryKeyJoinColumn`—Specifies a primary key that is also used as a foreign key column.

Inheritance Mapping

There are three ways to map inheritance hierarchies: *single table*, *table per class*, and *joined subclass*. When single table mapping strategy is used, a single relational table is used to store all instances of an entity type and its subclasses. The columns of this single table will be a union of all mapped columns of the entity type and its subclasses. A discriminator column can be used to identify the specific entity type of a database row. In the table per class mapping strategy, the entity type and each of its subclasses are mapped to a different table. The columns of a mapped subclass table include mapped columns of the parent class as well. The joined subclass mapping strategy is similar to table per class, in which each entity type and its subclasses are mapped to distinct tables; however, in the joined subclass strategy, the mapped columns of superclasses are not included in mapped subclass tables.

Each mapping strategy has its own merits and demerits. The single table strategy is nonnormalized and leaves redundant columns depending on the entity type being stored.

This approach provides good support for polymorphic queries and relationships because only one table needs to be accessed. Joined subclass mapping, on the other hand, is normalized but might present a performance issue especially with deep inheritance hierarchies because subclass-specific states are stored in separate tables. Table per class mapping is also normalized but has poor support for polymorphic queries and relationships. The developer must use the appropriate mapping strategy, based on the needs of the enterprise application. The following are some annotations that can be used to customize inheritance mapping:

- `@Inheritance`—Specifies inheritance mapping strategy (`SINGLE_TABLE, TABLE_PER_CLASS, JOINED`)
- `@DiscriminatorColumn`—Defines discriminator column for single table and joined subclass strategies
- `@DiscriminatorValue`—Specifies value of discriminator column for entities of a given type

An example of inheritance mapping is as follows:

```
@Entity
@Inheritance(SINGLE_TABLE)
@DiscriminatorColumn(name="PERSONTYPE")
@DiscriminatorValue("PERSON")
public class Person {
    // Definition of PERSON goes here
}

@Entity
@DiscriminatorValue("STUDENT")
public class Student extends Person {
    //Definition of STUDENT derived from PERSON definition
}
```

The preceding code snippet shows the creation of a `STUDENT` entity by inheriting the properties of `PERSON`. The annotations such as `@Entity`, `@DiscriminatorColumn`, `@DiscriminatorValue`, and so on help in an easier and more complete inheritance mapping of entities.

Summary

The new Java Persistence API provides a powerful, standard object-relational mapping facility usable by any component in Java Platform, Enterprise Edition. This API meets the key requirements for Enterprise components to persist or access data stored in relational databases. Entity objects in the new EJB technology are plain Java objects and can be used in detached mode, obviating the need for patterns such as Data Transfer Objects. The new API supports many object-oriented language features such as inheritance and polymorphism. This has resulted in more readable and maintainable domain object models. The Java Persistence API also includes support for several advanced features that are particularly appropriate in an Enterprise scenario, such as named queries and optimistic locking. In addition to the persistence mechanism, the latest Enterprise JavaBeans specification defines a much simpler model for writing Session EJBs and Message-Driven EJBs.

In the next chapter, we describe how the Java Platform, Enterprise Edition provides support for web services requirements of the Enterprise. Here, we provide an overview of several well-integrated technologies such as JAX-WS, JAXB, SAAJ, and so on and consider the details of how these technologies help in creating and consuming web services as part of the Enterprise application.

12

Java Web Services Overview

The Java Platform, Enterprise Edition includes an interoperable web services stack composed of several well-integrated technologies such as Java API for XML Web Services (JAX-WS), Java Architecture for XML Binding (JAXB), *and SAAJ. Web service endpoints can be defined as either web tier components or Enterprise JavaBeans components. The programming model is similar in either case. The newest version of the Enterprise Edition technology emphasizes simplicity, obtained by the careful use of Java language annotations. Another central feature is that any component can act as a client of web services, often without requiring a deployment descriptor. For maximal interoperability, the web services stack in the Java Platform, Enterprise Edition supports several standards, including SOAP, WSDL, WS-I Basic Profile, WS-I Attachment Profile, and the entirety of XML Schema. Furthermore, the JAXR client* Application Programming Interface *(*API*) provides access to standard-compliant registries and repositories.*

Implementing SOA through the web services route is the best option for any Enterprise. Web services provide a simple, intuitive, and elegant route for implementing service orientation. Delivering web services using Java EE technology constitutes the use of several web services-related APIs in composing part of or the whole Enterprise application. JAX-WS is the main web service rendering API in Java EE technology. It enables Java EE developers to access web services from clients and to implement web services on the server. With JAX-WS, the complexity of WSDL and SOAP message handling can be hidden completely from developers. The developers can instead program web services using the familiar Java concepts. Underneath, JAX-WS technology transparently handles the mapping between the Java representation of a web service and the web service definition in WSDL. JAX-WS APIs help in composing applications that process incoming SOAP messages, convert the XML data to Java objects, and invoke the appropriate Java method that represents the web service operation defined in WSDL. After the Java method completes the execution, JAX-WS technology converts any results back to XML format and sends the SOAP response back to the client. To ensure interoperability, JAX-WS technology is compliant with SOAP 1.1 and 1.2, WSDL 1.1, and WS-I Basic Profile 1.1.

Implementing a Web Service

Creating a new web service in Java EE from scratch is simple and straightforward. A developer first writes a Java class that represents the business logic of the web service. Appropriate annotations are incorporated into the class to indicate the class represents a web service and specifies and customizes mapping information between the Java class and WSDL. Based on the Java class and annotation information, the corresponding WSDL document can be generated automatically by the JAX-WS technology. The Java class is packaged as a Java EE application and, when deployed, the web service is available for use by web service clients.

Another scenario supported by the JAX-WS technology is mapping from an existing WSDL to Java object. In this case, JAX-WS generates annotated Java classes that map to the web services described in the WSDL document. Whereas annotations customize mapping in the Java to WSDL case, XML customizes mapping from WSDL to Java. The customization XML fragments can be embedded in the WSDL document directly, or they can be a separate customization file.

Mapping Between Java and WSDL

A WSDL document describes the format of the input and output messages that are required and understood by a web service. To create a web service or access a web service using Java EE technology, it is necessary to map the information contained in WSDL to corresponding constructs in Java language. Fortunately, this is handled transparently by JAX-WS technology and JAXB technology. For the most part, developers need to focus only on Java programming instead of handling WSDL documents directly.

Before going further, it is important to examine how the mapping is done between Java and WSDL. The main elements in a WSDL document are `<portType>`, `<message>`, `<port>`, and `<binding>`. A `<portType>` element or WSDL port describes a web service and the operations and messages that the web service accepts. A typical operation of a web service takes an input message and produces an output message. However, some web services might not require an input or output message. The format of a message is described by the `<message>` element. A message can contain one or more parts. Each `<part>` element has a data type, which is defined using XML schema. Up to this point, the web service is described in an abstract and protocol-neutral way. The `<binding>` element part of the WSDL defines the actual message format and protocol that would be used to communicate with the port. The most common binding used is the SOAP binding.

In a nutshell, the mapping of the preceding elements is rendered as follows:

1. The WSDL `<port>` is mapped to either a Java class or a Java interface.
2. The operations are mapped to Java methods, and faults are mapped to Java exceptions.
3. The input and output messages and the parts contained within the messages are mapped to the parameters of the Java methods.
4. The types of the message parts, specified in XML schema, are mapped to the Java types of the parameters.
5. Although there is no direct mapping of the binding specified in WSDL to Java artifacts, the specified binding in WSDL might affect how the messages are mapped to parameters of Java methods.

Here is an example of an annotated Java class and how it is mapped to WSDL:

```
@WebService(name="Warehouse", serviceName="WarehouseService")
@SOAPBinding(style = SOAPBinding.Style.RPC)
public class WarehouseImpl {
    @WebMethod()
    public int getInventory(String partNumber) {
       // Logic to obtain inventory count for the specified item
         // is included here
         ...
    }
}
```

`WarehouseImpl` is an annotated Java class that represents a web service endpoint. In this example, the `@WebService` annotation indicates the Java class that implements a web service. The `@WebMethod` annotation indicates that the Java method should be exposed as a web service operation. The `@WebMethod` annotation can be omitted if the user intends to expose all public methods of the class as web service operations. More details on the annotations will be revealed in the next section:

```
<message name="getInventory">
    <part name="arg0" type="xsd:string"/>
</message>
<message name="getInventoryResponse">
    <part name="return" type="xsd:int"/>
</message>
<portType name="Warehouse">
    <operation name="getInventory">
        <input message="getInventory">
        <output message="getInventoryResponse">
    </operation>
</portType>
<binding type="Warehouse" name="WarehousePortBinding">
    <soap:binding style="rpc"
                  transport="http://schemas.xmlsoap.org/soap/
http" />
    <operation>
        <soap:operation soapAction=""/>
        <input>
            <soap:body use="literal"/>
        </input>
        <output>
            <soap:body use="literal"/>
        </output>
    </operation>
</binding>
<service name="WarehouseService">
    <port name="WarehousePort" binding="WarehousePortBinding">
        ...
    </port>
</service>
```

Web Service Annotations

There are many annotations that help in describing and fine-tuning the web service description. Let's examine a few of the key annotations that can be used for describing the web services.

@WebService

This annotation indicates that the Java class is implementing web services. It can also be used with a Java interface to mark it as a web service interface. By default, the name of the Java class or interface is used as the name of the web service when mapped to WSDL. Customization of the mapping can be specified using member values with the annotation. For the example, the web service name can be customized using a syntax like `@WebService (name = "MyWebService")`. Further fine-tuning of the web services definition can be rendered using the mapping that includes the namespace, service name, port name, and location of WSDL.

@WebMethod

This annotation is used with a Java method to indicate it is a web service operation. By default, the name of the Java method is used as the operation name in WSDL. The operation name can be customized using a syntax like `@WebMethod (operationName = "myOperation")`.

@Oneway

This annotation indicates that a web service method takes only an input message but does not produce an output message. Because no return value is expected, a one-way method can return the control to the invoking client right away while server-side processing continues to execute in the background.

@WebParam

This annotation customizes the parameter of a web service method to the corresponding WSDL message part. It is possible to specify whether a parameter is intended to be an `IN`, `OUT`, or `INOUT` parameter. An `IN` parameter is provided by the client and cannot be modified by the target web service. Likewise, an `OUT` parameter is provided by the web service. An `INOUT` parameter, on the other hand, is provided by the client but can also be modified by the target web service. The name mapping to `wsdl:part` and namespace can also be specified.

@WebResult

This annotation specifies the mapping of the return type of a web service method. The available options are basically the same as those supported by `@WebParam`.

@HandlerChain

This annotation associates an external chain of handlers with a web service. More information about the handlers is described later in this chapter.

@SOAPBinding

This annotation specifies how a web service should be mapped to the SOAP message protocol. It is possible to specify the encoding style (`DOCUMENT` versus `RPC`), the formatting style (`LITERAL` versus `ENCODED`), and the parameter style (`BARE` versus `WRAPPED`) of the SOAP messages.

Accessing Web Services

In this section we describe how to access a web service from a client. The WSDL document of the target web service is the key piece of required information. Based on the WSDL document, JAX-WS technology tools generate annotated Java classes and interfaces that represent the target web service. An application can then invoke the web service operations by calling the Java methods just like invoking methods on an ordinary Java object. The following is an example of a client accessing the Warehouse web service previously defined.

```
public class MyProgram {
    public void myMethod() {
        WarehouseService svc = new WarehouseService();
        Warehouse warehouse = svc.getWarehousePort();
        System.out.println("Inventory count = " +
                               warehouse.getInventory("ES1543"));
    }
}
```

In the preceding example, the `WarehouseService` and `Warehouse` classes are generated by JAX-WS technology tools, based on the WSDL document describing the Warehouse web service. Within the Java EE technology, the example can be further simplified through the use of the `@WebServiceRef` annotation, which would inject the web service reference directly into a field.

```
public class MyProgram {
@WebServiceRef(WarehouseService.class) Warehouse warehouse;
    public void myMethod() {
        ...
        System.out.println("Inventory count = " +
                               warehouse.getInventory("ES1543"));
        ...
    }
}
```

In the preceding example, the `Warehouse` port is injected into the member variable warehouse by the Java EE container. The container takes care of instantiating the Warehouse service and obtaining the appropriate port from the service.

In both cases, the JAX-WS technology handles all the underlying communications between the client and server. It is important to note here that, due to the interoperability of web services, it is not necessary for both the client and server to be using JAX-WS technology tools. For example, it is possible to use JAX-WS tools on the client side to access a web service implemented using the .NET platform. Conversely, it is also possible for a .NET client to access a web service endpoint that is implemented using JAX-WS tools.

Protocol and Transport

In JAX-WS, the default protocol binding is SOAP 1.1 with attachments over HTTP. However, it is possible for a server-side web service to specify a different protocol binding. A web service client must use the binding specified in the WSDL. New protocols and transports can be plugged into the JAX-WS implementation. For example, it is possible to support additional bindings such as SOAP over JMS or XML or SMTP. Typical application code is protocol-agnostic, so it is not necessary to rewrite code to use a different protocol binding. The `@BindingType` annotation specifies the desired binding for a web service.

Advanced Features in JAX-WS

There are many advanced features within core JAX-WS technology that are crucial for delivering elegant and efficient web services. These include Handler Framework, Asynchronous Interaction capabilities, Messaging capabilities, and so on.

Handler Framework

The JAX-WS handler framework enables interception and processing of incoming and outgoing messages external to a web service implementation. On the server side, a handler can process incoming messages before the business logic of a web service is invoked. Similarly, a handler can process outgoing messages after a web service is invoked. The JAX-WS handler framework is also supported on a web service client and can process both outbound messages and incoming responses. Multiple handlers can be chained together to form a handler chain using an XML configuration file.

There are two types of handlers: *logical handler* and *protocol handler*. A logical handler can view and manipulate only the message payloads. It is independent of message protocol and cannot affect protocol-specific parts of the message. A protocol handler, on the other hand, is specific to a particular message protocol and can manipulate protocol-specific parts of the message in addition to the message payloads. The SOAP message handler is an example of a protocol handler.

Handlers are useful for applying similar logic across multiple operations of a web service so that it isn't necessary to incorporate the logic in each operation. One use case of handlers is to support auditing, which typically requires logging all the incoming requests and outgoing responses. Handlers can also transform or convert the data format of web service messages.

The following is an example of a protocol handler, which logs all the SOAP messages using the *Java logging API*.

```
public class SOAPMessageLoggingHandler implements
SOAPHandler<SOAPMessageContext> {
    private Logger logger = ...
    private String convertToString(SOAPMessage msg) {
        // private method to convert SOAP message to string
    public boolean handleMessage(SOAPMessageContext context) {
        String text = convertToString(context.getMessage());
        logger.info(text);
        return true;
    }
    public boolean handleFault(SOAPMessageContext context) {
        String text = convertToString(context.getMessage());
        logger.severe(context);
        return true;
    }
    public void close(SOAPMessageContext context) {
    }
}
```

The preceding class implements the `SOAPHandler` interface. The `handleMessage` method is called when the handler intercepts a regular SOAP message. Likewise, the `handleFault` is called when a SOAP fault occurs. The `close()` method is called after the completion of a web service invocation.

Asynchronous Interactions

The JAX-WS technology provides client-side asynchronous invocation support. Such asynchronous invocation helps avoid the blocking of client execution even if a web service operation requires a long period of processing time. Asynchronous invocation support is implemented completely on the client side in JAX-WS. As a result, a web service client can access any web service in an asynchronous fashion without having to modify the target web service implementation. The asynchronous invocation support can be used in two ways: *polling* and *callback*. In the polling model, a client first makes an invocation and continues processing. The client then requests the result when it is ready. In the callback model, a client registers a handler, and the handler will be invoked when the result is ready. The following is an example that shows a typical use of the polling model:

```
...
WarehouseService svc = new WarehouseService();
Warehouse warehouse = svc.getWarehousePort();
Response<Integer> response = warehouse.getInventoryAsync
("ABC123");
while (!response.isDone()) {
     // do some other work while waiting for the result
}
Integer result = response.get();
// process result
...
```

Similarly, the callback mode is exemplified in the following code snippet:

```
class MyHandler implements AsyncHandler<Integer> {
    ...
    public void handleResponse(Response<Integer> response) {
        Integer result = response.get();
        // process result
    }
}

WarehouseService svc = new WarehouseService();
Warehouse warehouse = svc.getWarehousePort();
warehouse.getInventoryAsync("ABC123", new MyHandler());
    // MyHandler will be invoked when result is ready
...
```

Messaging API

In addition to using regular Java classes and interfaces to implement and access web service, JAX-WS supports a low-level messaging API for implementing dynamic client and server applications. This requires more direct handling of messages that are sent over the network. *Dispatch API* and *Provider API* are the two main messaging interfaces.

On the server side, the Provider API enables a single class to implement multiple web service endpoints. This simplifies the implementation of a collection of web services that offers similar web service contracts or supports multiple versions of the same web service contract. The Provider API is also used to implement a proxy service that can transform incoming messages or route them to the appropriate destinations. The following is an example of Provider API usage:

```
@ServiceMode(Service.Mode.MESSAGE)
public class MyProvider implements Provider<SOAPMessage> {
    public SOAPMessage invoke(SOAPMessage request,
                                 Map<String, Object>context) {
        // process request using SAAJ
        SOAPMessage response = ....
        ...
        return response;
    }
}
```

On the client side, the Dispatch API provides a generic interface to invoke web services without having to generate type-specific classes or interfaces. This API can implement management or testing tools. For example, a development tool can provide a user interface to test and invoke web services by introspecting the supported operations of a web service. The following is an example of the use of a Dispatch API code snippet:

```
...
// create SOAP message
SOAPMessage requestMessage = ...;
Service service = ...;
// obtain reference to web service
Dispatch<SOAPMessage> dispatch =
service.createDispatch(portName,
                                 SOAPMessage.class, MESSAGE);
SOAPMessage result = dispatch.invoke(requestMessage);
...
```

There are several advantages of using the JAX-WS messaging API over the typical networking APIs. In addition to handling the web service communications between a client and server, the JAX-WS messaging API has JAXB support built in for marshalling between XML and Java objects. The parsing of MIME multipart packages is automatically handled, and it is possible to use JAX-WS handlers with the messaging API.

The messaging API can implement *Representational State Transfer* (*REST*)-style web services, in which services are exposed as resources based on the traditional web architecture and can be manipulated using HTTP. Some examples of REST-style web services include Yahoo! Search and Map web services. JAX-WS technology can also access REST-style web services using the Dispatch API and the XML/HTTP binding. The Provider API can implement a REST-style web service.

Java Architecture for XML Binding

In SOA, XML is the main language used in messages that are exchanged between multiple entities. However, XML is not actually a programming language and is not designed to implement the business logic of web services. Java EE and the Java programming language are better suited to implement such logic in web services. A web service implementation is now faced with data represented in two different systems: XML data and Java objects. It is imperative to convert between XML data and Java objects and vice versa, as a part of the web service exchange.

Multiple Java APIs can process XML documents. *Simple API for XML* (*SAX*) is an event-driven processing API that helps in processing XML documents. *Document Object Model* (*DOM*) can construct an XML parse tree. StAX, which we covered in Chapter 9, "Java Platform, Enterprise Edition Overview," is a pull-based streaming API. The JAXB API, on the other hand, provides direct mapping between Java objects and XML documents. JAXB integrated into JAX-WS and is the recommended way to support data conversion or binding between XML and Java. The architectural design of the JAXB is illustrated in Figure 12.1.

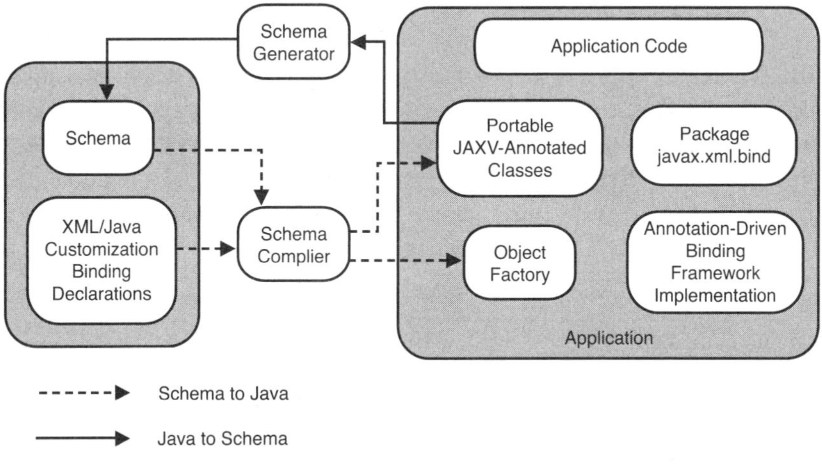

Figure 12.1 The Java API for XML binding architecture

The JAXB technology supports bidirectional mapping between Java and XML schema. It is possible to start with an XML schema because JAXB technology tools can generate the corresponding Java classes. Conversely, one can also start with a Java class, and the JAXB technology tools can generate the corresponding XML schema. After a mapping is established between Java and XML schema, JAXB can convert Java objects to XML documents (often termed *marshalling*) or XML documents to Java objects (often termed *unmarshalling*). During the process of marshalling and unmarshalling, the Java object or XML document can be validated against an XML schema to ensure proper formatting. Figure 12.2 shows the binding life cycle of the JAXB technology.

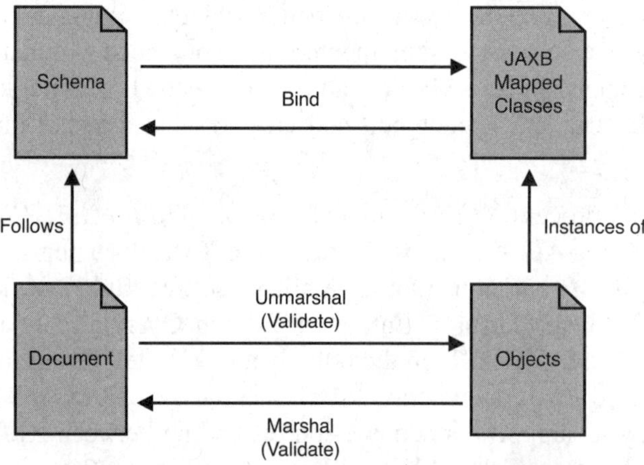

Figure 12.2 Illustration of JAXB binding life cycle

XML schema supports a number of built-in data types, such as `xsd:string`, `xsd:integer`, `xsd:boolean`, and so on. These built-in data types can be mapped in a straightforward way to Java types. For example, `xsd:string` can be mapped to the `java.lang.String` type in Java. Similarly, `xsd:int` can be mapped to the `int` type, and so on. Table 12.1 shows how the most common built-in data types are mapped between XML and Java.

Table 12.1 Comparison Between the XML Schema Java Data Types

XML Schema Data Type	Java Type
`xsd:string`	`java.lang.String`
`xsd:integer`	`java.math.BigInteger`
`xsd:int, xsd:unsignedShort`	`int`
`xsd:long, xsd:unsignedInt`	`long`
`xsd:short, xsd:unsignedByte`	`short`
`xsd:decimal`	`java.math.BigDecimal`
`xsd:float`	`float`

Table 12.1 Comparison Between the XML Schema Java Data Types

XML Schema Data Type	Java Type
xsd:double	double
xsd:boolean	boolean
xsd:byte	byte
xsd:QName	javax.xml.namespace.QName
xsd:dateTime, xsd:time, xsd:date, xsd:g	javax.xml.datatype.XMLGregorianCalendar
xsd:base64Binary, xsd:hexBinary	byte[]
xsd:anySimpleType	java.lang.Object
xsd:anySimpleType	java.lang.String
xsd:duration	javax.xml.datatype.Duration
xsd:NOTATION	javax.xml.namespace.QName

XML schema also supports complex data types. In this case, the data type is typically mapped to a Java class. The following is an example of a complex type and how it is mapped to Java.

XML Schema:

```
<complexType name="employee">
    <sequence>
        <element name="name" type="xsd:string"/>
    </sequence>
    <attribute name="id" type="xsd:int"/>
</complexType>
```

Java Class:

```
@XmlType
public class Employee {
    @XmlElement
    public String name;
    @XmlAttribute
    public int getId() { ... }
    public void setId(int arg) { ... }
    ...
}
```

XML Document:

```
<employee id="SM2342">
    <name>Joe Doe</name>
</employee>
```

In the preceding example, several Java annotations specify the mapping between Java and XML. The @XmlType annotation maps the class to an XML schema type. The mapped name of the schema type can be customized using a syntax such as `@XmlType(name="...")`. The `@XmlElement` annotation maps a field or a pair of `get/set` methods to an XML element. The mapped name of the XML element can be customized in a similar fashion. It is also possible to specify whether an element is required. If an element is required, the XML schema element will have a declaration with `minOccurs = 1`. If it is not required, the element declaration will have `minOccurs = 0`. The `@XmlAttribute` annotation maps a field or a pair of get/set methods to an XML attribute. Similar to the `@XmlElement` annotation, you can customize the mapped name of attribute and whether the attribute is required.

In addition to the basic mapping of data types, elements, and attributes, JAXB technology supports mapping of all concepts as defined in the XML schema. In other words, the JAXB technology can map all valid XML schemas to corresponding Java classes. Extensibility concepts in XML schema such as type substitution, element substitution group, and wildcard are also supported.

Not only can the JAXB technology bind an entire XML document to a Java object, it also supports binding a portion of an XML document. An application can then update the portion of the XML document without marshalling or unmarshalling the entire document. This is useful for performance optimization and in cases in which the web service might not understand or want to handle the unintended parts of an XML document.

Schema Evolution

As web services evolve, it might become imperative to update the format of the messages exchanged between client and servers. Due to the distributed nature of web services, it might not always be possible to guarantee simultaneous updates of all web service clients. As a result, it might become necessary to deal with different versions of messages being exchanged between client and web service endpoints. The JAXB technology elegantly handles such situations, which might not be uncommon in the enterprise scenarios. The JAXB technology provides schema evolution support through flexible unmarshalling of XML data. If the JAXB technology tools encounter missing elements or attributes during unmarshalling of XML data, their uninitialized values are assigned to the corresponding Java properties and the processing continues. For numeric properties, a value of zero is assigned, and for `boolean` data types, the value of `false` is assigned. For other Java properties, the value of `null` is assigned.

Suppose the preceding Employee binding is updated with an additional element salary.

Java Class:

```
@XmlType
public class Employee {
    @XmlElement
    public String name;
    @XmlElement
    public float salary;
    @XmlAttribute
    public int getId() { ... }
    public void setId(int arg) { ... }
    ...
}
```

XML Schema:

```
<complexType name="employee">
    <sequence>
        <element name="name" type="xsd:string"/>
        <element name="salary" type="xsd:float"/>
    </sequence>
    <attribute name="id" type="xsd:int"/>
</complexType>
```

If the JAXB technology tool attempts to unmarshall an XML document that is still using the previous schema (without the salary element), it automatically assigns `+0.0f` to the salary property and continues the processing without interruption.

Another situation that might be encountered during unmarshalling is unknown elements or attributes. In this case, JAXB technology tools skip these unexpected elements or attributes and will not map them to Java objects. Another way to handle unknown elements or attributes is to use the `xsd:any` type in XML schema. The mapped Java class includes a property with an `@XmlAnyElement` or `@XmlAnyAttribute` annotation. In this case, the unexpected elements or attributes will be mapped to the annotated property. The following is an example.

Java Class:

```
@XmlType
public class foo {
    public String alfa;
    public String beta;
    @XmlAnyElement
    public Object gamma;
}
```

XML Schema:

```
<element name="foo">
    <complexType>
        <sequence>
            <element name="alfa" type="xsd:string"/>
            <element name="beta" type="xsd:string"/>
            <element name="gamma" type="xsd:any"/>
        </sequence>
    </complexType>
</element>
```

XML Document:

```
<foo>
   <alfa> ... </alfa>
   <beta> ... </beta>
   <delta> ... </delta>
</foo>
```

During unmarshalling of the preceding XML document, the unknown XML element `delta` will be stored in the generic property `gamma`.

Summary

The Java Platform, Enterprise Edition includes an interoperable web services stack composed of several well-integrated technologies such as JAX-WS, JAXB, and SAAJ. The focus of this newest edition has been on simplicity, time-to-market, and ease-of-development compared to the Java 2 Enterprise Edition. Web services annotations and other advanced technologies such as JAXB, XML Schema, and so on have rendered the development of web services applications simple, easy, and straightforward. For enhancing the interoperability, the web services stack in the Java Platform, Enterprise Edition supports many standards, including SOAP, WSDL, UDDI, WS-I Basic Profile, WS-I Attachment Profile, and the entirety of XML schema.

In the next chapter, we overview the technology of *Enterprise Service Bus* (*ESB*) and explain the importance of the service bus in integrating enterprise applications and web services as loosely coupled composite applications. We also describe the technology of *Java Business Integration* (*JBI*) and indicate how it addresses the challenges of integrating application components and orchestrating application services.

13

Enterprise Service Bus and Java Business Integration

The Enterprise Service Bus *(*ESB*) is a technology that is increasingly being adopted by Enterprises for business integration purposes. An ESB provides a standards-based integration platform that combines messaging, web services, data transformation, and intelligent routing in an event-driven SOA. The ESB also provides services for transforming and routing messages and has the capability to centrally administer the distributed system.* Java Business Integration (JBI*) is a means for constructing service containers—in which the integration happens and IT assets are turned into providers and services, consumers of services, or both.*

Enterprises today need a mantra that renders ubiquitous integration. The evolution of *Java Message Service (JMS)* specification and services is seen by the business analysts and researchers in the Enterprise maze as the first step in reaching this goal. The introduction of XML as an interoperable communication language coupled with the arrival of the web services standards for services definition, discovery, invocation, and other advanced XML vocabularies encouraged the hopes of inducing the interoperability and service orientation in such business integration solutions. These events signaled the arrival of what is now called the ESB. There are important advantages of middleware solutions; this chapter chronicles their influences and limitations, indicating how these technologies pave the way for promising new solutions in business integration. The chapter also notes how Java and the related Enterprise specifications and technologies are evolving to meet the new challenges and the needs of the Enterprise businesses.

The Service Bus and Enterprises

Having witnessed a series of paradigm shifts in the Enterprise IT environments in the past decade, many business and IT analysts opine that the early middleware products, such as *Message Oriented Middleware (MOM)*, are making way for the new technologies that promise superior features and meet the demands of the nonfunctional requirements of the Enterprises. A careful observation of the market and technologies and their growth over the past few years indicates that the arrival of new technologies such as *web servers*, *application servers*, and *integration servers*, combined with the XML-based *web services* as a route to better interoperability, resulted in the steady decline of the heritage middleware technologies, including MOM. Researchers also note that the newer technologies not only possess the functionality of the heritage middleware but also can effectively handle the processes asynchronously and in real time. They also can provide superior *quality of service* (*QoS*) and performance options for the dynamically changing demands of the Enterprise. This new infrastructure-based architecture is termed the ESB.

With the help of the new breed of servers, the new infrastructure consists of a set of service containers that help in the integration of various types of IT assets of the Enterprise. The architecture of ESB enables the connecting of these service containers with reliable messaging bus. Furthermore, the service containers adapt the IT assets to the standardized services model based on XML messaging standards using the standardized *message exchange patterns* (*MEP*). This new infrastructure and the architecture also helps provide services for transforming and routing of messages and can handle multiple protocols to meet the business process requirements of the Enterprises. ESB also enables legacy or packaged applications to be plugged into the Enterprise infrastructure using adapters (such as JCA).

ESB—A Business Perspective

The term Enterprise Service Bus was coined at the University of Stamford, in a report from a leading business analyst, Gartner. Gartner describes ESB as follows:

An Enterprise Service Bus (ESB) is a new architecture that exploits web services, messaging middleware, intelligent routing, and transformation. ESB acts as a lightweight, ubiquitous integration backbone through which software services and application components flow.

According to Gartner, ESB will supersede traditional communication middleware before the end of this decade. ESB is a new architecture for Enterprise integration. This architecture can be described as a lightweight integration broker based on XML and web services standards stack. As illustrated in Figure 13.1, ESB is a combination of messaging and other related middleware, basic transformation, and content-based routing. ESB is best used to leverage web services and messaging technologies that facilitate the development of flexible SOA. The ESB infrastructure acts as the universal Enterprise integration backbone and can even be referred to as the Enterprise Digital Nervous System.

The arrival of ESB has been an evolutionary process, influenced by a number of events, vendors, research, and development efforts by business researchers and academicians, and so on. Development of ESB efforts has drawn positive influences from the heritage middleware along with attempts to avoid the pitfalls of the middleware approaches and solutions. The introduction of *Java Message Service* (*JMS*) and the adoption of the Java technologies in the message-oriented middleware has resulted in significant positive influences on the evolution of ESB. Development and use of web services as a standardized way of interoperability and the need for a services-oriented architecture has nurtured the development of ESB.

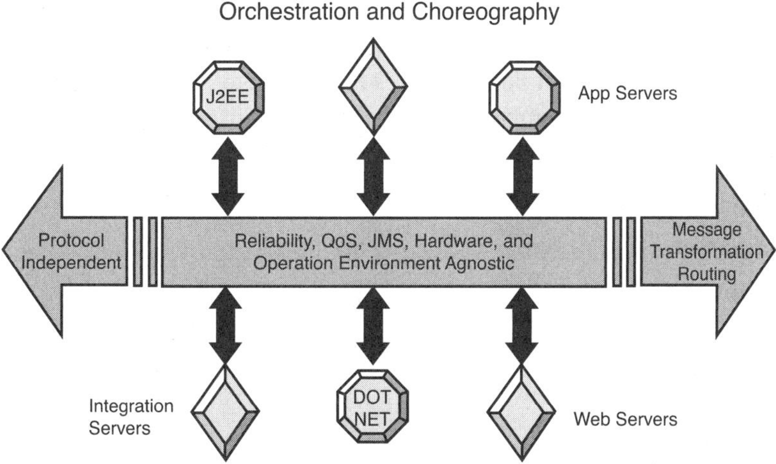

Figure 13.1 The backbone of the Enterprise: Enterprise Service Bus

Salient Features of ESB

ESB is dubbed an encompassing solution to all the problems of any Enterprise. Although it might seem a sweeping statement, the features and characteristics of the new architectural infrastructure of the ESB make it seem feasible. The following is a list of some of the characteristics of the ESB:

- Operating environment agnostic and programming language-independent
- Uses XML as a standardized communication language
- Supports web services standards for SOA implementation
- Allows loose coupling
- Reliable and supports all possible QoSs
- Supports synchronous and asynchronous communication
- Provides messaging transformation services
- Supports service orchestration and choreography
- Provides standardized message routing services
- Supports standardized web service definition for service delivery and invocation
- Distributed but centrally administered
- Supports event-driven services
- Enables standards-based adapters for legacy integration

Although the list of salient features and characteristics seems to be long and is still growing, not all the features are necessary for all the Enterprises and all business needs of any particular Enterprise. Many other technologies also offer a smaller or a larger subset of these features and characteristics. That said, only the ESB infrastructure undeniably meets some of the most important and common needs of any Enterprise:

- Intelligent routing
- Transformation
- Multi protocol transport
- Reliable messaging
- Security

Intelligent Routing

The ESB infrastructure enables a flexible and efficient routing mechanism and provides intelligent, content-based routing services or itinerary routing.

Transformation

In the ESB infrastructure, a service component does not need to know the request format of the service it is interested in invoking. Based on the requester and the target service, the ESB infrastructure should apply the requisite transformation to the service request to enable the target service provider to understand it.

Multiprotocol Transport

An ESB implementation should communicate with any Enterprise application. For example, the different islands of automations in an Enterprise could use different solutions in their localized environment. Each of these applications could use a different set of communication protocols. Although one business unit could use JMS-based message exchange as the primary process, another business unit could use state-of-the-art web services for communication. An ESB infrastructure should bring all these islands of automations into the common fold.

Reliable Messaging

Messaging technologies have provided a stable business process platform for most of the Enterprises for a long time. This technology is unlikely to go away any time soon. However, ESB provides standards-based reliable messaging communication for the messaging needs of the Enterprise—delivered at most once, delivered exactly once, and delivered at least once.

Security

Security is undeniably the most important requirement for any Enterprise. ESB enforces the fundamental security requirements such as authentication, authorization, access control to different service components, and integration infrastructures.

Java Business Integration—Java and ESB

You might recall from Chapter 10, "Web Technologies in Java EE," that Java and the Enterprise specifications of Java have induced a paradigm shift in the way Enterprise solutions are built, implemented, and deployed. Thus, Java, as a set of specifications and as a portable and interoperable solution continues to play a crucial role in providing improved solutions to the IT needs in general and Enterprise needs, in particular. This trend is seen in the recently introduced *Java Specification Request (JSR) 208* by *Java Community Process (JCP)*.

JSR 208 is referred to as the *Java Business Integration specification* (*JBI*). Many leading industries and individuals alike have come together to propose this Java specification. Some key companies include Apache Software Foundation, Sun Microsystems, SAP, Novell, Red Hat, Sybase, TIBCO, Nokia, and Oracle. The proposed JBI Specification attempts to extend the Java technologies (Java Platform, Standard Edition and the Java Platform, Enterprise Edition) with business integration *Service Provider Interfaces* (*SPI*). These SPI enable the creation of an environment for specifications such as WS-BPEL for business process and WS-CDL for choreography working groups.

In essence, the JBI specification is an industry-wide initiative to create a standardized integration platform for Java and business applications. JBI addresses SOA needs in integration by creating a standard meta-container for integrated services.

JBI is a messaging-based plug-in architecture. JBI specifications employ concepts similar to the Java Platform, Enterprise Edition to extend application packaging and deployment to include the business integration components. These components are called JBI components. JBI components are an open-ended class of components based on *JBI Abstraction Business Process Metadata*. JBI components describe their capabilities through standard *Web Service Definition Language* (*WSDL*). The JBI specifications do not define how developers need to code the JBI components. JBI enables both standardized and proprietary coding components to coexist in such an environment. Different components might be developed to meet the different needs of the Enterprise solution. Some components might provide rich business functionality, whereas other components can provide rich integration functionality.

The primary goal of JBI is to provide architecture and an enabling framework that facilitates dynamic composition and deployment of loosely coupled composite applications and service-oriented integration components. It enables anyone to create JBI-compliant integration plug-in components and integrate them dynamically into the JBI infrastructure. Figure 13.2 shows the key pieces of the JBI environment.

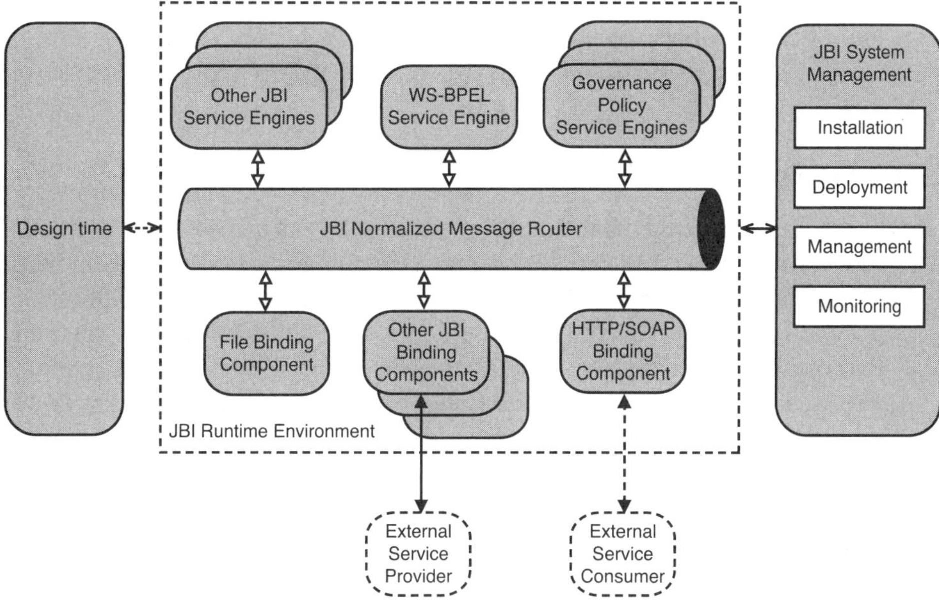

Figure 13.2 The Java Business Integration Infrastructure Bus and the Enterprise Service Bus

There are several key components of the JBI environment: *service engines*, *binding components*, *normalized message router*, and *JBI runtime environment*.

- **Service engines**—*Service Engines* (*SE*) are JBI components that enable pluggable business logic.
- **Binding components**—*Binding Components* (*BC*) are JBI components that enable pluggable external connectivity.
- **Normalized message router**—The *normalized message router* (*NMR*) directs normalized messages from source components to destinations according to specified policies.
- **JBI runtime environment**—The JBI runtime environment encompasses the JBI components and the NMR. Because of its container characteristics, it is sometimes called the JBI meta-container.

Binding components and service engines can act as containers, and *service units* can be deployed to installed JBI components. This arrangement enables the deployment (and undeployment) of component-specific artifacts (for example, concrete WSDLs). Service units can describe which of the services are provided and consumed by the JBI component. In addition to the standard descriptor, the JBI component is responsible for interpreting the contents of the service unit jar file. Multiple service units can be packaged in a *service assembly*. In turn, the service assembly defines the target JBI components that deploy the service units.

Summary

IT trends have affected the nature and function of Enterprises all over the world. The former stable and reliable middleware solutions can no longer meet the needs and ever-changing demands of the Enterprises today. Evolution of the ESB infrastructure and the related technologies holds a lot of promise to the Enterprises in meeting these new demands of the dynamically evolving businesses. Java technologies and the Enterprise Edition specifications continue to evolve to meet these new demands by introducing a new layer (or stack) called the Java Business Integration (JBI), which attempts to extend the Java technologies with business integration Service Provider Interfaces (SPI). In turn, these SPIs enable the creation of an environment for related specifications such as WS-BPEL for business process and WS-CDL for choreography working groups.

In the next part, we dive deep into the implementation aspects of the SOA. Having chosen the Java Enterprise Edition as the appropriate implementation platform for service orientation, we reveal the crucial advantages of this technology that support in the implementation of Enterprise solutions. We also discuss how services can be delivered by components in different tiers of Enterprise architecture for service orientation.

Part IV

Implementing SOA Using Java EE Platform

14

Service Oriented Architecture and the Web Tier

Large enterprises need to offer and deliver services to complete all critical processes and workflow. Naturally, tasks must be completed to the satisfaction of the intended Enterprise. Through the use of the Internet and the World Wide Web, Enterprises can implement this important strategy, using web services frameworks to design and deliver services over the Internet.

Web components such as servlets, filters, JavaServer Pages *(*JSP*), and so on and frameworks such as* JavaServer Faces *(*JSF*) of the new Java EE technology can help reorient the architecture for services delivery. These components along with the aid of Design Patterns on the web tier can help the services to be easily and elegantly designed for service delivery.*

Clearly, web technologies are a critical part of the Java Enterprise Edition technology framework. The web tier might be the most important of all the tiers of any enterprise solution. Java EE provides a solid web component foundation to build a robust, scalable, and extensible web application. Servlets, JSP, Servlet filters, *JSP Standard Tag Libraries* (*JSTL*), and HTML components can be created to build the features required by the Enterprise applications, and design patterns can be applied on them to build the web-based services for the Enterprises. Although these components are necessary for building the Enterprise applications, a mere combination of components is not sufficient for the Enterprise application to work as per the nonfunctional requirements of the organization. Web-based frameworks are necessary because they help the architects and developers to effectively and quickly build, test, and deploy the applications. Apache Struts and JSF are two such popular web-based frameworks that help in building components, applying design patterns, and achieving quick time-to-market for completing the web-oriented Enterprise applications. These frameworks also help in realizing the web services for the Enterprise application so that the service orientation is suitably achieved.

In this chapter, we provide an overview of design patterns of the presentation tier and sneak a peek into the web frameworks that help in the creation of services for delivery. We then focus on the JSF technology and framework and discuss in detail how these services can be weaved into the Enterprise process/workflow to deliver services.

Delivering Services Through the Web Tier

The IT architects and business analysts of the Enterprises, intending to automate the collaborative activities with partners and business associates, are realizing that the best way to implement the business collaboration is by providing and availing business services. With the advent of the Internet and World Wide Web, services are exchanged between the partner organizations over the web. The web tier or the Presentation Tier, therefore, assumes immense importance in the Enterprise architecture. Although the components in this tier focus on presentation aspects of the Enterprise solution, these components can also offer a variety of business-related services. The role of the web tier, therefore, is considered important in SOA for any Enterprise.

The Servlet, Filter, and the JSP components of the Java EE technology help in developing web applications that can render appropriate services. These components encapsulate presentation logic and business logic and data access logic capability to the services. Furthermore, these web components are essentially lightweight, scalable, and reliable Java EE components.

Recall from Chapter 9, "Java Platform, Enterprise Edition Overview," that a number of web tier components make up web application technologies. The roles and responsibilities of these web components are different, and they help in meeting a variety of the Enterprise business services and business process needs. In the next section, we explore how the business components of the Java Platform, Enterprise Edition involve availing and providing services as part of SOA.

The Overall Picture

Figure 14.1 illustrates the tiered structure of the new Java EE architecture, with different tiers and components shown communicating with each other. The focus here is essentially the presentation tier. This figure highlights the role of the web tier and the components that participate in delivering and availing the services on the web. In this chapter, we focus on the communication of presentation tier components and how they help to manage the business goals of the Enterprise as part of the service orientation.

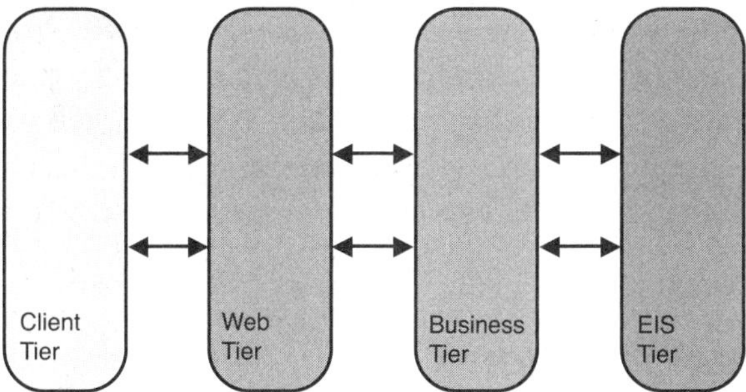

Figure 14.1 The tiered structure of the Java Platform, Enterprise Edition Architecture

As discussed, there are three main types of web tier components: Servlets, Servlet filters, and JSP. In addition to these components, other components are commonly referred to as Helper Classes or Utility Classes. Among these components, the Servlets (together with helper/utility classes) are best suited for providing business services. These components can exchange SOAP-based messages over the *Hypertext Transfer Protocol* (*HTTP*); however, these services are essentially synchronous web services.

Since their introduction, Servlets have been used for enabling business operations such as online insurance, Internet banking, and so on over the web. These components can deliver services to *Business-to-Consumer* (*B2C*) Enterprises that depend heavily on web tier components. Servlets, together with other participating components in the web tier, such as helper/utility classes, can now be considered a perfect fit for exposure as web services.

These web tier components, along with the other colocated components in the web tier, help developers create design patterns that solve the standard problems encountered in the development of web technology applications. Some of these design patterns have evolved into Java frameworks. In the next section, we explore the web tier design patterns and discuss two of the frameworks that are considered important in the present context.

Web Tier Design Patterns and SOA

In Chapter 10, "Web Technologies in Java EE," we indicated that MVC is an architectural pattern that helps in decoupling for the high-level domain abstractions. Such abstractions at the architecture level consist of a number of low-level components at the design level, called *design patterns*. The design pattern might be described as a common repeatable solution to a problem that recurs in the design of software applications.

Design patterns, as applied to Java Platform, Enterprise Edition technology, can be broadly classified in three ways: *presentation tier design patterns*, *business tier design patterns*, and *integration tier design patterns*. Some patterns can be applied strictly within the scope of a particular tier, whereas some of the patterns include components (or patterns) from the adjacent tiers as well. In this section, we limit our discussion to the high-level aspects of the presentation tier design patterns.

Presentation Tier Design Patterns

The purpose of presentation tier design patterns is to manage the change and flexibility of web-based Enterprise applications. A majority of changes in the Enterprise applications take place in this tier due to the dynamic nature of the web in the Enterprise businesses. Furthermore, the patterns in this tier help support some of the Enterprise Application QoS attributes.[1] The five important patterns that can be identified in this tier are

- **Front controller**—Helps provide a mechanism to manage a user request that results in different views of the data that are per the user requirement. A front controller is the first component to intercept the user request.
- **View helper**—Helps retrieve a specific view along with the logic to build the view or subviews.
- **Composite view**—Helps construct a larger view from many different subviews.
- **Dispatcher view**—Helps build the views. It is not uncommon to find many patterns that are formed by combining two or more patterns in a suitable manner. The dispatcher view design pattern is one such example. The dispatcher view design pattern is essentially a combination of two other patterns: front controller design pattern and view helper design pattern. In this case, while the front controller part of the design pattern manages the user request, the view helper part of the pattern helps in building the views.

- **Service to worker**—Similar to that of dispatcher view pattern. The front controller part of the pattern, in this case, takes up more responsibilities than in the dispatcher view scenario.

As these patterns emerged and their utility in the enterprise world became widespread, some of them evolved into frameworks. These frameworks essentially leveraged the advantages of the design patterns and best practices for building Enterprise applications.

Frameworks and Service Delivery

The term *framework* is considered by many to be enormously hyped. An appropriate definition for this term would be *frameworks = software components + design patterns*. The reason for using frameworks is to enhance QoS, such as modularity, improve productivity, impart extensibility, and increase reusability. Frameworks help the developer to quickly develop, test, and deliver the Enterprise software applications.

Many frameworks that help in developing the web applications are based on J2EE.[2] The most important of them are

- Apache Struts
- JSF

Apache Struts can be described as an open-source framework for building web applications based on the MVC architectural pattern. This framework helps architects create application architectures based on the MVC pattern and provide services commonly required by most web applications. The Apache Struts framework is used for building web applications using Servlet and JSP components. The Struts framework, created in 2000 by Craig R. McClanahan,[3] had initially become the de facto standard framework for architecting web applications using J2EE technologies.

JSF, on the other hand, is an advanced, yet simple, framework that helps in building web applications through its well-defined component, state, and event framework. The JSF-based application consists of a set of reusable JSF components, a set of JSP, and an XML-based configuration file. Unlike Struts, JSF uses *render kits* to present the user interface in a markup language such as HTML. The JSF framework also provides specialized *conversion* and *validation* support that helps verify the correctness of the user input.

Recall the technological aspects of JSF discussed in detail in Chapter 10. In the next section, we focus on this new framework and describe in detail how to develop and deliver services on the web tier using the Java Platform, Enterprise Edition. As a part of this effort, we discuss the architectural aspects of the JSF framework and describe the functional aspects of the framework and its role in services delivery.

Services Delivery Using JSF

Conceptually, the JSF technology can be visualized as a combination of the two popular Java frameworks: Apache Struts on the web application development aspects and Java Swing on the user interface-based desktop application development aspects. Similar to the Apache Struts framework, the JSF framework provides web application life-cycle management through the use of a controller Servlet. And, like the Swing framework, JSF provides a rich component model, including event handling and component rendering. Together, these features make the JSF technology framework simple, intuitive, and elegant for use in building Java Platform, Enterprise Edition-based web applications.

Figure 14.2 presents the top-level architectural view of the JSF framework. It is important to note here that JSF pages, together with front controller, help to provide a superior web application development environment.

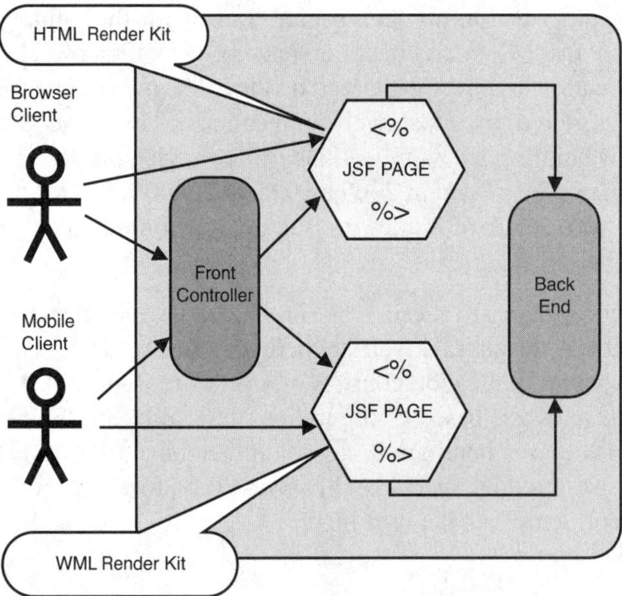

Figure 14.2 The JSF architecture

Functional Aspects of JSF Framework

As indicated in Chapter 10, the JSF framework is essentially an event-driven application. In Figure 14.3, we exemplify the processing schema of a typical JSF application. A JSF application functions by processing the events triggered by the components on the JSF pages. These events are caused by the typical user actions on the web pages. For example, when the user clicks an OK button or the Submit button, this triggers an event. Event listeners are coded to address the respective events. When an event transpires (such as clicking on the button, for example), the event notification is sent as an HTTP request to the web server. On the server side, a special servlet called the `FacesServlet` intercepts this request. (Note that there can be many JSF applications on a web server, and each JSF application in the Web container has its own `FacesServlet`.)

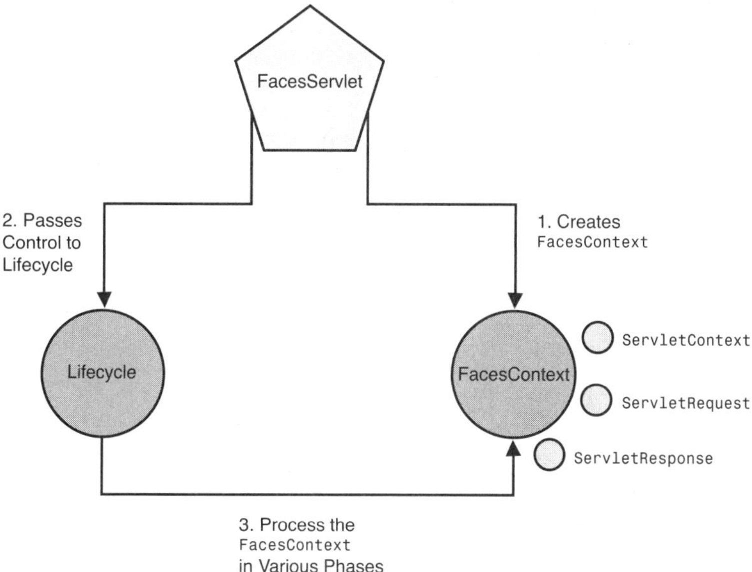

Figure 14.3 Functional aspects of JSF architecture

Upon the interception of the request by appropriate client, `FacesServlet` creates an object called `FacesContext`, which contains information necessary for request processing. In fact, `FacesContext` contains three objects, namely `ServletContext`, `ServletRequest`, and `ServletResponse`. These objects are passed to the service method of `FacesServlet` by the web container. During processing, the `FacesContext` object is modified.

Next is the processing aspect of the framework. The processor is an object called `Lifecycle`. The `FacesServlet` servlet hands over control to this `Lifecycle` object. The `Lifecycle` object processes the `FacesContext` object in six different phases in a predetermined order.

The JavaServer Faces Lifecycle

The manner in which the JSF handles an HTTP request is distinctly different from that of frameworks such as Apache Struts. JSF handles HTTP requests with the following six phases:

- Reconstitute component tree
- Apply request values
- Process validations
- Update model values
- Invoke application
- Render response

These phases are outlined in Figure 14.4, along with the flow control lines. The solid arrows represent the normal processing in the JSF environment; the dotted lines represent alternate paths (demonstrating a processing problem has occurred). These phases are discussed next.

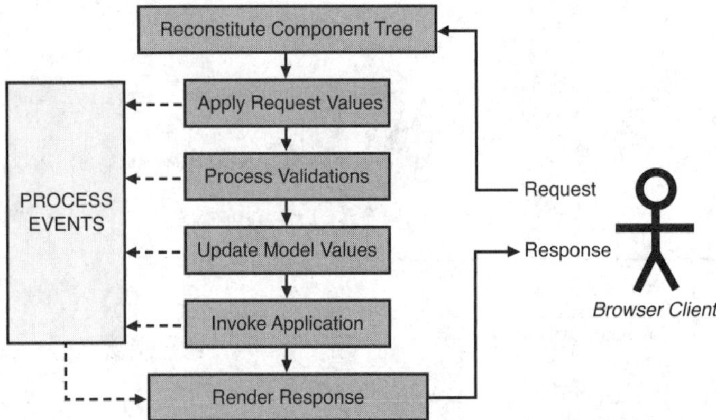

Figure 14.4 Life-cycle phases in JSF architecture

Reconstitute Component Tree Phase The *reconstitute component tree* phase creates a component tree for the page requested. If that page was previously displayed and JSF has saved the page's state information, the state information will also be added to the request. Such a feature enables the JSF to automatically retain the form information when a form is redisplayed, for example, when the requester does not fill out a form correctly.

Apply Request Values Phase During the next phase, the JSF implementation iterates over the components in the component tree, calling each component's `decode()` method. The objective here is to extract the information from the request and store it in the component. In addition to decoding request information during this phase, components or their renderer can create request events. The request events usually signal a visual change for one or more components. Or an event in one component can update the visual representation of another component. In such situations, a request event will be generated and added to the JSF context.

Process Validations Phase During the reconstitute component tree phase, the JSF implementation can register one or more validators for the components in the component tree. In the process validations phase, the JSF implementation invokes the `validate()` method for each validator. The validator performs correctness checks and returns a Boolean value from the `validate()` method. At this stage, if method returns `true`, the life cycle of the JSF application proceeds normally. Otherwise, the JSF implementation invokes the render response phase directly.

Update Model Values Phase Each JSF user interface component can be associated with a field in a model object (a Java object). During the update model phase, values of the component are copied to the component's model object. The component's `updateModel()` helps in effectuating the data transfer. There can be problems here, too. The conversion errors, for example, can occur during this phase because of the mismatch in the type of request parameters. Occurrence of such errors will make the JSF implementation invoke the *render response* phase directly.

Invoke Application Phase When an activity such as form submission or clicking on a URL is performed in an application created using JSF, the JSF implementation results in the creation of a *Form Event* or a *Command Event*, respectively. These events are handled during the *invoke application* phase by an application-specific handler.

Render Response Phase This is the final phase, which creates a response component tree and forwards the response to the requester. If this is for an initial request, the components represented in this page are populated in the component tree. If not, the component tree remains unchanged. If the request is a *post back* and errors were encountered in any of the earlier phases, the original page is rendered. After the view is rendered, it is saved for subsequent requests.

Web Services Delivery Using JSF Framework

JSF complements SOA by essentially enabling a desktop-based user interface in the architecture. JSF is a standard Java EE technology that provides a component-based approach to user interface development. This technology also adheres to the MVC architecture and provides an easy-to-deliver web services strategy. The JSF technology can configure the web application to deliver web services as part of SOA in a variety of ways. For the sake of simplicity, we focus on two of the direct ways to deliver web services: *simple route* and *involved route*.

Simple Route Figure 14.5 provides a rather simplistic representation of the web tier in which JSF can directly interact with the web/business tier components to deliver web services. The JSF is essentially communicating with components deployed in either the web tier or the business tier. The web tier components could be JavaBeans, and the business tier components providing web services could be session Enterprise JavaBeans.

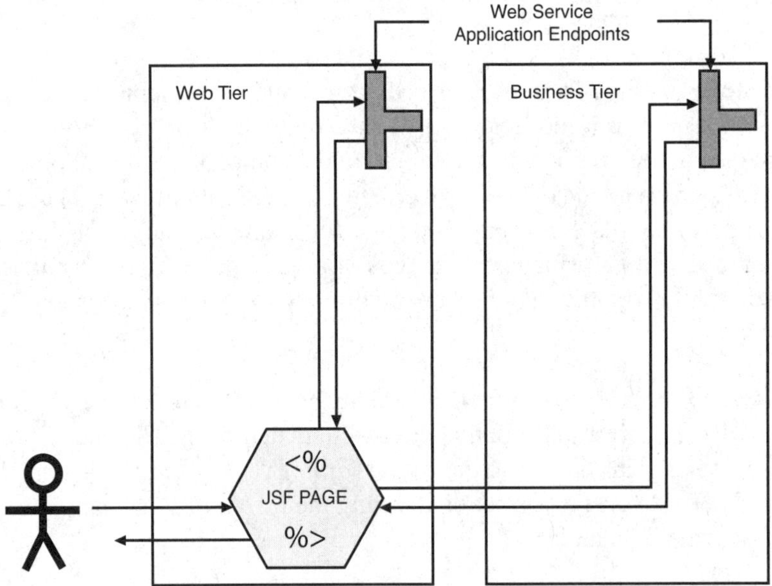

Figure 14.5 Delivering web services through a simple route

Involved Route A more sophisticated way to offer web services is to orchestrate a set of web services into a business process. This route is more complete and more elegant in conforming to the SOA paradigm of web services. A process that is modeled through language such as BPEL can not only invoke a web service, it can also automate the web services execution based on several process/workflow parameters. BPEL's engine, based on the SOA process model, can orchestrate the web services based on the business needs of Enterprise requirement.

Consider the following example that constitutes a JSF application and a BPEL process flow. The JSF user interface could include a user form that requests some user-related information. Let's consider that the JSF enables the user to submit a request for an airline reservation from San Francisco to New York. The JSP page could prompt the user to input the departure location, arrival location, date, and time. Based on the user input, the JSF application submits the request to the BPEL service engine. The BPEL engine, based on the requirement and the process model, submits the request for a quotation to two or more web services endpoints of different airlines, as shown in Figure 14.6. These airline web services, in turn, could independently report the best rate quote. Further upon, the process engine can opt to choose the best airline for confirming the reservation, based on the specific requirement.

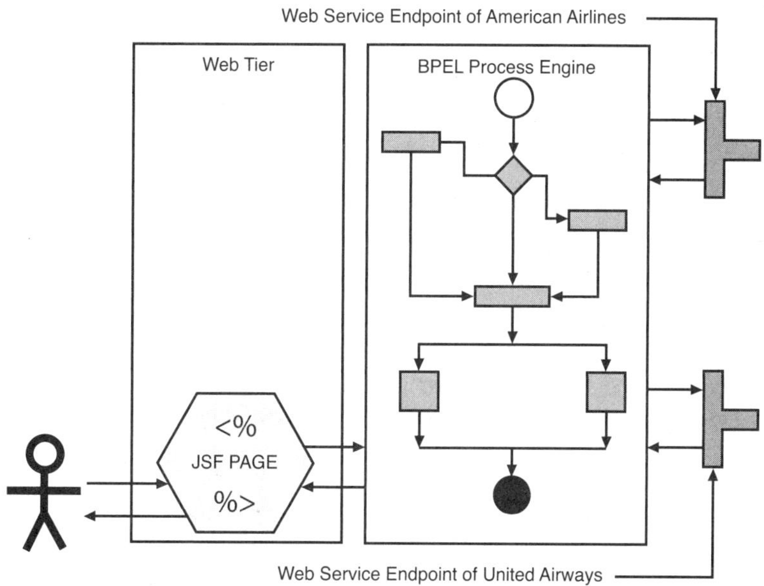

Figure 14.6 Delivering web services through orchestration of process model

In essence, the Enterprise requirement governs the process model, and the application service endpoints offering services can be properly and effectively orchestrated to suit the SOA requirements for the Enterprise.

Deciding on the Right Framework

There are many frameworks that are available to developers. Many are available for purchase, whereas other frameworks and tools are open-source and therefore free. Although it can be difficult for a developer to choose the right package for any given situation, here we compare two web-based frameworks: Apache Struts and JSF. Both are widely used by the developer community around the world.

Apache Struts is an open-source framework used for developing J2EE-oriented web applications. It uses and extends the Java Servlet API, enabling developers to adopt an MVC architecture, and it has already gathered a large user community worldwide. Apache Struts is a feature-rich, flexible, and expendable framework. Over the last nine years it has helped developers and architects to develop and deploy Java EE-based solutions to a variety of Enterprises.

While the Apache Struts framework is not completely unique, it nevertheless provides many key benefits to the developers and architects:

- Implements Model 2 MVC architecture
- Java-based and an important constituent in web technologies
- Supports internationalization (I18N)
- Includes a rich set of JSP tag libraries for presentation purposes
- Boasts features that are extensible and customizable
- Supports different presentation implementations (JSP, XML, XSLT, and even JSF)

More recent developments in web technologies, combined with the emergence of advanced frameworks such as JSF, have changed the scenario for aging frameworks such as Struts. Furthermore, several limitations in the Apache Struts have surfaced due to the changes in business demands on the framework requirements. There are some notable limitations of Struts frameworks:

- Despite its popularity, it is not an industry standard.
- Struts frameworks do not support the built-in UI component model.
- There is no built-in support of multiple renderer applications.
- Struts frameworks do not provide an event model for UI components.
- They do not support state management for UI components.

JSF technologies and frameworks, on the other hand, ease web-based application development by providing the developer and the architect with the following important features:

- Allows the developers to create UIs from a set of standard, reusable server-side components
- Provides a framework for implementing custom components
- Provides a set of JSP tags to access JSF components
- Saves state information transparently and repopulates forms when they are redisplayed
- Encapsulates event handling and component rendering, enabling the use of standard JSF components or custom components to support markup languages other than HTML
- Allows tool vendors to develop IDEs for a standard web application framework

The JSF framework can be considered a conceptual combination of Apache Struts and Java Swing, and is, in fact, seen as a direct competitor to Microsoft's WebForms. Although both these frameworks are similar in concept and implementation (and because JSF represents a standard for Java-based web application frameworks), tool vendors can focus on developing IDEs for JSF instead of developing an IDE for one of more than 40 existing Java-based web application frameworks, including Apache Struts.

Summary

The web tier is a critical component in the Enterprise solution. For many Enterprises, a web application can be the overall Enterprise solution. The web tier plays a crucial role in presentation and web services. Although Java Platform, Enterprise Edition technology has been established as the best and most productive way of configuring the architecture for a given enterprise solution, the multitude of frameworks that use Java EE technologies have helped to make this so. The JSF technology is emerging as the most powerful way to develop and deliver web-based Java EE solution for the enterprises. JSF frameworks help in delivering services, either as a stand-alone web services endpoint strategy or as part of the Enterprise business process/workflow in providing service orientation to Enterprise applications.

In the next chapter, we delve into the details of delivering SOA through the business tier. We'll explain how the business components in the business tier—namely, Session EJBs, Entity EJBs, POJOs, and MDBs—can engage in building services for addressing the needs of the Enterprise workflow.

Endnotes

1. Enterprise application QoS attributes are essentially the nonfunctional aspects of the Enterprise application. Scalability, Reliability, Availability, Security, Performance, and so on are some of the examples of Enterprise Application Quality attributes that are important to any Enterprise business. A few of these quality attributes were presented briefly in Chapter 9.
2. We are specifically referring to the J2EE technologies here, as many frameworks based on these technologies are still used. Although some of these frameworks are applicable to the new Java EE technologies scenario, many more are emerging to exploit the advantages of the new Java EE technologies.
3. He was a part of the expert group that defined Servlet 2.2, Servlet 2.3, JSP 1.1, and JSP 1.2 specifications. He is also the architect of Tomcat's Servlet container popularly known as Catalina.

15

Service Oriented Architecture and the Business Tier

Strategically developed business components deployed in application servers can successfully deliver services in the Enterprise framework. Session Enterprise JavaBeans *(*EJB*) in the business containers can be considered suitable candidates for delivering services because these business components can host the appropriate business logic and related services. These session EJBs are also session builders and therefore deliver services that help in building the workflow. These session beans are capable of delivering services using SOA-based messages. Business tier design patterns further help to provide optimal service-building capability to the Enterprise SOA.*

The business tier and the business components occupy a significant and strategic position in the Enterprise application. These components help in controlling the business logic and can address crucial operations such as transactions, data persistence, and so on. These business tier components are also capable of delivering web services. Session EJBs, for example, can be configured as web services endpoints to deliver service (or services). The new Java Platform, Enterprise Edition technologies enable easier, quicker ways to compose services as part of the SOA. The business methods defined in the session EJBs can now be exposed as web services, and these services can be suitably invoked by partners/collaborators. This chapter outlines the steps for exposing the methods of an EJB as web services and describes some of the design patterns session EJB components for SOA.

Delivering Services Through the Business Tier

The previous chapter detailed that enterprises with the intent to collaborate with partners and associates are realizing that the best way to meet that goal is through providing/availing services. Many of these services operate on business information as a part of meeting the service demands. The role of the business tier, therefore, is critical in SOA for any Enterprise. The EJB specifications of the Java EE technology help develop business components that can render the appropriate services. These components encapsulate business and data access logic capability to the services. The EJB technology ensures that the services are scalable, secure, robust, and transaction-oriented in nature. Furthermore, these business components are portable, reusable, and container-managed.

Recall from Chapter 9, "Java Platform, Enterprise Edition Overview," that there are three varieties of EJBs: *Session EJB*, *Entity EJB*, and *Message-Driven Bean* (*MDB*). The roles and responsibilities of these business components are different and meet different needs of the enterprise business services and business processes. Here, we discuss how business components of the Java Platform, Enterprise Edition provide services as part of SOA.

Business Tier Overview

Figure 14.1 illustrated the overall picture of the tiered structure of the new Java EE technology scenario, complete with different tiers and components communicating with each other. The focus here is the business tier. (The ways and the means in which the client communicates with the presentation tier are detailed in Chapters 10, "Web Technologies in Java EE," and Chapter 14, "Service Oriented Architecture and the Web Tier." Please refer to those chapters to review, if necessary.)

In this chapter, we focus on the communication of presentation tier components with the business components and analyze how they help in managing the business goals of the Enterprise, as part of the service orientation.

Among these three business components, we see that the session EJBs are ideally suited for providing services. Since their inception, session beans have been used for a variety of session-oriented business operations such as online banking, online shopping, and so on, and these operations become a perfect fit for exposure as web services. Furthermore, these EJBs have already been used to accomplish transaction-oriented business operations by accessing a persistence layer such as Entity EJBs or an ORM framework such as *TopLink*, or even sending a message to a *Java Message Service* (*JMS*) queue that would, in turn, activate an MDB to process the business logic. These session EJBs become a natural web services gateway. The business methods defined in the session EJBs, indicated as the Web Service endpoints in Figure 15.1, can now be "exposed" as web services so that partners/collaborators can invoke these web services as part of *Business-to-Business* (*B2B*) transaction.

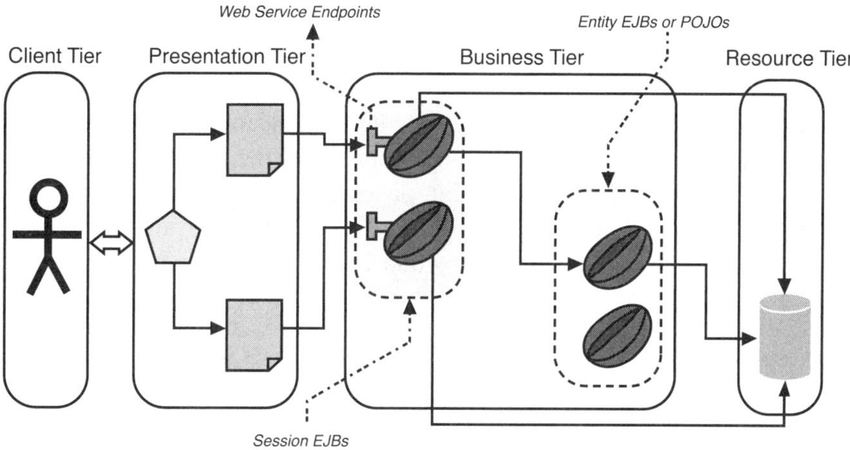

Figure 15.1 The business tier in the new Java Platform, Enterprise Edition technology

When a web service on the session EJBs is invoked, it can render the services by carrying out the appropriate business task and returning the response to the service invoker. The service invocation is a SOAP request message to the session EJB. The response to the service consumer is a SOAP response message. Before the SOAP response message is constructed, the session EJB will carry out the business transaction that can involve things such as data persistence, message delivery to a JMS queue, and so on. When performing the data persistence, the session EJB can interact with the entity EJBs or the new POJOs for carrying out the data persistence operation. These EJBs can directly communicate with the underlying database for carrying out the data persistence operations.

Because there are a myriad of possibilities of service invocation sequence from the client and business components performing business tasks, it is critical to exercise proper care in architecting the Enterprise solution for optimum performance. Architecting the Enterprise application for service orientation, along with designing the tiers, components, and communication for meeting the *quality of service* (*QoS*) standards, helps Enterprises transact business in a normal, satisfactory fashion.

Design patterns in the field of software architecture and design have gained increased importance over time. Patterns basically reflect the experience, knowledge, and insights of developers who have successfully used and cataloged these patterns to share them with the developer community. Although these patterns are reusable, they need to be properly adapted to the current needs of the Enterprise problems.

If the business tier is present in the architecture of an Enterprise application, it likely plays a critical role in meeting the needs of the Enterprise. It is therefore necessary to apply appropriate design patterns in this tier so that the application behaves expectedly and smoothly during the operation. In the next section, we explore the variety of design patterns that can be applied to the business tier.

Business Tier Design Patterns and SOA

Unlike the presentation tier components, the business tier components are not directly exposed to clients. Clients normally establish connection to these business components via the web tier components. For example, when a client intends to transact with the business components, he initiates an HTTP session with the presentation tier components such as Servlets and JSP. These components build a session for the client and then route the communication to the business tier components. The business tier components, in turn, carry out the intended task/transaction. This transaction could be leading to persisting the data in a database or triggering a sequence of persistence tasks in the EIS tier.

The increased popularity of the web services, along with the requirement to reorient the services for SOA, led to changes in the EJB specifications. These changes enabled the business components to be web services-oriented. The previous J2EE specification, J2EE 1.4, focused heavily on the world of web services. At that time, it was a JAX-RPC route to define web services and enable the EJB components to exchange SOAP messages via *remote procedure call* (*RPC*) communication mode.

The new Java EE technology and specifications have eased the development and deployment of the business tier components. Now, these components are not only lightweight and efficient, they are also easier to develop and deploy. These components can also persist the data, carry out important business transaction tasks, and participate in the workflow of the Enterprise. The current version of Java EE technology application servers and tools also supports the components developed for the earlier versions of the Java Enterprise Edition technologies. Moreover, the new components can coexist and communicate with earlier versions of the components. This option enables the developers to transition to the newer technology easily and quickly. It also helps the enterprise application smoothly transition to the newer technology.

Business Tier Design Patterns

Typically, the presentation tier components act as the *facade* to the business tier components. In fact, facade is a pattern in the presentation tier. Likewise, the business tier components communicate with the EIS integration tier components and resource adapters for persisting the information. Moreover, a number of business components such as EJBs, POJOs, JavaBeans, helper classes, utility classes, and so on are typically present in the business containers. This situation also demands that patterns be incorporated within the business tier so the components in the business tier function smoothly and efficiently while delivering services.

The following are the most common business tier design patterns:

- Presentation tier-to-business tier design patterns
- Integration tier design patterns
- Business tier patterns

In the next section, we briefly discuss the first two patterns, and later in the chapter we explore business tier design patterns.

Presentation Tier-to-Business Tier Design Patterns

Recall that the presentation tier acts as a facade to the business tier. Any service components in the business tier are accessible to the presentation tier components only. Components within the web tier frameworks, such as Struts or JSF, invoke the service request on the business tier service components.

The overall architecture of the presentation tier-to-business tier design pattern is depicted in Figure 15.2. The component-level interaction among different components between presentation and business tiers are depicted as a class diagram in Figure 15.3. We have focused only on the parts relevant to our discussion. Also, the components that are shown only represent the typical components that are present in that tier. Furthermore, this diagram is conceptual in nature. Different design patterns belonging to this category can be suitably mapped on to this figure to reveal this class diagram for the specific design pattern in question.[1]

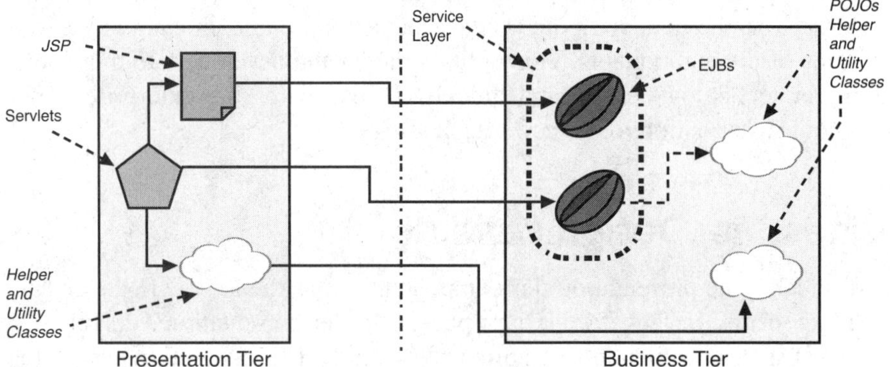

Figure 15.2 The presentation tier-to-business tier scenario

There are four major patterns that belong to this category of design patterns:

- Session facade pattern
- Business delegate pattern
- Transfer object pattern
- Service locater pattern

To illustrate the behavior of different components in the presentation tier and business tier, we will choose the transfer object as a typical design pattern.

Transfer Object Design Pattern

Transfer objects are simple POJOs that transport data across the different tiers. In this particular design pattern, the data transport is between the presentation tier and the business tier. The main advantages of transfer objects are as follows:

- They reduce coupling between the presentation layer and the business layer.
- They reduce the number of remote method calls, which are expensive.

To reduce the coupling between the presentation tier components and the business tier components, it would be advisable to avoid communicating with these business objects directly on the presentation layer. Introducing a transfer object helps in reducing this coupling.

The interaction between different components in the presentation tier and business tier can be better expressed with the help of a component diagram and sequence diagram. The component diagram for the transfer object design pattern is represented in Figure 15.3.

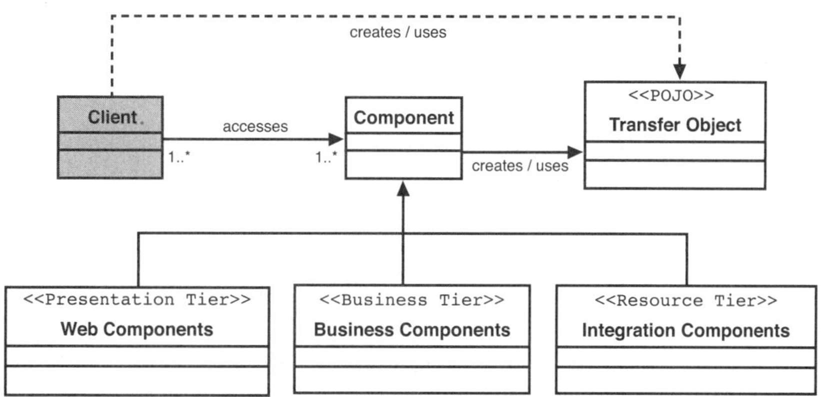

Figure 15.3 The class diagram showing the component-level interaction among different components

Here, the class named `Client` essentially represents the browser client. The class named `Component` essentially creates and uses the transfer objects that are, in essence, POJOs. These POJOs can get the data from any or all of the tiers by suitably interacting with the components.

In this case, we have mapped the sequence of the interaction of different components in different tiers using a sequence diagram in Figure 15-4. For the sake of simplicity, we have shown the sequence of events that transpire between the client and the two transfer objects.

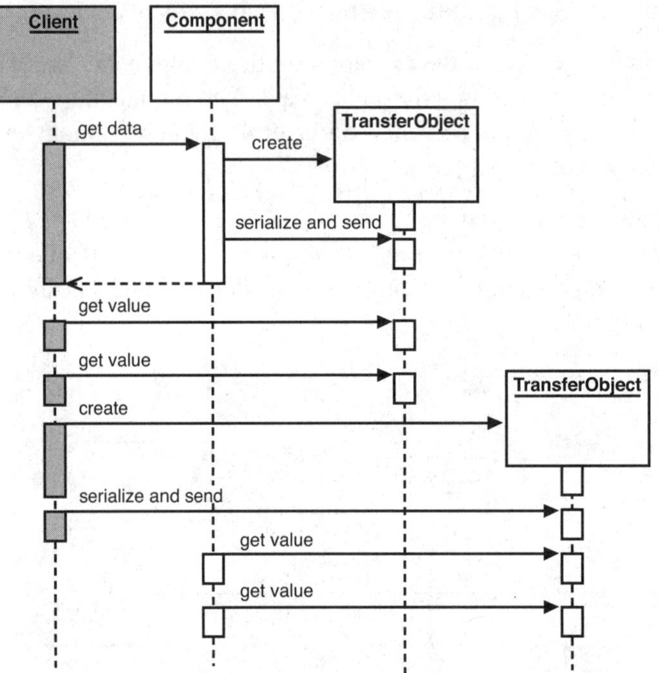

Figure 15.4 The sequence diagram indicating the sequence of method invocation/creation/use of different objects in a transfer object design pattern

In Figure 15.4, we see that the client is initiating the request on the component. The component, in this case, is creating two transfer objects that fetch the data from different tiers.

Integration Tier Design Patterns

The overall architecture of the integration tier design pattern, in association with the business tier design pattern, is depicted in Figure 15.5. For our purposes, we have focused only on the relevant portions of the tiers involved, leaving out the finer details for the sake of brevity. Also, the components that are shown represent only the typical components that are present in that tier. Furthermore, this diagram is conceptual in nature, and different design patterns belonging to this category can be suitably mapped on to this figure to reveal this class diagram for the specific design pattern in question. These patterns can also be referred to as *business tier-to-integration tier design patterns*.

There are four major design patterns in this tier:

- *Data access object (DAO)* design pattern
- Service activator design pattern
- Domain store design pattern
- Web service broker design pattern

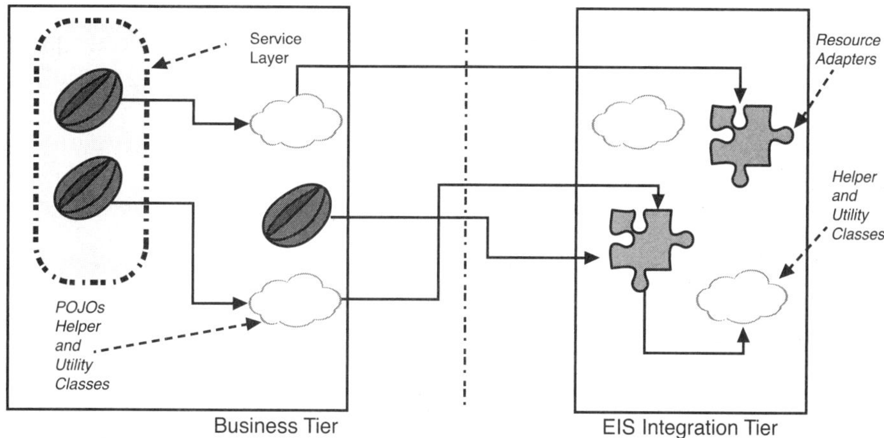

Figure 15.5 The integration-tier pattern scenario

To illustrate the behavior of different components in the business tier and integration tier, we will choose DAO as a typical design pattern for detailed discussion in the next subsection. This pattern is very close to (as well as related to) the transfer object design pattern we discussed earlier in the "Presentation Tier-to-Business Tier Design Patterns" section of this chapter.

The Data Access Object Pattern

The class diagram of this pattern is shown in Figure 15.6.

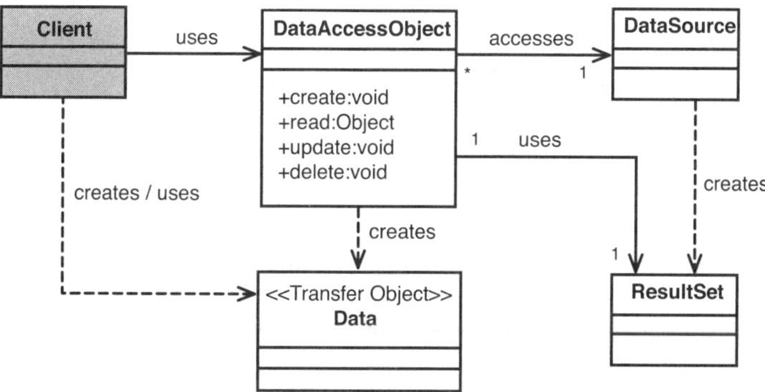

Figure 15.6 Class diagram representing the data access object design pattern

The classes involved here are essentially the data source object, the DAO, and the data object itself. The DAO uses (looks up) the data source object to create the data, and this normally would be a result set from the database query. The DAO uses this result set object to extract the data. The DAO then creates the transfer object and populates the data. Ultimately, the client uses this transfer object.

This sequence of events is illustrated in Figure 15.7. This figure presents just one set of interactions that result in the exemplification of the DAO design pattern.

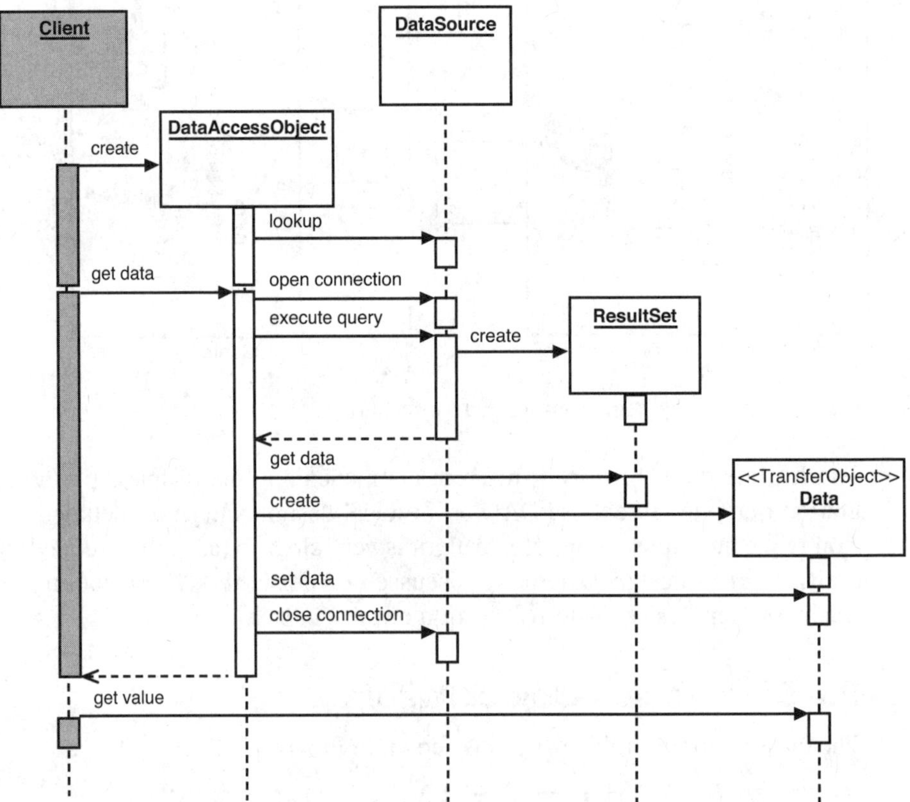

Figure 15.7 Class diagram representing the DAO design pattern

To review, the client creates the DAO, and the DAO performs a lookup to access the data source object. After the connection is established, the DAO executes a query on the data source object, resulting in the creation of a result set object. The DAO now creates the data object (which is the transfer object) and populates the fields from the result set object. This transfer object is now available to the client object.

Intrabusiness Tier Design Patterns

The overall architecture of the intrabusiness tier design pattern is depicted in Figure 15.8. For our purposes, we have focused only on the relevant components and portion of the tiers, leaving out the finer details for the sake of brevity. Also, the components that are shown represent only the typical components that are present in that tier. Furthermore, this diagram is conceptual in nature, and different design patterns belonging to this category can be suitably mapped on to this figure to reveal this class diagram for the specific design pattern in question.

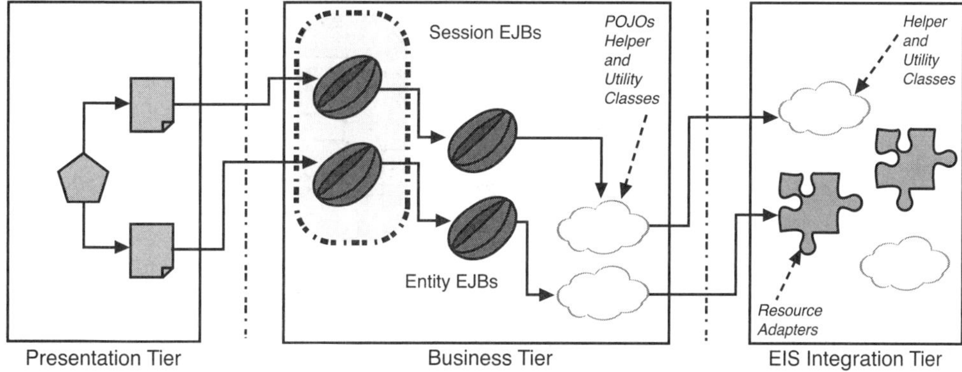

Figure 15.8 The intrabusiness tier design pattern scenario

Intrabusiness tier design patterns are basically the business tier design patterns as documented and cataloged elsewhere. The business tier design patterns assist in effectively handling business logic and data persistence functions effectively and efficiently. These design patterns also help improve performance, tighten security, and promote modularity to the Enterprise application. There are eight design patterns identified in this tier that help in achieving these QoS:

- Business delegate
- Service locater
- Session facade
- Application service
- Business object
- Composite entity
- Transfer object
- Transfer object assembler

To illustrate the behavior of different components in the intrabusiness tier, we choose *application service* as a typical design pattern for a detailed discussion on the intrabusiness tier design pattern.

Application Service Design Pattern

Application service design patterns essentially help centralize and aggregate behavior to provide a uniform service layer. This pattern essentially uses an application controller that invokes the business and data access methods from the *business objects* (*BO*) or DAO. The class diagram showing the interactions among different components in this design pattern is shown in Figure 15.9.

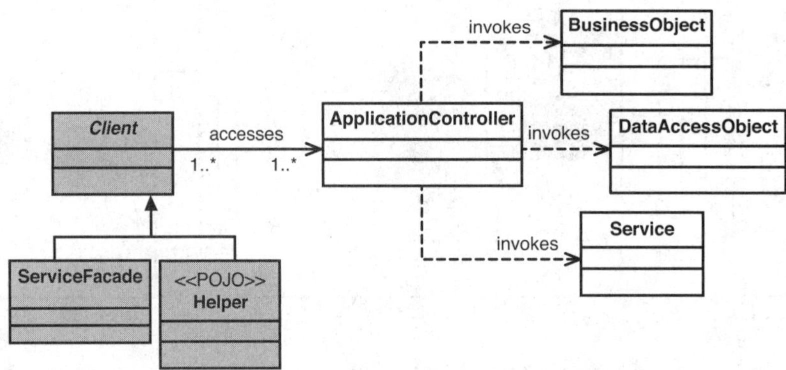

Figure 15.9 Class diagram showing interactions among different components in application service design pattern

The client accesses the application controller, which now is a centralized repository to access business logic and services. Based on the requirement, the client invokes the BO, the DAO, or a service. The application controller is essentially the application service. There could be any number of application services deployed in the business tier. These application services handle the logic and service requests from the clients and process them accordingly.

Consider a situation in which a client is attempting to access services from two applications: Application Service 1 and Application Service 2, as shown in Figure 15.10. Initially, the client invokes the Application Service 1, which sets things into motion. The Application Service 1 invokes a business method on Business Object 1 first and then on Business Object 2. Next, the client invokes Application Service 2 for services. This sets things into motion, this time, in Application Service 2, which invokes methods on DAO and another service object, respectively.

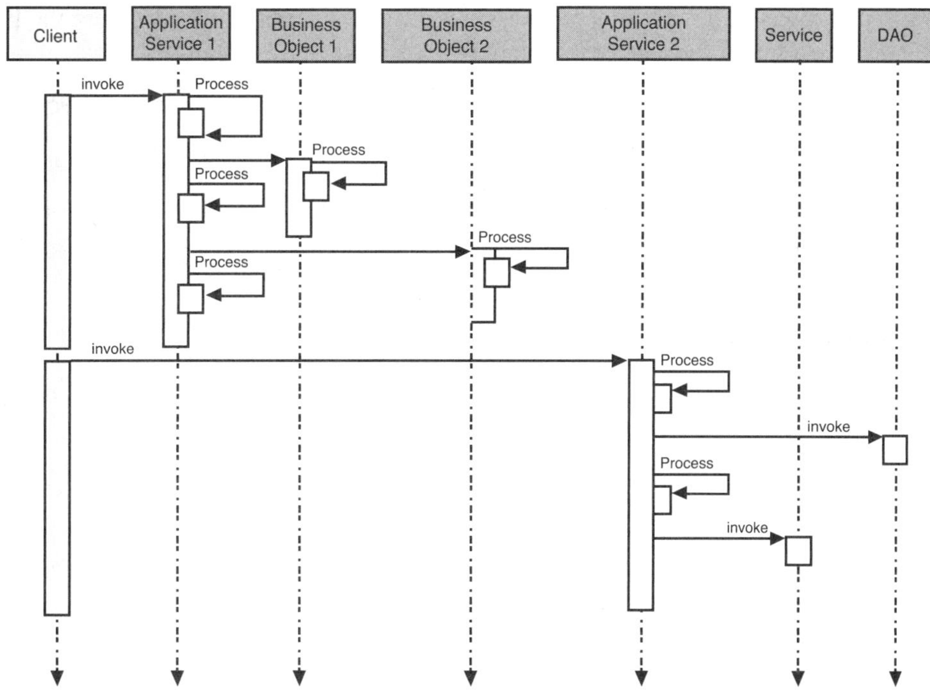

Figure 15.10 Sequence diagram indicating the sequence of events taking place between the application controller and other business objects in the application service design pattern

Summary

The business tier plays a significant role in the enterprise application tiers. The components in this tier not only control the business logic, they are capable of addressing critical operations, including transactions, data persistence, and so on. The arrival of web services technology and the motivation for service orientation have significantly influenced the functionality of the business components. These components are now ready for delivering web services.

It is now quicker and easier than ever to create and deploy business components in the new Java EE technologies. The business services in these components can be exposed as web services. The new technology also supports the older business components created as per the earlier EJB specifications and can interact with the new components, as well. If present in the overall architecture, the business tier significantly affects the QoS of the Enterprise application. It is, therefore, important to carefully consider business tier design patterns while designing the Enterprise solution for service orientation.

In the next chapter, we describe briefly how the new Java Enterprise technology addresses the QoS aspects of the services in SOA. We essentially cover some of the important QoS aspects such as reliability, availability, and security and indicate how these nonfunctional requirements affect the nature of solution in service orientation.

Endnote

1. The patterns are usually presented using sequence or class diagrams. When we deal with specific patterns, we present the appropriate diagram.

16

Advanced Service Oriented Architecture

Because Enterprises deliver services, and the Enterprise applications should be service-oriented in nature. These applications can clearly be designed to deliver services using technologies such as web services. Although First Generation Web Services technologies can help create and configure the business services, the Second Generation Web Services technologies can meet the nonfunctional requirements such as scalability, availability, reliability, security, and so on. The quality of services *(*QoS*) of the Enterprise application is a particularly important consideration. Although they are not devoid of problems, Java Platform, Enterprise Edition technology and all its specifications and APIs enable the implementation of key aspects of these advanced service-orientation aspects for implementing SOA.*

The realm of SOA elevates Enterprises to a different level of requirements. Patterns are emerging in the world of SOA to deal with the process and workflow issues. These patterns are collectively referred to as SOA patterns. The SOA patterns are essentially the patterns that manage the processes or orchestration. In this chapter we highlight the importance of the workflow/process modeling and indicate how these patterns can deliver SOA using Java EE technologies.

Patterns in SOA

Patterns introduced by the *Gang of Four* (*GoF*)[1] were revolutionary in nature and attempted to simplify solutions for a variety of common problems. Classified according to one of the three categories—*creational*, *structural* and *behavioral*—patterns essentially helped the developers and architects to organize and streamline the components in such a way that they avoid the usual problems encountered during the software application development. With the arrival of the newer technologies, such as J2EE, newer patterns emerged, and the nature of classification of the new patterns changed. On the J2EE technologies front, the patterns gained momentum, and the classification of the patterns was essentially based on the tiers. For example, *presentation tier design patterns*, *business tier design patterns*, and *EIS tier design patterns* were commonly used to solve the tier-level issues. Additional patterns emerged that used an approach of the combination of two or more patterns; *service to worker* and *dispatcher view* are two of the most frequently encountered patterns that belong to the category of combination patterns. Some of the other combinations spanned across the tiers as well. *Business delegate* and *transfer object* are two of the common examples of the combination patterns that spans across different tiers.

The GoF and the related patterns are essentially user-to-user communication patterns that have been extended to *user-to-computer* or *user-to-application* communications. These patterns are essentially expressed in the underlying programming environment. They have been largely successful and continue to provide solutions for similar kinds of problems. Now that service orientation is gaining importance and architectural issues have begun to emerge, newer paradigms have appeared on the horizon of Enterprise architectures. Business process or workflow, choreography, web services, messaging middleware, Enterprise Service Bus, and so on present new challenges for delivering the QoS for the Enterprise application. This new way of thinking is giving rise to new sets of patterns called *SOA patterns*.

SOA patterns can be classified into a variety of categories. For our purposes we focus on the following patterns:

- Message exchange patterns
- Asynchronous messaging patterns
- Conversation patterns
- Orchestration patterns
- Process or workflow patterns
- Endpoint patterns
- Security patterns

Our emphasis in this chapter is on *asynchronous messaging*, *conversation*, *orchestration*, and *process (or workflow) patterns*.

Asynchronous Messaging Patterns

In any Enterprise application situation, there can be many service providers and service consumers. The communication between these participants can be in the form of messaging, and there can be many combinations of service provision and service consumption. For example, multiple service consumers could be seeking services from multiple service providers. And a service consumer could be sending multiple service requests to one or more service providers. Likewise, a service provider could be providing multiple services to one or more consumers. The situation could be complicated enough that each service consumption (or service provision) could mean an exchange of one or more messages between the consumer and provider. Such situations could be handled using the following patterns:

- Request-reply
- Return address
- Correlation identifier

To keep things in check, we briefly describe each of these patterns in the following subsections.

Request-Reply

Request-reply is the simplest of the asynchronous messaging patterns. In this case, there is just one service consumer and one service provider. This is similar to the synchronous *request-response* MEP discussed in Chapter 8, "Advanced Web Services Infrastructure for Implementing SOA." The difference here is that *asynchronous MQ systems* are used to exchange communications. Under such circumstances, we have a pair of message channels per consumer/provider combination. The channels are unidirectional in nature and, as shown in Figure 16.1, they form a pair of asynchronous point-to-point channels. One channel is used for sending the request message, and the other channel is used for receiving the response message.

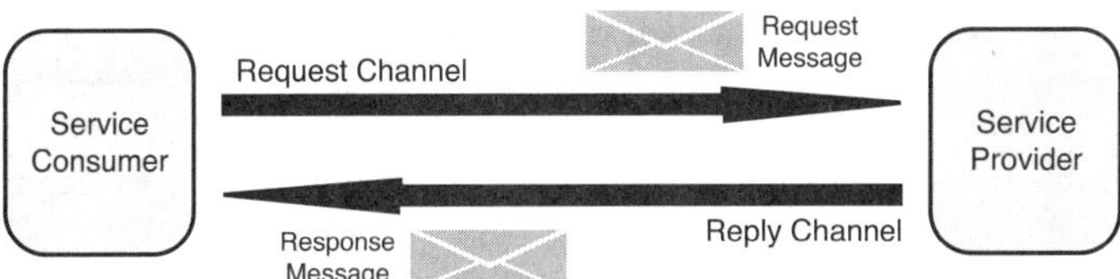

Figure 16.1 Asynchronous request-reply oriented point-to-point channels

Request-reply patterns help in solving the simplest of the provider-consumer situation—one-on-one. The situations in the Enterprise scenario will hardly be that simple. In some Enterprise situation, there could be the possibility of a single service provider providing services to many service consumers. Under such circumstances, it is possible to configure the provider to use one request channel for receiving requests from multiple consumers and use independent reply channels for each of the service consumers. Such a situation is taken care of by the return address pattern.

Return Address

In this pattern, we can configure the provider to use just one request channel for receiving requests from multiple consumers and use independent reply channels for each of the service consumers. In fact, this situation, represented in Figure 16.2, is not at all uncommon in the Enterprise scenario. This dictates us to configure a robust pattern for handling precisely these situations. To illustrate this, let's consider a common travel-related example. Several travel agents around the world are planning to use the reservation service of a particular airline. Under such circumstances, the service provider is besieged with the problem of which channel is to be used for which consumer. One quick-fix solution could be that the service provider sends the same reply message to all the consumers on their individual reply channels. This solution would be appropriate, provided all consumers are looking for the same reply message. However, such occurrences in the enterprise scenario are likely to be rare; we therefore need to look for a more efficient and robust pattern that efficiently handles multiple consumers simultaneously.

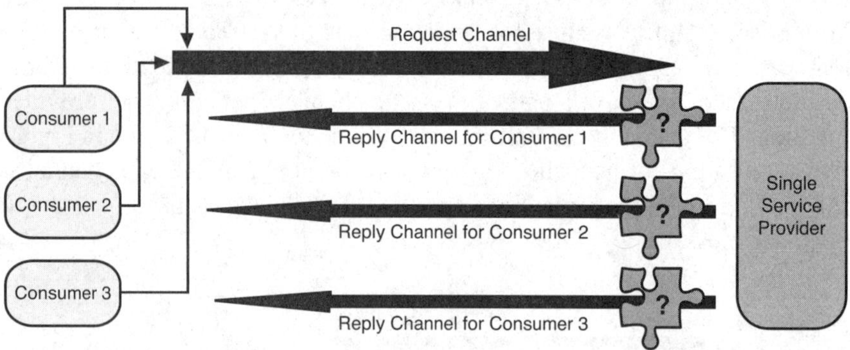

Figure 16.2 Multiple service consumers communicating with a single service provider

A more robust and efficient solution would require that each of the consumers tag a *reply-to* address while sending the message to the service provider. The provider knows the consumer's needs and the reply channel address, as presented in Figure 16.3.

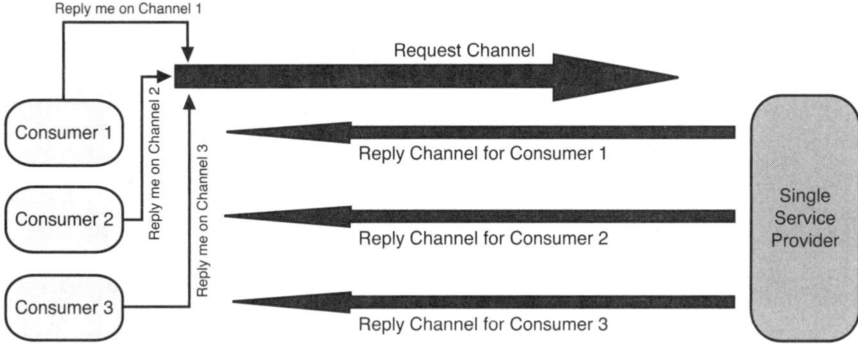

Figure 16.3 Multiple service consumers reply to return address pattern

Correlation Identifier

Next, we analyze an Enterprise situation in which there are multiple service providers. Again, using the airline reservation scenario, a service consumer is trying to get a service from multiple service providers. The difference here is that the consumer is seeking the reservation from multiple airline reservation systems for travel between two different cities, as shown in Figure 16.4. The objective is that multiple airlines are tapped for optimization purposes.

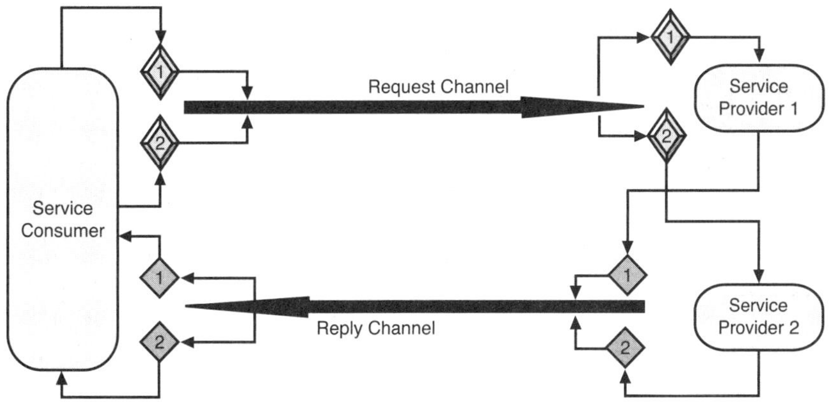

Figure 16.4 Single service consumer communicating with multiple service providers

In certain situations, when a consumer seeks a service from multiple providers, the consumer might not expect a reply message from all the providers at the same time. That said, it is possible that the message from Service Provider 1, the first provider to reply, will be consumed by the consumer (see Figure 16.5).

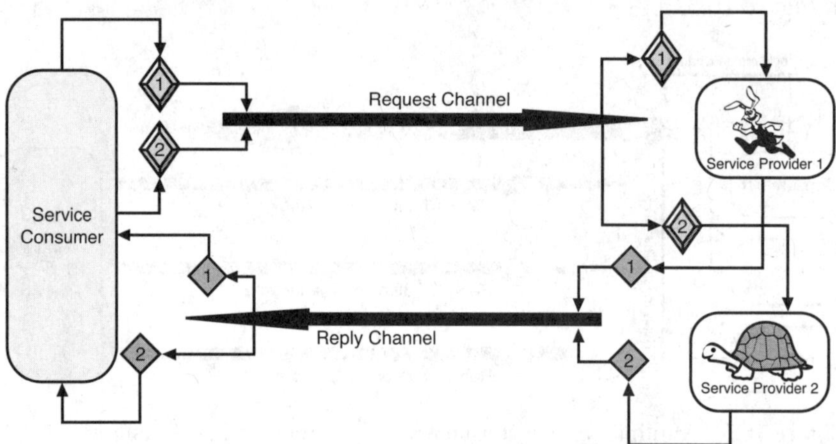

Figure 16.5 Different service providers could provide services at different response times.

We can envision a more complicated scenario in which a single consumer requests multiple services from multiple service providers. The complications arise when it is important for the consumer to wade through the requests and replies from many service providers and correlate the responses.

Situations such as these can be handled by equipping different messages to different service providers with a unique identifier called the *correlation identifier*. When a provider receives a service request from a consumer that contains an identifier, the provider copies the identifier to the reply message. When the reply reaches the consumer, the identifier attached to the reply is used to *identify*, *correlate*, and *retrieve* the message state, as shown in Figure 16.6.

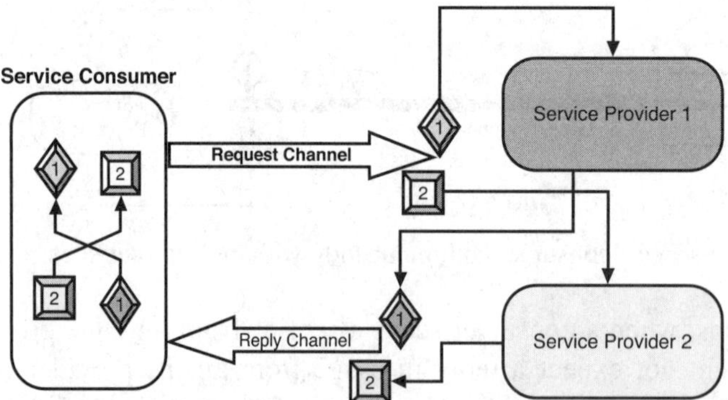

Figure 16.6 Using the correlation identifier to track and identify the providers and the conversation state

Conversation Patterns

In the previous section, we covered a few different message exchange patterns based on the following situations:

- Consumer–Provider
- Consumers–Provider
- Consumer–Providers

Recall when we outlined the simple scenario of consumer and provider, we referred to the request-reply pattern. A request-reply pattern is suitable when there are two fixed partners exchanging messages. Such message exchange is referred to as *conversation*, which is essentially the exchange of messages over time between two communicating partners. The exchange could involve just one message or multiple messages. When multiple messages are exchanged between two such partners, these messages need to be described and coordinated. This is essentially the concept of choreography.

Choreography (and the concept of WS-Choreography Definition Language)[2] is essentially the coordination of message exchange between multiple partners engaged in conversations. When just two such fixed participants are engaged in such conversation, they can, ideally, demand any pattern in conversations because there are no issues. However, the situation is hardly ever straightforward when there are multiple partners engaged in multiple conversations. Patterns to handle situations under such circumstances are referred to as *conversation patterns*. Some of the commonly encountered conversation patterns encountered in the Enterprise situation are *request-reply*, *subscribe/notify*, and *process pattern*. We briefly describe them in the following section.

Request-Reply

Request-reply is the simplest of the conversation patterns. The consumer makes a request for service, and the provider sends a response. There are no issues or problems; this ideal conversation is represented as a sequence diagram in Figure 16.7.

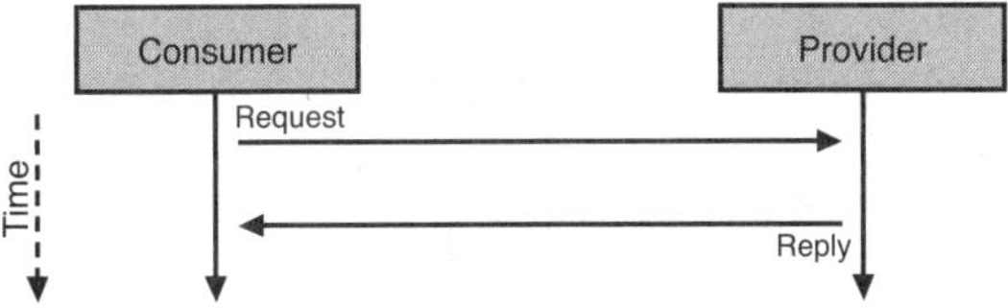

Figure 16.7 Sequence diagram showing request-reply conversation between two isolated partners

Realistically, the situation is hardly ever that straightforward. Many requests might need resending or retrying. The provider might reply after a *single retry* or *multiple retries*. It might be important to configure such retries for the conversations between two communicating partners. A simple retry situation is shown in Figure 16.8. Here the consumer sends a request and waits for a predetermined amount of time. A retry is attempted by the consumer after ΔT1. However, there is no reply from the provider. The consumer will attempt a second retry after ΔT2. The provider then sends a reply to the request. What is desirable under such circumstances is that the provider needs is idempotent. *Idempotent* essentially means that processing the same request two (or more) times has the same effect as processing it just once.

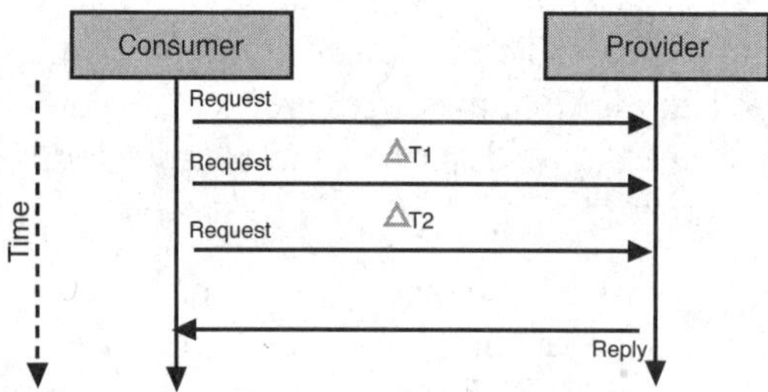

Figure 16.8 Request-reply conversation with retry option due to failure in request/provider processing

It might well be that the consumer submits many retries and eventually gives up. Still, the provider could respond after repeated retries.

Subscribe/Notify

Subscribe/notify (Figure 16.9) is a common occurrence in the Enterprise world. The consumers essentially register themselves with the service providers by expressing interest in a desired service (subscribe). The providers, in turn, communicate with the registered consumers to provide the services (notify).

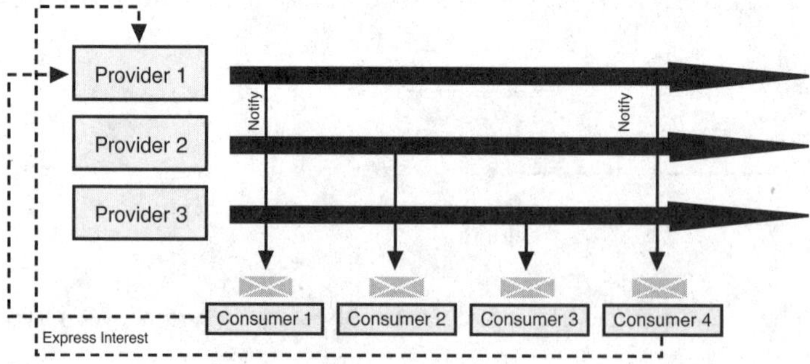

Figure 16.9 Subscribe-notify pattern. Observe Consumer 1 and Consumer 4.

In Figure 16.9, Consumer 1 and Consumer 4 have registered with Provider 1. When appropriate, these consumers are notified by Provider 1. Likewise, Consumer 2 and Consumer 3 will be notified by Provider 2 and Provider 3, respectively, when appropriate.

Process Patterns

Processes (commonly referred to as *workflow*) are fundamentally the neural network of the Enterprise application. For an organization to function successfully, an Enterprise must appropriately manage several sets of processes.

These processes could be long- or short-running, and many processes are composed of other subprocesses. At any point of time, there could be many processes running concurrently in an organization. Each process, large or small, could either complete a specific task or invoke a service to complete a part of the process. These services could be web services, and as part of the Enterprise requirement, the processes could be invoking the *service endpoints* to complete the business task. *Orchestration* is the ability to handle, manage, and execute processes across multiple services (that are known as *composite services*). The orchestration fundamentally describes the automated arrangement, coordination, and management of business processes and services. Orchestration addresses the management of multiple processes and multiple conversations (choreography). Although the process description and modeling might appear outwardly simple, internally it typically requires the completion of numerous complex tasks to meet the business goals of the organization. Currently, *WS-Business Process Execution Language (WS-BPEL)*[3] is the industry standard; this specification helps in standardizing the process description and modeling using a dialect of *Extensible Markup Language* (*XML*).

The top-level pattern classification is simple and straightforward: *workflow patterns* and *orchestration patterns*. In the following sections we explore these two major classification systems of the SOA patterns.

Orchestration Patterns

Orchestration is managing the multiple processes and multiple conversations as one complex conversation. WS-BPEL is the accepted standard used to manage orchestration, and this is essentially the XML dialect to express processes in terms of predefined XML elements. To manage the process, we need a process-oriented engine, the *orchestration engine*.

Although the process is expressed in BPEL language, the management aspect presents unique challenges. Patterns[4] are proposed to address these challenges. There are nine orchestration patterns, as follows:

- Orchestration engine
- Orchestration language
- Orchestration builder
- Evaluator
- Rule Builder
- Orchestration context
- Conditional transitions
- Engine monitoring and control
- Compensating action

Orchestration Engine

This pattern essentially suggests using an *engine* capable of managing the processes and conversations wherever the need for managing the process is crucial. This pattern is also essential when orienting and reorienting the architecture. Using an orchestration engine for managing the process helps greatly in the matters of *separation of concerns*. The process code is at last separate and distinct from the business logic, and this is instantly beneficial.

Services are separate from the process flow, and the entire process can run separately and efficiently. This pattern explicitly recommends using a separate and specialized *process modeling language*. The orchestration functions by executing the process model expressed in the new specialized language. This pattern also recommends that this language be fundamentally different from the other general-purpose programming languages.[5] At minimum, the pattern recommends the language must provide a means for transferring control to a *business process actor* and receiving data from the same. The language must also provide *activity execution points*. These represent a point at which the control flow crosses the boundary between the *orchestration realm* and the *application realm*. An orchestration language must also provide a means of composing primitives, variables, and so on so that the process modelers can define more realistic business processes. This language must also provide all the necessary process/workflow-oriented features: *sequence*, *conditional*, *looping*, *forking*, *joining*, *merging*, *synchronizing*, and so on.

Orchestration Builder

This pattern suggests that the process building is enabled by a graphical tool. This builder tool provides a level of abstraction above the orchestration language. The process modeler enables nontechnical users to define the coordination aspect through combining graphical representations of the different elements of the orchestration language. This pattern also recommends that the builder can carry out tasks like drag-and-drop, cut-and-paste, copy-and-paste, and so on. A typical graphical modeling tool is shown in Figure 16.10.

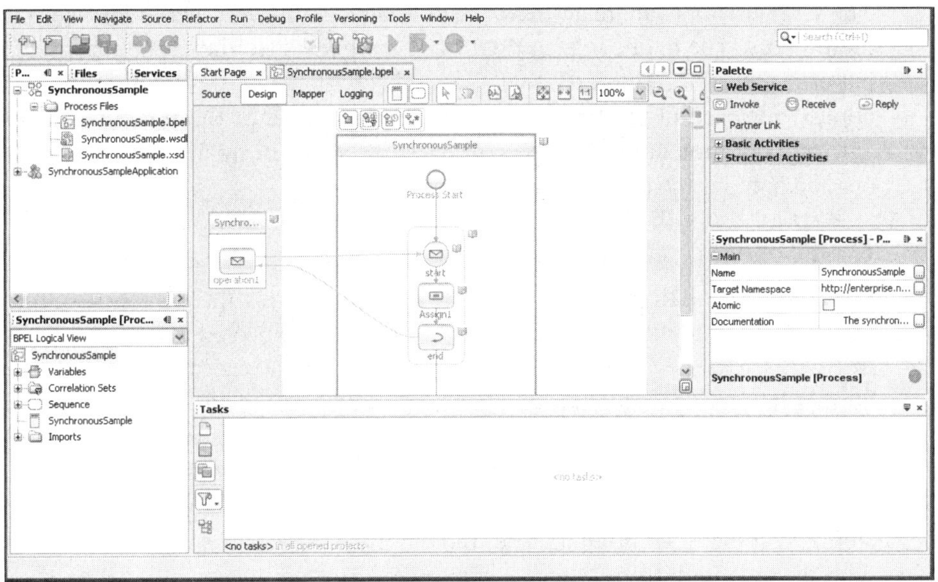

Figure 16.10 NetBeans Enterprise pack showing graphical process modeling capabilities

Evaluator

Evaluation is essentially the process of testing. Any and all process models should be tested and evaluated for different things—from simple arithmetic evaluation to complex looping and conditional evaluation. This pattern recommends prescribing a specialized language for defining test conditions and delegates the processing to an evaluator[6] who is specialized in evaluating conditions.

Rule Builder

Often nontechnical users become involved in building the rules for process modeling. In fact, this is more likely to happen than not. These users should function in this capacity without having to master the intricacies of the process definition language. This pattern recommends creating a *builder tool* that provides a level of abstraction above the rules specification language.

Orchestration Context

When a process is executed by an orchestration engine, it should be possible for this engine to pass the outputs from each preceding activity to the next activity. The engine should manage the data flow across different activities as a part of the process. The data can also flow from a requester to the process activity. The pattern, therefore, suggests that the orchestration engine create orchestration context for each orchestration throughout the course of the process executions. The orchestration context carries all the necessary information between requesters and handles the data and the state.

Conditional Transitions

Processes essentially constitute a series of steps. During the execution of the process, after one activity is cleared successfully, it is expected that the process control will seamlessly jump to the next step. Realistically, certain conditions must be met before the execution of the next stage begins. This is termed the *conditional transition*. The pattern suggests augmenting the activities with conditions that determine when they should execute. Under such circumstances, the orchestration engine no longer transfers control from one activity to another when a step is complete. At this juncture, the engine evaluates the condition associated with the transition from *previous step* to *next step* and waits until the condition is satisfied. This conditional control mechanism could easily handle activities that do not require conditional transitions.

Engine Monitoring and Control

This pattern stresses the monitoring and control aspects of the orchestration engine. The engine should be designed in a way that utilizes both *instrumentation* and *control points*. Although the instrumentation points let you capture engine-level orchestration information, the control points enable the control orchestration execution. When designing the orchestration engine, it should be possible to provide and implement *data capture hooks*. These hooks should enable administrators to customize the data capture mechanism and even provide new implementations. For example, a hook designed with modifiability in mind enables users to customize the engine so that it augments the information with a time stamp and then logs it to a database. The instrumentation and control points should provide a programmatic way to control the orchestration engine. This could include commands such as *Abort* to terminate execution of an orchestration, *Stop* to stop the engine, or *Resume* enabling the engine to resume the process execution, and so on. Engines must also either expose the control points as an API or enable users to implement various tools.

Compensating Action

In an Enterprise scenario, any processing must be planned from compensating action. The role of a compensating action is to negate a planned executed action. The granularity of the process definition is also an important part of the compensating action. Consider that one situation in the Enterprise scenario could call for cancellation of part of or the whole executed process. This pattern suggests the orchestration engine should address such scenarios using the compensating actions. Compensating or canceling a certain activity should invoke corresponding actions in an appropriate order. If the granularity is course in nature, a compensating action results in reversing several executed processes (or subprocesses). If the granularity is fine in nature, several compensating actions might need to be forced on the orchestration engine. While planning for compensating actions, it should be noted that the grouping should not mix the nontransactional steps with transactional steps because the transactional compensating actions result in rollback on databases.

Workflow Patterns

In the world of process modeling or workflow, the patterns are, in essence, termed *perspectives*. These perspectives are subdivided into four different categories:[7]

- **The Control-Flow Perspective**—Captures aspects related to control-flow dependencies between different tasks, such as parallelism, choice, synchronization, and so on
- **The Data Perspective**—Deals with the passing of information, scoping of variables, and so on
- **The Resource Perspective**—Deals with resource-to-task allocation, delegation, and so on
- **The Exception-Handling Perspective**—Deals with the causes for different types of exceptions and the actions that need to be taken as a result

The Control-Flow Patterns

The terms *control* and *flow* are the essence of the processes. This perspective defines more than 40 different patterns that cover different aspects of control and flow. Although a full discussion of these categories is beyond the scope of this chapter, we have attempted to nonetheless provide a brief description of each. The six categories under this perspective follow:

- Basic control flow patterns
- Advanced branching and synchronization patterns
- Structural patterns
- Multiple instance patterns

- State-based patterns
- Cancellation patterns

Basic Control Flow Patterns This class of pattern expresses the basic aspects of process flow and contains five basic patterns:

- **Sequence pattern**—The tasks are executed in a predefined sequence, one after the other.
- **Parallel split pattern**—The processes are split into two or more branches, and the tasks place in each of the branching in a parallel manner. A simplistic representation of the parallel split pattern of process flow is shown in Figure 16.11.

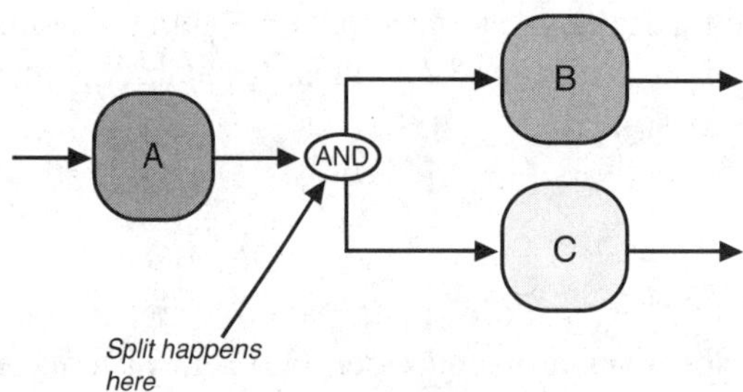

Figure 16.11 Parallel split pattern exemplified

- **Synchronization pattern**—This enables the subbranches to combine in such a way that the new branch will get the control only when all the subbranches have successfully executed their predefined tasks. A simplistic representation of the synchronization pattern is portrayed in Figure 16.12.

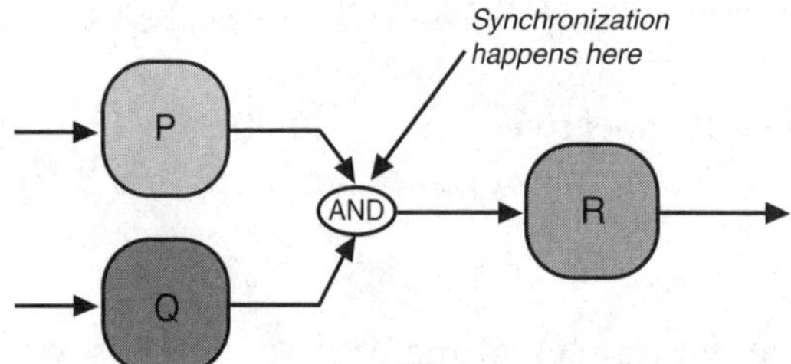

Figure 16.12 Synchronization pattern exemplified

- **Exclusive choice pattern**—This can also be called the *Exclusive OR (XOR)* pattern. As in the case of the XOR definition, the exclusive choice pattern results in the divergence of a control flow into two or more branches. When the incoming branch is enabled, the thread of control is immediately passed on to *precisely one* of the outgoing branches. This decision is based on the outcome of business logic associated with a branch.

- **Simple merge pattern**—This enables clubbing two or more subbranches to one subsequent branch. Unlike the synchronization pattern, the business logic associated with the branch does not evaluate preconditions when a process flow is encountered in a subbranch.

Advanced Branching and Synchronization Patterns Unlike the basic control flow patterns, these characterize more complex branching and complicated merging concepts prevalent in many business scenarios. Some of these patterns are also a combination of the basic patterns just discussed:

- **Multichoice pattern**—In simplest terms, this is a combination of the parallel split, an exclusive choice, or a simple multiple choice pattern. An incoming process, depending on the business logic at the branch, can choose one or more parallel executions in the subsequent branching. This pattern is shown in Figure 16.13.

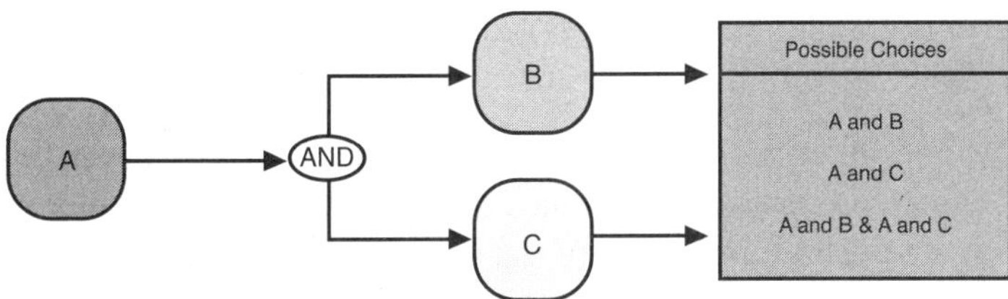

Figure 16.13 Multichoice pattern exemplified

- **Structured synchronizing merge pattern**—This is a combination of the parallel split and synchronization patterns. It enables the convergence of two or more branches into a single subsequent branch. The converging branches are essentially the divergence branch at the earlier process step, which is a uniquely identifiable point. The control of execution is passed to the subsequent branch when each active incoming branch has been enabled.
- **Multimerge pattern**—This is similar to the structured synchronizing merge pattern, although there are some differences. The multimerge pattern enables the convergence of two or more branches into a single subsequent branch; however, each enabling of an incoming branch results in the flow control being passed on to the subsequent branch.
- **Structured discriminator pattern**—This pattern is structurally similar to the structured synchronization merge, but functionally different. In this pattern, two or more subbranchings can converge to a single subsequent

branch. The subbranching is essentially a divergence (or split) from the previous step in the process path. In this pattern, the control flow is passed to the subsequent branch when the *first incoming branch* has been enabled. Subsequent enabling of incoming branches does not result in flow control being passed on. Here, the structured discriminator construct is reset when all incoming branches have been enabled. A simple flow diagram of this pattern is shown in Figure 16.14.

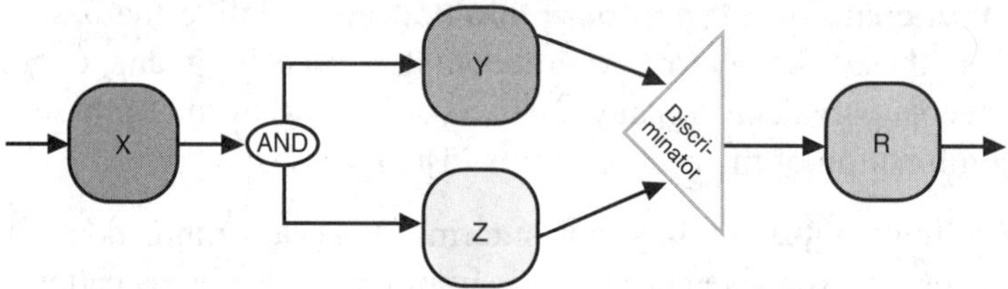

Figure 16.14 Structured discriminator pattern exemplified

Multiple Instance Patterns In this classification, patterns enable the execution of multiple process threads (or instances) in a process model that relate to the same activity. There are four different patterns in this category:

- **Multiple instances without synchronization pattern**—At any time within a given process instance, multiple instances of a particular activity can be created. These instances of the activity are independent of each other and could run concurrently. The need for synchronization among these instances is not a requirement.
- **Multiple instances with a priori design-time knowledge pattern**—At design time, multiple instances of an activity can be created within a given process instance. The required number of instances is decided at design time. These process instances are independent of each other and run concurrently. It is important to synchronize the activity instances at completion before any subsequent activities can be initiated.
- **Multiple instances with a priori run-time knowledge pattern**—According to this pattern, within a given process instance, it should be possible to create multiple instances of an activity. The required number of instances, however, depends on a number of runtime factors, such as state data, resource availability, interprocess communications, and so on. That said, *the number of instances* is known before the activity instances must be created. When initiated, these process instances are independent of each other and can run concurrently. Again, it is necessary for these instances to be synchronized at the end before any subsequent activities are triggered.

- **Multiple instances without a priori run-time knowledge pattern**—According to this pattern, within a given process instance, it should be possible to create multiple instances of an activity. The required number of instances depends on a number of runtime factors, such as state data, resource availability, inter-process communications, and so on. It is important to note that *the number of instances is not known until the final instance has completed.* At any time, while instances are running, it is possible for additional instances to be initiated. Again, it is necessary that these instances are synchronized at the end before any subsequent activities are triggered.

The Data Patterns

These patterns are also called *workflow data* patterns. They aim to capture the various ways in which the data is represented and utilized in enterprise processes. There are more than 40 different patterns in the data patterns category. For a better understanding, these patterns are subclassified into four different perspectives:

- Data visibility
- Data interaction
- Data transfer mechanisms
- Data-based routing

Data Visibility The data visibility patterns address the distinct ways in which the data elements can be defined and utilized within the context of a workflow engine. These variations relate to the manner in which the data elements are declared and the process to which they are anchored. These variations directly influence the way in which the data element can be used.

Data Interaction For our purposes, the term *interaction* refers to the exchange of the data between components in a process. The patterns described under this category enable a variety of ways in which data elements can be passed between components in a particular process. These patterns also deal with how the characteristics of the individual components can influence the manner in which the trafficking of data elements takes place. Two major data interaction subsets can be identified here. They are internal data interaction and external data interaction. The internal data interaction subset deals with the communication of components within a process. The external data interaction subset deals with the communication of a process element with that of the external environment.

Data Transfer Mechanisms Although the data interaction pattern deals with the exchange of data between the components of a process, the data transfer mechanisms patterns essentially address the manner in which the actual exchange of data elements occurs between one process component and another. These patterns also attempt to capture the mechanisms by which data elements can be exchanged across the interface of a process component.

Data-Based Routing These patterns capture the various ways in which data elements can interact with perspectives and influence the overall operation of the process such as control, resource, data-based routing, and so on within an enterprise. The essential difference between the data-based routing set of patterns from that of the other data patterns is that the latter set of patterns essentially deal with the characteristics of data elements in isolation from other process perspectives.

The Resource Patterns

These patterns are also known as the *workflow resource* patterns. They aim to capture the variety of ways in which the enterprise resources are represented and utilized by process items during the execution of a process in the Enterprise scenario. There are more than 40 different resource patterns classified into 7 different perspectives:

- Creation patterns
- Push patterns
- Pull patterns
- Detour patterns
- Auto-start patterns
- Visibility patterns
- Multiple resource patterns

We describe briefly some of these perspectives in the following sections.

Creation Patterns These patterns are different from the *creational patterns* of the GoF design patterns. The rationale for creation patterns is to provide a degree of clarity about how a process item should be handled at different stages—after creation, during the offering and allocation stages, and prior to processing an item being executed. These patterns ensure that the operation of a specific process conforms to its intended design principles and operates as deterministically as possible. The creation patterns are specified at design time in relation to a specific process task. These patterns serve to restrict the range of resources that can undertake work items that correspond to the task being executed.

Push Patterns These patterns enable different ways to allocate resources in a proactive manner to the process items when they are created during any state in a particular process. In this situation, the proactive allocation is essentially identical to the *push technology* identified in the MEP in Chapter 8. The push can occur indirectly by advertising work items to specific resources through a shared work list or can occur directly with work items being allocated to specific resources.

Pull Patterns These patterns work in fashion opposite to that described in push patterns. Pull patterns enable different individual resources to be aware of different work items that require execution, either directly or indirectly. The commitment to undertake a specific task, as part of the process, is therefore initiated by the resource itself rather than the system.

Detour Patterns Detour patterns, as the name suggests, help to change the normal course of events for any process. The change from the normal course could be instigated by either the workflow system or by the resource. These changes could result from unexpected events that could occur during any business transaction.

Auto-Start Patterns The auto-start patterns help in triggering the execution of one or more work items automatically during the life cycle of a specific work item or the related process definition. These specific triggering events can include the creation or allocation of the work item, completion of another instance of the same work item, or even a work item that immediately precedes the one in question.

Summary

The process or workflow in any Enterprise involves exchange of information among many partners and collaborators. Any large Enterprise could be dealing with a number of processes in a regular manner. Such processes in the Enterprises are often complex in nature because the partners and collaborators will be contributing in an intricate way in terms of producing and consuming business information. Moreover, the dynamics of the business could further pose challenges to the Enterprise in handling such multifarious and multifaceted conversation among such participants in the business scenario. Process and workflow patterns often help the architects to properly identify the problems and take care of such issues in the Enterprise world. Asynchronous message patterns, conversation patterns, orchestration patterns, and workflow patterns are recognized as the most important SOA patterns that address the bulk of the process/workflow issues in a complex Enterprise.

In the next part, we take up the case study of a typical large Enterprise engaged in the business of tours and travels. Presence of multiple partners and collaborators are a common scene in such an environment, and the nature of interaction and exchange of business information is complex and dynamically changing. In this case study, we help identify and deal with a typical set of problems that necessitate service orientation in such a business scenario. We also present an architectural solution to alleviate the problems and arrive at a high-level design. Further, we present some of the steps to arrive at a solution for a typical business use case using Java Platform, Enterprise Edition technology. We also show how quickly and easily the solution can be arrived at for this use case using NetBeans IDE.

Endnotes

1. Erich Gamma, Richard Helm, Ralph Johnson, and John Vlissides, who were responsible for initiating work on the design patterns, are referred to as the Gang of Four (GoF).
2. We have dedicated Chapter 5, "Web Services and WSDL," to the description of WS-Choreography Definition Language.
3. Chapter 7, "Orchestration and Choreography," describes, in detail, the big picture of orchestration under the W3C umbrella specification—WS-BPEL.
4. The orchestration patterns and workflow patterns are also expressed in the good-old GoF way. Each of the patterns is cataloged with information such as context, problem, forces, solution, and so on. Although it is not impossible to provide this information here, the scope and the vision of this book curtails us of such details. We have therefore limited ourselves in just describing the functionality of the pattern and provide a graphical view where it is deemed fit.
5. Notice that this pattern does not explicitly mention that the language has to be expressed in XML.
6. An evaluator is a component in the orchestration environment.
7. An exceptional and comprehensive treatment on workflow patterns can be found at `www.workflowpatterns.com/`.

Part V

Case Study

17

Developing Service Oriented Applications—A Case Study

To exemplify the successful implementation of SOA in a typical Enterprise, we focus on the requirements of an Enterprise engaged in providing travel and related services. The goal is to present the business application scenario of the requirements of SOA for a travel services-based company. Before considering the case study of a hypothetical enterprise, we provide a concise background of the Open Travel Alliance *(*OTA*), a successful alliance of many companies, organizations, and groups. The alliance includes many organizations and companies that represent various aspects of travel, including airlines, railways, ground transportation, restaurants, and so on. While presenting a high-level architecture as a suitable solution, we focus on various aspects of a travel service company, analyze, and architect the application for services orientation. We will also discuss how the various features of the new Java EE technology can meet different aspects of services development.*

The OTA is composed of several service-oriented industries—airlines, major hotels, automobile rental companies, leisure providers, travel and transport agencies, global distribution systems (GDS), IT services providers, and other parties. These organizations collaborate to create and implement industry-wide, open e-business specifications that cater to the travel needs of a variety of end users. The objective of this collaboration is to establish a common electronic business language to support and encourage development of systems related to a variety of travelers, in particular, and the travel industry, as a whole. The OTA is also a nonprofit organization working to establish a common electronic vocabulary, represented in *Extensible Markup Language* (*XML*) format, for use in the exchange of travel information. The travel specifications developed by the OTA alliance group are intended to create new opportunities for all organizations related to the travel industry to greatly reduce the communication cost and to normalize the communication using a common and proven protocol.

The OTA's open specifications are supported and effectively used by the organization and the members of the Alliance. The OTA provides working groups for each of the main activities: air travel, hotel reservation, car rentals, and integration, as shown in Figure 17.1. The *Air Working Group* (*AWG*), the *Hotel Working Group* (*HWG*), the *Car Working Group* (*CWG*), and a *Travel Integration Working Group* (*TIWG*) constitute the core-working group of the OTA. The TIWG includes travel agencies, a variety of *Internet service providers* (*ISP*), and other entities that provide direct or indirect travel-related services. These working groups share all the necessary information through an umbrella group called the *Interoperability Committee* (*IO*) made up of representatives of each working group.

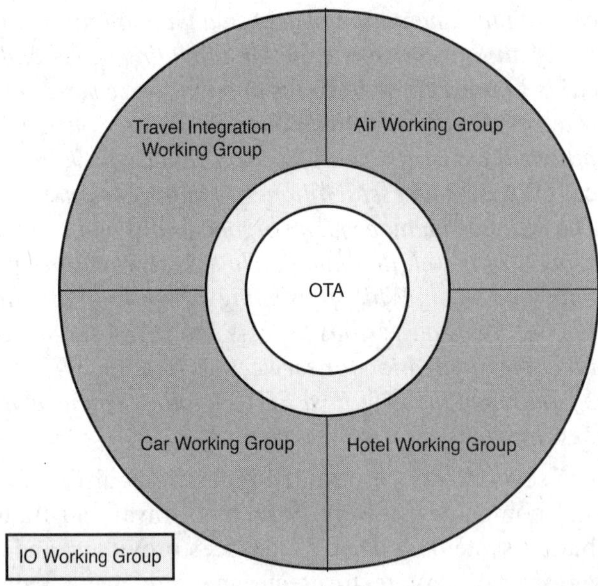

Figure 17.1 Variety of working groups contributing to the OTA's efforts

The Industry Perspective

The travel industry business and technology leaders responsible for product distribution are working in collaboration through the OTA to transform the travel industry into a global supermarket of travel-related products and services. The OTA provides an essential platform in which all vertical and horizontal sectors of the travel industry unify toward the common goal—creating unified and integrated information exchange specifications. The unification of the OTA members aims to effectively promote electronic commerce and serve travelers effectively and efficiently, lessen the duplication efforts, and build upon the experience and expertise of each other.

Another important goal is to leverage the new technology for optimizing the end consumer travel costs and benefit the other stake holders of the associated organizations and industries.

Messaging Distribution in the OTA

Messaging and message distribution among the involved partners and collaborators form the lifeline of the members of the OTA. Currently, a vast majority of travel messaging distribution takes place through one of the two protocols: *Res-Teletype* and *UN/EDIFACT*. The ResTeletype protocol is a complete 64-character sentence containing a minimal data set of information in a set order. For example, the details of the itinerary of a person in ResTeletype will contain the following:

```
Name/Date/Origin/Destination/Carrier/Flight#
```

The UN/EDIFACT protocol is considered more robust than ResTeletype; however, it is still text-based. This protocol requires two parties to agree on a set message they plan to exchange for a particular transaction. For example, the UN/EDIFACT communication resembles a sentence-based communication message:

```
What flights and seats are available at 2:00 on Friday between
A and B?
```

Both these standards have been serving the industry very well and will continue to do so. However, unfortunately, they require near unanimity at the highest industry level to create a new set of messages or change an existing message standard. This indeed calls for a lowest common denominator approach for creating required standards.

The Goals of the OTA

The OTA aims to help the travel industry along with all its ancillaries take full advantage of the near universal access to the technologies such as the Internet and web and related technologies, such as XML, by creating a consensus-driven XML schema and documentation to support them. By collaborating in cross-industry sectors, each industry (or organization) within the OTA identifies its own particular industry-appropriate needs and terms.

The OTA's specifications are open in nature and are supported by the organizations of the Alliance. The working groups are under the OTA umbrella, namely *Air Working Group*, *Hotel Working Group*, *Car Working Group*, and the *Travel Integration Working Group*. The Travel Integration Working Group essentially includes members from all the agencies, such as travel agencies, IT service providers, communication service providers, and other entities that provide direct/indirect travel-related services. These groups, along with the help of an IO, will strive to achieve the set goals of the OTA.

The Plans and Specifications of the OTA

The organizations belonging to the travel and its ancillary industries have been using the same systems, protocols, and code that were developed more than 30 years ago. Clearly, things have changed enormously over the past three decades. These old systems and applications are complex in nature and often expensive to operate and maintain. The proprietary nature of the code used in these systems and ancient architecture render these systems closed and limited for use for the current market conditions, which is dynamic and explosive in nature. By opting for open specifications and making them widely available to the alliance organizations, all the related organizations operate efficiently and cost-effectively. Also, by opting for the new and advanced technologies, it is possible to render convenient ways for the organizations to communicate smoothly and effectively.

The OTA recommends an open syntax specification that simplifies the communication at the core level. This specification takes communication syntax down to the individual data element level and enables the two partner organizations, for example, to communicate using the individual data elements. These parties can use these individual data elements in any order and quantity that they want. Using the TCP/IP infrastructure of the Internet and World Wide Web, partner organizations (essentially the service providers) can communicate with consumers directly or through numerous intermediaries, efficiently and economically. It is up to the partner organizations to use a particular data element as part of the exchanging information.

For the travel and ancillary industry, which thrives on the delivery of services, it is more than necessary to form an alliance and participate in the ongoing service orientation paradigm shift. The travel suppliers, their intermediaries, and their consumers alike are embracing the World Wide Web and Internet as a new communications and distribution channel. XML technologies have been proven to be the best way of interchanging the messages between the partner organizations. The OTA specifications take advantage of this nearly ubiquitous infrastructure to communicate efficiently and effectively at a lower cost but adding a higher value.

The Alliance Members

There are more than 150 members in the OTA currently, comprised of the "who's who" from industries such as airlines, hotels, automobile rentals, cruise and leisure, and other travel industry sectors. We have divided these alliance members according to the following classification: *travel and transport-related*, *automobile rental*, *hotel*, *IT services and allied industry*, *cruises*, *leisure*, *and holidays*, and the *GDS*.

Travel and Transport-Related Industry

The travel and transport classification essentially groups the partner organizations that belong predominantly to the airline and railroad transport industry. The members included in this category are American Airlines, AMTRAK, Continental Airlines, Delta Airlines, United Airlines, US Airways, and more. Most of these airline and railroad transport companies cover essentially the entire continents of North America and Europe.

Hotel Industry

The hotel industry is one of the most important industries for the travel and ancillary industries. A few of the important members of these groups represent the most important and leading hotel chains throughout the world. Some of these are American Hotel and Motel Association, Best Western International Inc., Hilton Hotels Corporation, Hotel de AG, Hyatt Hotels Corporation, Marriott International, Omni Hotels, and Starwood Hotels and Resorts.

IT Services and Allied Industry

These industries represent the new and advanced technologies that are promising to take the travel industries to the next level of service efficiency and sophistication. Some of the important members from these industries are EDS Technologies, IBM, IBS Software Services Americas, Inc., Microsoft Corporation, SAP AG, Sun Microsystems, Datalex Communications, Friend Communications, and more.

Cruises, Leisure, and Holiday-Related Industry

The components of this particular force are important drivers for the travel industry as a whole. Many worldwide companies plan packages for a variety of end customers—individual business traveler to leisure and holiday groups. Some of the important members from this industry are HRG (Earlier known as BTI Canada), Expedia, The Norwegian Cruise Line, The Royal Caribbean Cruises, The SITA, Inc., and so on.

The Global Distribution Systems

There are currently four major GDS systems: Amadeus, Galileo International, Sabre, and Worldspan. They essentially cater to the global bulk of the travel service requirements. In addition, there are several regional GDSs that include SITA's Sahara, Infini, Axess (both for Japan), Tapas (for Korea), Fantasia (for the region of South Pacific), and Abacus (region of Asia/Pacific) that serve interests or specific regions or countries.

The Case Study

Silhouette Tours is a Michigan-based airline and hotel reservation agency providing services to customers primarily in the region of the northwest and the lake region of the United States. Serving its customers for more than a decade, Silhouette Tours' focus is providing airline ticket reservations and hotel accommodation reservations to its customers; it has maintained a steady growth and development in the region. Silhouette is also engaged in providing services at the local level in many tourist attraction locations to international tourists.

To provide elegant services, Silhouette maintained a computer systems network—a telephone, fax, and a tele-text-based messaging services. Silhouette also developed and maintained a set of computer applications to store travel-related services information, including data such as the records of the existing customer base, agents, and train, road, airways, and sea travel information for the local region. Some of the applications that were developed in Silhouette could communicate with the agent's airline and hotel reservation system to a limited extent.

A few years ago, things at Silhouette Tours began to change. Emergence of the Internet and World Wide Web changed the business scenario for many enterprises worldwide. Soon, things at Silhouette Tours, too, began to change. Businesses all over the world saw a major upswing. The management of Silhouette Travels was observant of this upward trend. To exploit the current market conditions, Silhouette decided to play a major role in the region. It decided to play the key role of international travel facilitator to the main GDS player in the region and offer a whole new suite of services to existing locals and international clients. The proposed services included a local air/train/road reservation system, hotel reservations, and leisure and holiday packages to the interior regions of tourist spots in the United States and to other regions such as Europe, Asia-Pacific, Australia, and South America.

As a result, Silhouette invested in a major way in the company's infrastructure and expanded its network. The investment included the opening of branch offices at many locations in the United States, Europe, Asia-Pacific, Australia, and so on. Silhouette wanted to make the best use of the power of the Internet and the World Wide Web to bring in the much-needed boost to the company in terms of business, market coverage, and expansion. Silhouette believed in carefully planned growth of the company in terms of procuring a variety of application software, middleware, desktops, and servers throughout the organization network. Although this investment yielded handsome dividends to Silhouette in terms of growth and expansion within the United States, Silhouette realized its penetration into other regions around the world—particularly in Europe and Asia Pacific—was largely not coming through, as these markets saw the presence of already well-established organizations that had dominated the market for many years.

As a strategy to expand the business in potential markets, the management at Silhouette aimed at achieving a phenomenal growth path for the next few years, which was to be largely facilitated through acquisitions. Silhouette planned to acquire Cyber Tours PLC, UK, and Green Pastures Travels Pte. Ltd. of Singapore.

Cyber Tours PLC is headquartered in London, UK, and like Silhouette, was also a player that had charted an impressive growth pattern and had a tremendous reach into the tourism markets in Europe, the Mediterranean, and the regions of North Africa.

Green Pastures Travels Pte Ltd. is a Singapore-based tours and travels company that had built an excellent network in the Asia-Pacific region, including Malaysia, China, Hong Kong, Thailand, Japan, and South Korea. Green Pastures was also a well-known name in the U.S. and European markets.

These acquisitions were strategically sound for Silhouette's expanding market coverage, revenues. and profitability.

Challenges

Although these acquisitions were well timed and strategically sound, Silhouette had to deal with a completely new set of issues, largely pertaining to the legacy systems of both Cyber Tours and Green Pastures Travels. These issues, coupled with Silhouette's already existing legacy systems, caused a great deal of integration problems. There were also issues with reference to redundant services that were part of the legacy systems that came with acquisitions.

Silhouette's organizational goal at this point was to leverage the power of the Internet. This could be achieved only by bringing all the group companies under the umbrella of a unifying system that facilitated the business in achieving its lofty growth plans. This clearly required Silhouette to upgrade and integrate the legacy systems to an environment capable of handling its current and future business needs.

After taking stock of the requirements from both the group companies, namely Cyber Tours and Green Pastures, and after discussions with various IT experts, Silhouette is seriously considering harnessing the power of web services to provide its customers with superior service. It was found that a complete overhaul of the legacy applications was not viable. Therefore, Silhouette decided to minimize the imprint of legacy systems and utilize web services in a major way. The next challenge for Silhouette was to translate the existing services into web services.

Silhouette's strategy in this regard was simple. They required web services to be meshed into an SOA that would be well integrated into the organization's envisaged workflow. This would ensure that Silhouette would achieve its organizational objectives of market dominance and superior service to its customers.

Solution Implementation Strategies

Silhouette's implementation strategy of the SOA was also simple and elegant. Accordingly, the IT division drew up an implementation with the following important implementation guidelines and framework:

- Minimize the legacy footprint.
- Retain existing web services irrespective of their implementation.
- Use the new Java Enterprise Edition technology for defining services as web services in lieu of the legacy services wherever possible.
- Use the new Java Platform, Enterprise Edition technology for defining the new services.
- Use a service bus for unifying the message communication across all divisions and geographies.

In the next section, we explore Silhouette's proposed top-level design and implementation details of one of the services and describe in detail several aspects of the solution. We choose to implement one of the most important and frequently used services in this industry: travel reservation service. As a part of the details, we also discuss some of the important implementation strategies such as the Java Platform, Enterprise Edition technology and use of service bus as part of the whole solution.

Travel Reservation Service

Consider the familiar travel reservation scenario in Silhouette. A customer requests that the travel agency books a particular tour package that consists of three reservations: air travels, hotel accommodations, and car rentals. The process for this tour package request might be simplistically represented in the form of a sequence diagram in Figure 17.2.

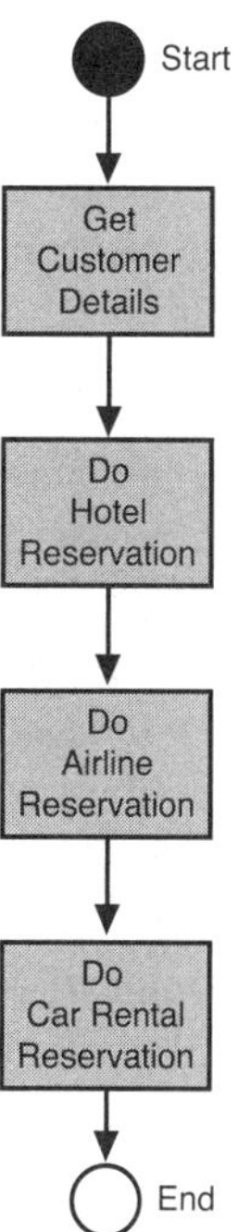

Figure 17.2 A simple activity diagram indicating the way hotel reservation and air travel reservation could be initiated

Although the scenario might seem simple at first glance, there could be many situations possible, and the customer might have preferences that can allow him to choose an optimum package. For example, the airline reservation step itself could offer many possibilities for the client in terms of the choice of airlines, price, time, connectivity and hops, and so on. However, the client preferred choice may or may not be immediately available for confirmation. Likewise, the hotel reservation scenario could offer different possibilities for the customer in terms of choice of hotels, room preferences, room rate, location of the hotel, and so on. Again, the customer preferred choice may or may not be immediately available for confirmation. Similar possibilities can be extended for the other services such as the local sightseeing package, car rental, and so on.

In such a situation, a standard tours and travel company could attempt the following course of action: attempt the airline reservation, hotel reservation, and car rental reservation in a particular sequence. The agency might also wait for the reservation confirmation from one service provider before attempting the next service provider. Or the agency could go ahead and confirm the reservation from some service providers, while waiting for the other service providers to confirm. Alternatively, the agency could attempt to process all the reservations in parallel and process the reservation from the individual service provider as it happens. Processing such requests could easily turn into a complicated affair for the customer and the agency if the tour package requested by the customer has multiple location visits, a range of hotel preferences, price constraints, choice of locations, and so on.

In the dynamic world of tours and travel, we can no longer afford the hassle and inconvenience of managing travel itineraries the standard way. Moreover, partial or incomplete itinerary confirmations are not acceptable to customers. Furthermore, the situation could be complicated enough that the customers might want to change the itinerary during the course of the reservation process, request additional benefits, and indicate that the package needs to be attractively priced. If the travel agency is not flexible to incorporate these requests into the tour package and competitive enough to offer an attractive pricing, it could easily lose customers to the competitor. Under such circumstances, a travel Enterprise, such as Silhouette, must be equipped with all the ways and means to meet such business challenges. Enterprises with efficient and robust networking, equipped with state-of-the-art systems and services, communication protocols, message routers, and middleware with an Enterprise application architected on the principles of service orientation, will be in a unique position to deal with such challenges.

In the service-oriented world, Silhouette now offers a network-accessible service for customers to submit their travel itineraries. Silhouette will employ a suitable business process to fulfill all these tasks. The business process, in turn, will utilize appropriate web services that might provide bookings for multiple suppliers (for a range of search and filter options) connecting to multiple reservation systems. A range of applications thus providing a loosely coupled environment can consume this service.

Specifically, in given scenario, the reservation itinerary gets filed with the travel reservation business process employed by Silhouette. Upon receiving the reservation itinerary, the business process first checks to see if the airline reservation has been made. If it has not, the business process makes the airline reservation by invoking the airline reservation web service. The business process then checks if the vehicle reservation has been made. Likewise, the car rental reservation web service is invoked if the rental car reservation has not been made. Finally, the process is repeated for the hotel accommodation reservation. Each of the airline, car rental, and hotel accommodation reservation web services confirms the reservation by sending a callback message to the business process.

Figure 17.3 illustrates the travel reservation scenario, with Silhouette Travels invoking the web services-based business process. It is important to remember that many different types of clients can access the end-to-end development of an enterprise solution that employs SOA.

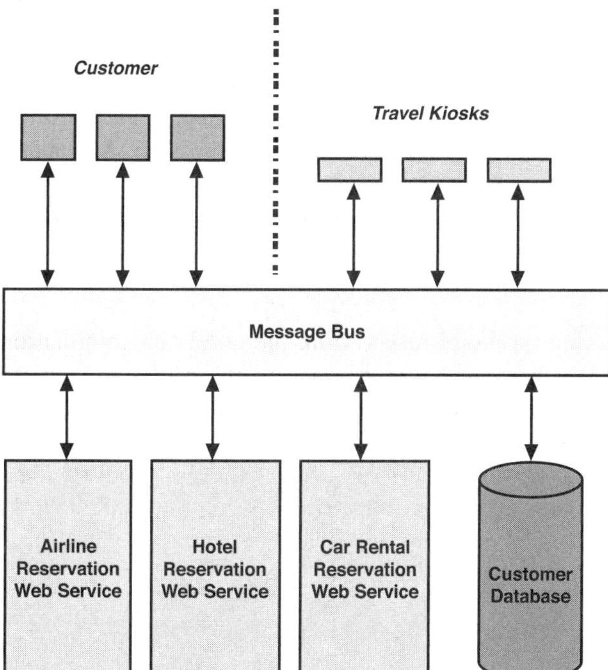

Figure 17.3 Travel reservation scenario for Silhouette Tours

The Workflow or the Process Definition

Recall from the previous section the travel package for a particular customer who required a set of three reservations: hotel accommodations, airline travels, and car rental reservations. A customer who would be requesting such a set of reservations could also insist on certain restrictions in the travel package. For example, the customer could indicate that if the hotel accommodation is not available, the entire trip should be canceled. Or if the airline and hotel accommodation are available, the car rental reservation is mandatory. Implementation of such activities is essential in such service-oriented enterprises, and such requirements become the basis for the use of the *Business Process Execution Language* (*BPEL*) or the *Choreography Definition Language* (*CDL*), as described by the new generation of web services,[1] in the SOA.

In the present context, Silhouette proposes two scenarios of the travel reservation schemas for the customer's requirement discussed in the previous section. In the first scenario, Silhouette will allow a sequencing of the individual business process. In this case, the agency first receives the travel itinerary request from the customer. The next step is to finalize the airline reservation. Upon successfully booking the airline reservations, Silhouette will initiate the hotel accommodation reservation process. After this step is successfully completed, Silhouette will finally initiate the rental car reservation. In each of the cases, the system will initiate an appropriate web service from the respective service provider. For example, while processing the reservation from the airline, the airline reservation web service will be invoked.

Similarly, while processing the hotel reservation, the hotel accommodation web service will be invoked. Likewise, while processing the rental car reservation, the car rental web services would be invoked. The sequences of events that would transpire in such a scenario are depicted in Figure 17.4.

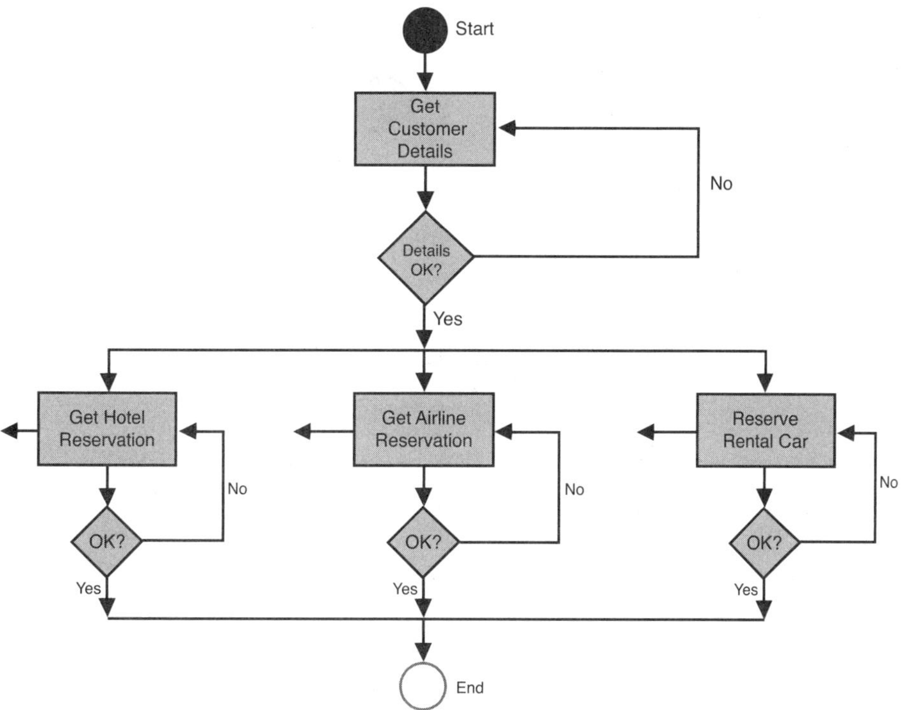

Figure 17.4 Sequential processing of itinerary travel requests

In the second scenario, Silhouette will facilitate for a simultaneous or parallel processing of the travel itinerary. As in the first scenario, the first step is to get the travel itinerary request from the customer. Silhouette will then simultaneously submit the processing of airline reservation, hotel accommodations reservation, and car rental reservation process. Each of these processes will invoke the appropriate web services. The sequence of events in the second scenario is presented in Figure 17.5.

Upon confirmation of the appropriate reservations, the service application may be designed to generate the appropriate confirmation ID numbers and trigger other related operations such as payments, credit card processing, and so on.

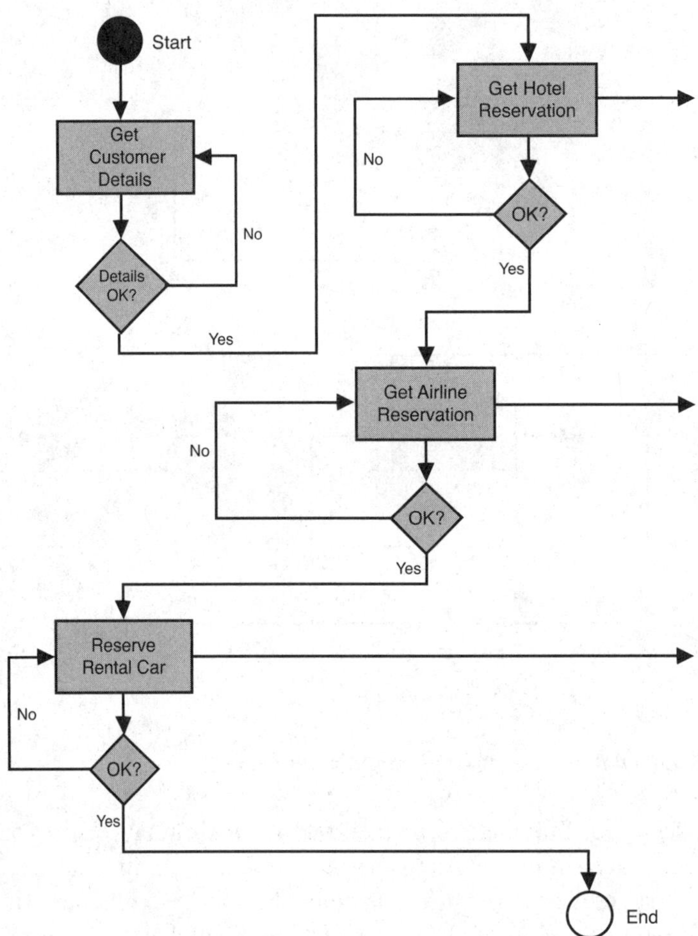

Figure 17.5 Sequential processing of itinerary travel requests

Architecting such an Enterprise application using the principles of service orientation, in combination with suitable service engines such as web services and other constituents such as service bus, BPEL, and so on will provide a loosely coupled and flexible services environment for the Enterprise.

Solution Platform Considerations

Recall that Silhouette had opted to choose The Java Platform, Enterprise Edition as one of the main technologies for implementing the service orientation solution. The new Java Platform, Enterprise Edition technology plays a crucial role in appropriately implementing many activities and processes that collectively participate in the service orientation along with service providers, collaborators, and partners of the travel ecosystem. In such an ecosystem, a variety of activities would be taking place on many systems—partners systems, collaborators systems, and more—distributed geographically and performing under different time zones and on different platforms. The application could be web-based applications and Enterprise applications. Furthermore, recall that some of the service providers/partners could be using legacy systems, processing the information on mainframe systems as well as their back-ends. A few of the possible Java EE solution scenarios for Silhouette include web applications, enterprise applications, and web services applications.

The Web Applications

The web application could address the airline, hotel accommodation, and car rental reservation part of the process. The reservation process of the individual service can further be broken into subprocesses. For example, a hotel reservation might require searching and zeroing in on a set of hotels based on the criteria specified by the customer. For instance, a customer could request a hotel reservation based on the hotel rate, not to exceed $160 per night. The customer could also insist on a specific hotel and might request priority booking based on some type of membership, such as AAA or AARP. Applications carrying out such services can be appropriately modeled using a set of web components such as Servlets, *JavaServer Pages* (*JSP*), Servlet filters, JavaBeans, JSTL, Custom Tag Libraries, and so on.

A set of robust web application can be built using all these components using a web-based framework such as *JavaServer Faces* (*JSF*).[2] As discussed in preceding chapters, the JSF framework helps the developer to easily develop and deploy the web application that helps reflect Enterprise application requirements. Using such web frameworks, it is also possible to easily modify and extend the application based on the dynamic nature of the Enterprise application requirements.

The Enterprise Applications

The Enterprise applications hold and process all the necessary business logic and the persistent data for the Enterprise application. The Enterprise application components[3] could also take care of maintaining sessions for a customer who is processing part of or a whole travel itinerary; there are many options available for the developer to configure Enterprise applications. Session *Enterprise JavaBeans* (*EJB*) could be considered for creating client sessions. The developer can maintain the state of Session EJBs by creating stateful or stateless session EJBs. For communicating with the messaging middleware part of the Enterprise application, the developer might create and use Message-Driven Beans. Furthermore, the developer may consider using Entity EJBs or POJOs for taking care of the persistent data in the Enterprise application. These components are not directly exposed to the client request such as HTTP requests. Web application components usually act as a facade for these components.

Normally, such Enterprise applications communicate with legacy systems or EIS systems for data persistence. This can be achieved through the use of appropriate resource adapters. The communication between the Enterprise components and databases/resource adapters could be either RMI/IIOP or another commonly accepted protocol.

The Web Services Applications

The new Java Platform, Enterprise Edition makes creating and using web services an easy task. Recall that the web and Enterprise applications could constitute several services, and only a few of the services would qualify for web services. Such services in the components of web applications and/or Enterprise applications could be turned on to reflect the web services. Essentially, these services accept and respond to the SOAP protocol communication. For example, in web applications, either selected services (method calls) in the servlets or JavaBeans can be turned on as web services. The containers holding these components will take care of the remaining communication mechanism to complete the request/response. Such web components in the web applications accept the SOAP request over HTTP protocol.

Likewise, a particular method (or a set of methods) from one or more Session EJBs could be identified for rendering the web services. These components, as indicated earlier, will accept SOAP messages as requests and send SOAP messages as response.

The Java Platform, Enterprise Edition technology provides a rich set of APIs and libraries such as JAX-WS (Java AIP for XML Web Services), Java API for XML Binding (JAXB), SOAP with Attachments API for Java (SAAJ), and so on. Rendering any component web service-oriented is a simple and quick task using these APIs and libraries in the new Enterprise Java environment.

Summary

The alliance formed by the OTA sets a solid example of different Enterprises connecting and communicating together to achieve common business goals. The specifications simplify the process in a cost-effective manner and save time, and the costs are passed to the consumer. The end results benefit all involved.

Orienting the Enterprise architecture to offer services in a loosely coupled manner has been beneficial for complex and dynamic business requirements of Enterprises engaged in, for example, the tour and travel business. Together with web services route and process management using BPEL/CDL and new age middleware such as service bus, today's Enterprises are in a better position to handle the current and futuristic challenges faced by the industry.

Java Platform, Enterprise Edition technologies help in meeting almost all the business aspects of the travel and ancillary industries. Presentation components such as servlets, JSP, JavaBeans, JSTL, and so on can be used as part of JSF framework to create web applications. Similarly, business components such as Session EJBs, MDBs, or POJOs can be created and used in conjunction with the web application to meet the requirement of the Enterprise application. Specific and special services from these web and Enterprise applications can be identified and exposed as web services to cater to the needs of service orientation.

In the next chapter, we explore the use of Java Platform, Enterprise Edition technology to implement the services-oriented architecture for an Enterprise that is engaged in tours and travels. We also discuss the use of NetBeans IDE and related tools to show how quickly and easily the whole or parts of the solution can be implemented.

Endnotes

1. The details about WS-BPEL and WS-CDL were discussed in detail in Chapter 8, "Advanced Web Services Infrastructure for Implementing SOA." We request the reader's attention to the process part of the service orientation.
2. Recall that these components and frameworks were discussed in detail in Chapter 10, "Web Technologies in Java EE."
3. Recall that the Enterprise components such as Session EJB, MDB, Entity EJB, and POJOs were discussed in detail in Chapter 11, "Enterprise JavaBeans and Persistence."

18

Delivering SOA Using NetBeans SOA Pack: Case Study—Solution

It is well evident that there is an increasing convergence of business strategy and the IT platform; it is important for the organization to make sure that the business services are suitably and appropriately delivered through the IT platform. Although the IT platform delivered such services as a piecemeal approach, as functions or procedures of stand-alone applications, they essentially missed the important requirements of the business services environment that demand loosely coupled, dynamically changing, process-oriented, and time-to-market environments. The services provided in a typical business environment can run synchronously or in an asynchronous manner. Also, the messages/information exchanged could be conversational-centric or document-centric in nature.

In the previous chapter, we analyzed the needs of business environment of Silhouette Travels, a typical case study articulating the need for service orientation. We also explained how Silhouette arrived at the architectural and high-level design details and implementation strategies for service orientation. As noted, the travel reservation and other related services, under the SOA umbrella, are composed of related services that are loosely coupled, process-oriented, and web services-enabled. Also, several aspects of the services orientation have been addressed through different aspects of the new Java Platform, Enterprise Edition.

Using Silhouette Travels as our business model once again, we suggest an approach to implement SOA using the new Java Platform, Enterprise Edition with the help of NetBeans *Integrated Development Environment* (*IDE*). As part of this exercise, we explore a familiar use case of airline reservation as an example and indicate how easily an implementation can be accomplished intuitively using NetBeans IDE. The current version of NetBeans Enterprise Pack is bundled with a sample Travel Reservation Service prototype application. The Travel Reservation Service in this prototype acts as a logical aggregator of related services such as airline reservation, hotel reservation, and vehicle reservation. We will use parts of this prototype in the implementation exercise.

Implementation Strategy—An Overview

In the service-oriented world, Silhouette Travels offers a network-accessible service for customers to initiate their travel itineraries. Silhouette Travels will typically employ a business process to fulfill the tasks. The business process will utilize web services for reservations that, in turn, might provide bookings for multiple suppliers (for a range of search and filter options) connecting to multiple reservation systems. This service, in turn, can be consumed by a range of applications, thus providing a loosely coupled environment. Keep in mind that the reservation service described here does not need to be aware of the different applications that use the service.

Specifically, the reservation itinerary is filed with the travel reservation business process employed by Silhouette Travels. Upon receiving the reservation itinerary, the business process first checks to see if an airline reservation has already been made. If it has not, the business process initiates the airline reservation by invoking the airline reservation web service. The business process then checks if any vehicle reservation has been made. If no vehicle reservation has been made, the vehicle reservation web service is invoked. A similar process is repeated for the hotel reservation. Each of the airline, car, and hotel reservation web services confirms the reservation by sending a callback message to the business process. Figure 18.1 illustrates the high-level architectural requirement for Silhouette Travels. There are different types of clients that can access the end-to-end development of an Enterprise solution that employs an SOA as the appropriate architecture and solution.

In the previous chapter, we reviewed how different enterprises can connect and communicate to achieve the common business goals of travel-related enterprises. We also indicated how the components and technologies of the Java Enterprise Edition can help in meeting most or all the business aspects of the travel and ancillary industries.

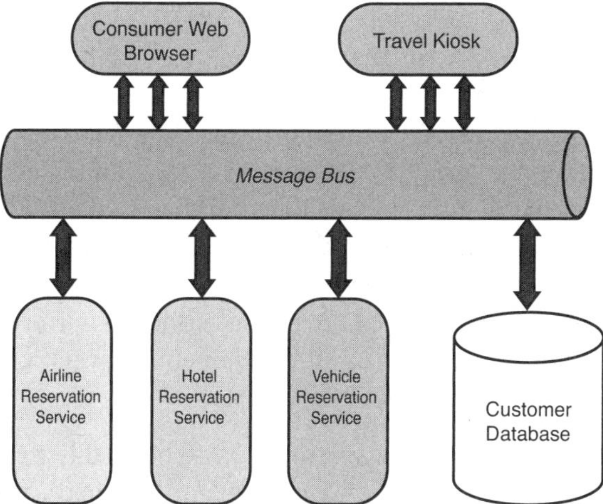

Figure 18.1 Travel reservation scenario for Silhouette Travels, Inc.

In the previous chapter, we reviewed how different enterprises can connect and communicate to achieve the common business goals of travel-related enterprises. We also indicated how the components and technologies of the Java Platform, Enterprise Edition can help in meeting most or all the business aspects of the travel and ancillary industries.

In this chapter, we describe the way a composite application such as a travel reservation is built using the tools and process suites of NetBeans IDE that employs Java Platform, Enterprise Edition technology. The steps described in the following section essentially highlight the ease of implementation of such an application and show how NetBeans IDE can help in creating an end-to-end application environment of an Enterprise solution that employs SOA.

NetBeans IDE

NetBeans is a free, open source IDE for software developers. It provides developers all the tools needed to create professional desktop, Enterprise, web, and mobile applications with a variety of programming languages such as Java, C/C++, PHP, JavaScript, Groovy, JavaFX, and Ruby. NetBeans IDE is easy to install and is ready to use straight out of the box. It can be used on many platforms including Windows, Linux, Mac OS X, and Solaris. The latest platform, NetBeans IDE 6.7, provides several new features and enhancements, such as rich PHP, JavaScript, and Ajax editing features, improved support for using frameworks such as Hibernate, and the *Java Persistence API* (*JPA*). NetBeans is also tightly integrated with the GlassFish Enterprise server V2, Enterprise server prelude V3, Apache Tomcat application server, and MySQL database server.

The NetBeans IDE is also equipped with SOA Pack, which enables the developer to learn and jump-start building SOA applications quickly and easily. The documentation on the SOA pack is replete with tutorials, articles, and demo programs for developing, deploying, testing, and debugging a variety of SOA-related applications. Some of the demo packs include building composite applications, building BEPL oriented SOA applications, WSDL editing tools, JBI component development tutorials, and so on. We have chosen the "Travel Reservation Service" demo project under the BPEL category of the SOA pack of the NetBeans IDE to enunciate how a case such as the Silhouette Travels, Inc., can be easily and efficiently treated using the NetBeans IDE.

The most recent version of NetBeans IDE is version 6.7.1. The installer package for an appropriate operating system can be downloaded and executed for installation on the desktop system. For a detailed description on installation and configuration instructions on NetBeans IDE, refer to the NetBeans.Org website.[1]

Invoking NetBeans

After installation is complete, run the NetBeans application (on the Windows XP operating system) by double-clicking on the NetBeans 6.7.1 icon on the desktop. Alternatively, you can choose **Start > All Programs > NetBeans > NetBeans IDE 6.7.1** to invoke NetBeans.

Exploring the IDE

Launching the NetBeans IDE opens up the development environment in a new window. The entire window of the IDE can be divided into four main areas. These areas can be called panes and are referred to as

- Left pane
- Main pane
- Right pane
- Bottom pane

The Left Pane

The left pane is also known as NetBeans Explorer. It hosts the following environments:

- **Files tab**—Enables access to files and directory structures, and so on. Driver files necessary for application development are accessed here.
- **Runtime tab**—Displays servers, databases, database drivers, processes, registries, debuggers, and so on. These can all be controlled from this tab.
- **Projects tab**—Enables control of project-level activities. *Project compilation*, *project building*, *project debugging*, and so on can be easily done here.
- **Services tab**—Enables access to the UML design and modeling activities.

The Main Pane

The main pane is essentially a multiview editor. The content usually depends on the selection of the chosen activity in the left pane. For instance, if the developer is working on an Entity EJB business method updating activity, the main pane displays the content of the corresponding bean file so that the developer can incorporate the code. This pane can show multiple related files that can be accessed through tabs. These tabs are accessible at the top of the main pane.

The Right Pane

The right pane supports multiple activities. When selected during development activities, things such as collaboration, GUI design, and so on are displayed in the right pane. Based on the component selected in the left pane, appropriate content is displayed in this pane. For example, when a database is selected in the Runtime tab of the left pane, the database table views can be displayed in the right pane. Similarly, under the Files tab in the left pane, when an EJB or a JSP file from a specific project is chosen in the left pane, the developer can visualize one or more of these files in the right pane. Likewise, this pane enables the Design view and the Code view of the BPEL process activity that is designed as part of SOA.

The Bottom Pane

The bottom pane is intended for a variety of output display activities. This pane displays activities such as results of program execution, output of application, search results, to-do list, and so on. Outputs from the activities such as compilation, execution, verification, and so on are displayed on this pane.

Project Basics

NetBeans IDE provides wizards in the IDE with the help of which project can be created. There are two wizards available: The New Module Project Wizard and the New Project Template Wizard. The Project Wizards are very useful because they help in reducing the coding efforts in the application development work. Creating a project in NetBeans results in the creation of a set of files and directory structure, a few of the basic components, configuration files, and so on based on the nature of the application chosen. For example, when a web application is created, the project will contain the basic view files such as `index.jsp`, configuration files such as `web.xml`, and so forth.

Server Startup

In the IDE, click the **Services** tab and expand the Servers node. Right-click on **GlassFish V2** and choose **Start**. If the *Start* option is disabled and the *Restart* and *Stop* options are enabled, the server is already running. This is shown in Figure 18.2. When the project is ready, the application server will be used for activities such as compilation, deploying, testing, and so on.

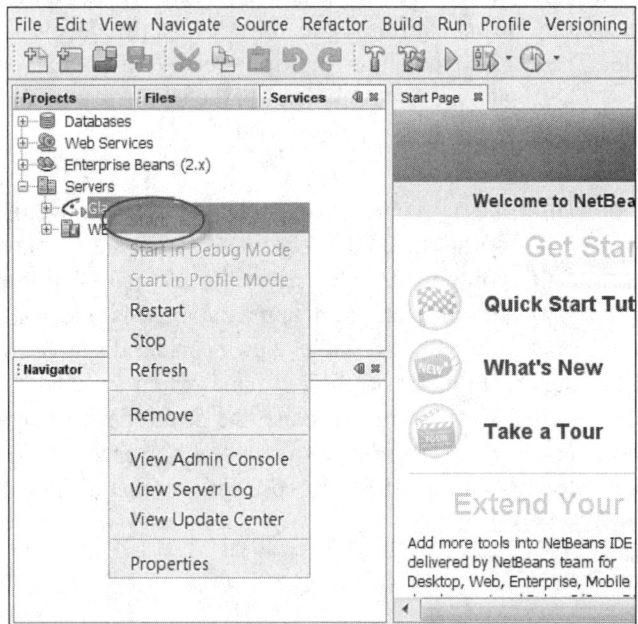

Figure 18.2 The IDE indicating that the GlassFish application server is running

Project Creation

Any major development activity using NetBeans IDE should be initiated through Project workspace. This is done by creating a new project using the IDE as the first step. By creating a Project workspace, the IDE creates an appropriate programming environment for the developer, based on the type of the intended development activity. For example, if the developer intends to create a JSF-based web application, NetBeans IDE generates an environment (such as Faces Servlet, configuration files, Helper files, directory structure, and so on) through the use of an appropriate Project Creation Wizard. The wizard helps the developer to fill in appropriate information regarding the Project Name, workspace location, environmental conditions, resources locations, and so on.

In the following sections, we show how quickly and easily a developer can create an SOA project through the use of an appropriate Project Creation Wizard and sift through different aspects of the life cycle, including testing and debugging aspects of the SOA using the NetBeans IDE.

Creating the TravelReservationService Sample Project

In the IDE, from the main menu, choose **File > New Project**. This launches a wizard for project creation. This wizard helps in the initial settings and configuration of the project. This action is shown in Figure 18.3.

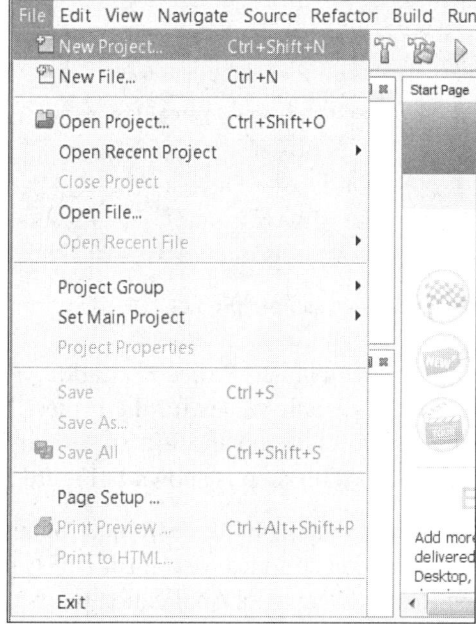

Figure 18.3 Creating a new project

In the New Project dialog box, under Categories, expand **Samples** and select **SOA**. The wizards in NetBeans IDE are helpful and informative. Information on the selected options is provided as shown in Figure 18.4. Now, under Projects, select the **Travel Reservation Service** project and click on the **Next** button in the wizard.

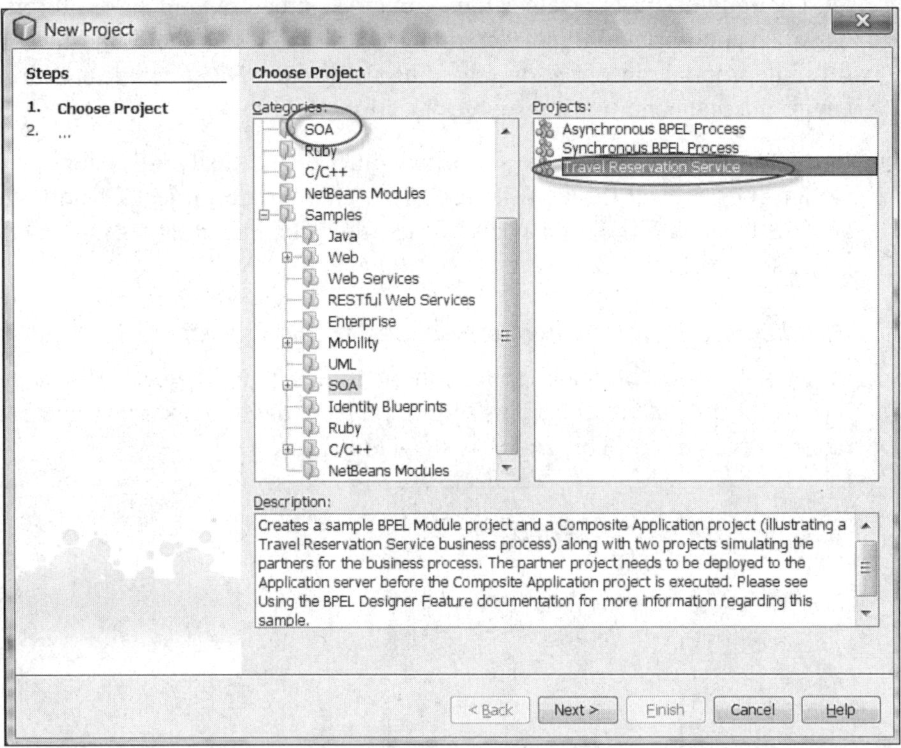

Figure 18.4 Create the TravelReservationService sample project

Provide appropriate values such as Project Name, Project Location, Project Folder, and so on. Alternatively, accept the default values for the Project Name, Project Location, and Project Folder fields. Click on the **Finish** button in the wizard to complete the project creation step. This step is shown in Figure 18.5.

The creation of the project results in the creation of three project nodes. The Projects tab in the left pane reveals three project nodes: one for a BPEL project called *TravelReservationService*, one for the Composite Application project called *TravelReservationServiceApplication*, and one for *ReservationPartnerServices*, a bundled EJB project, as presented in Figure 18.6.

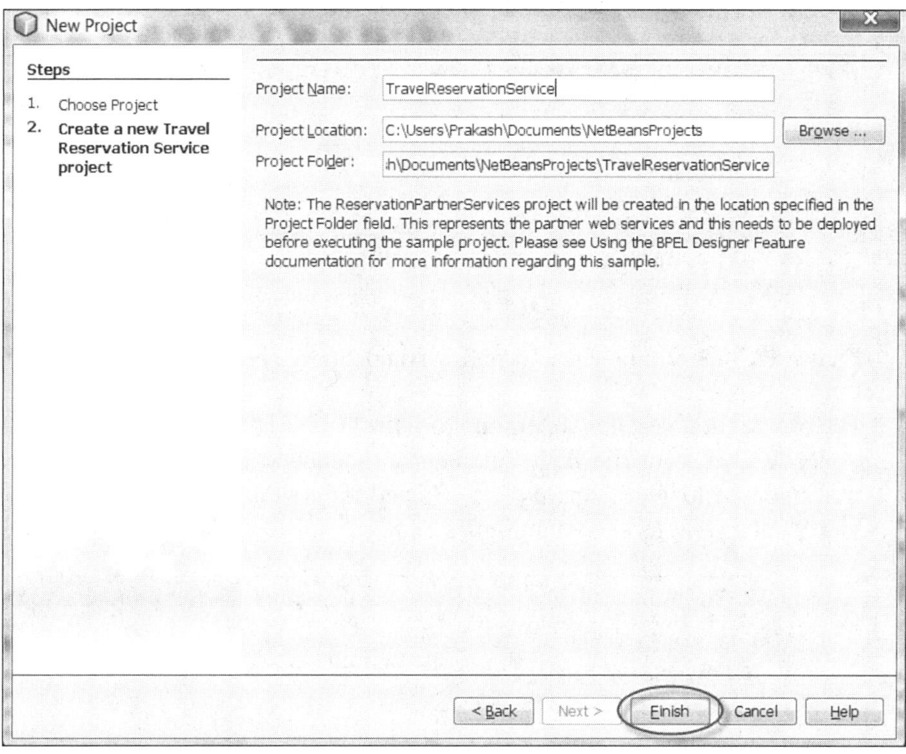

Figure 18.5 Finalizing the name and location of the sample project

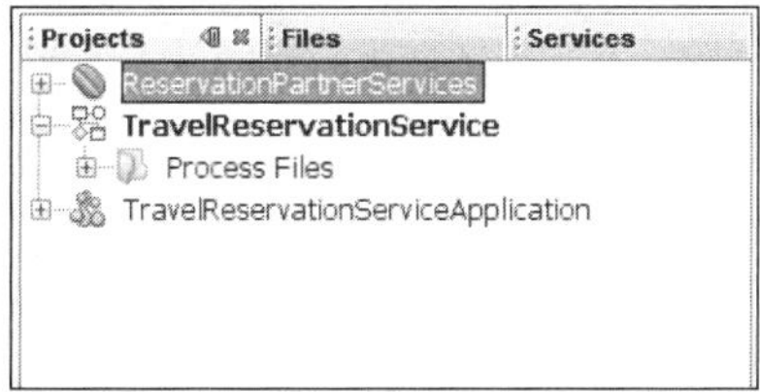

Figure 18.6 Completing the creation of the TravelReservationService project

Exploring the TravelReservationService BPEL Project

In the Projects tab, expand the Process Files node under the *TravelReservation-Service* node, and you see it contains the following items:

- `TravelReservationService.bpel`, the BPEL process
- Some `*.wsdl` files, which are the web service interfaces for the project
- `OTA_TravelItinerary.xsd`, an XML Schema document

These three nodes and the corresponding process files are displayed in a structured format in Figure 18.7.

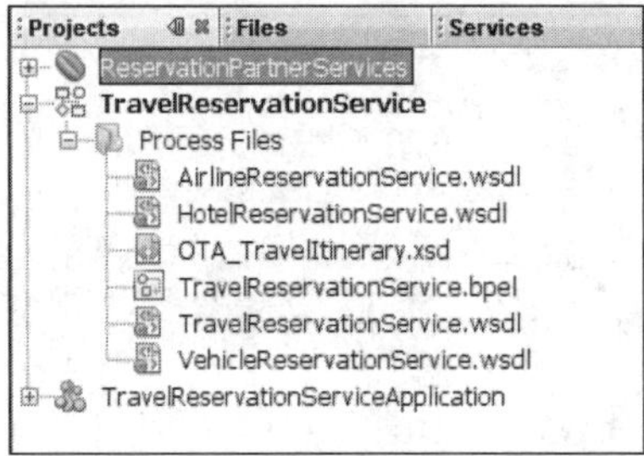

Figure 18.7 Structure of the TravelReservationService project

Perform a double-click operation on the `TravelReservationService.bpel` node. A palette[2] of the BPEL element is opened with a Navigator view and a multiview editor in the main pane. This editor contains two views: *Design View* and *Source View*, as shown in Figure 18.8.

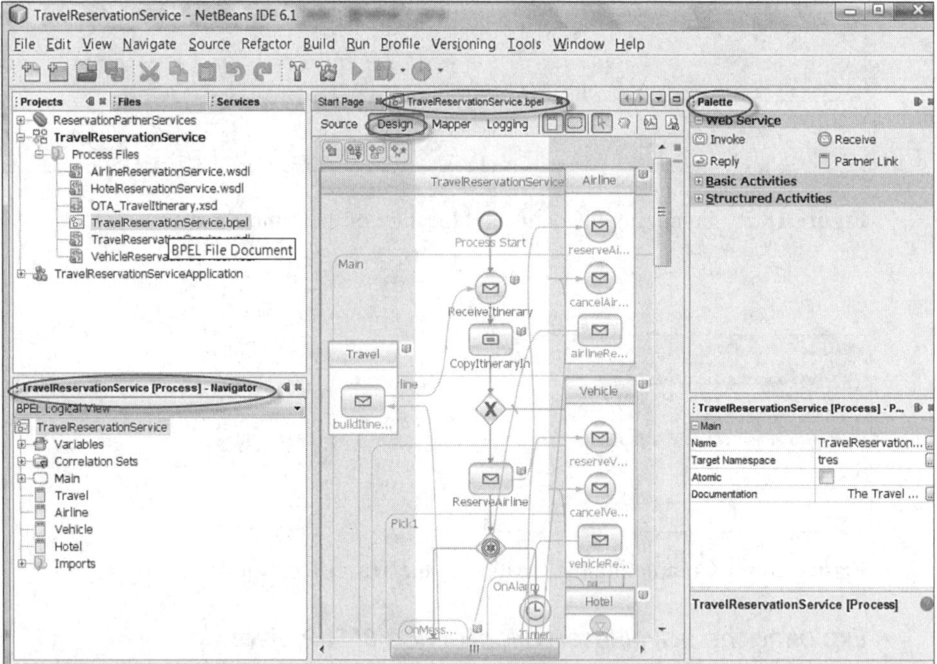

Figure 18.8 Using the multiview editor, Navigator, and BPEL palette for process modeling

Examining the TravelReservationService Project

Click on the **Design** tab to switch back to the Design view. Double-click the `TravelReservationService.bpel` tab to enlarge the editor. In the Design view, at the top of the diagram, a client initiates the process by sending a message containing a travel itinerary document. The TravelReservationService receives it. The details are shown in Figure 18.9.

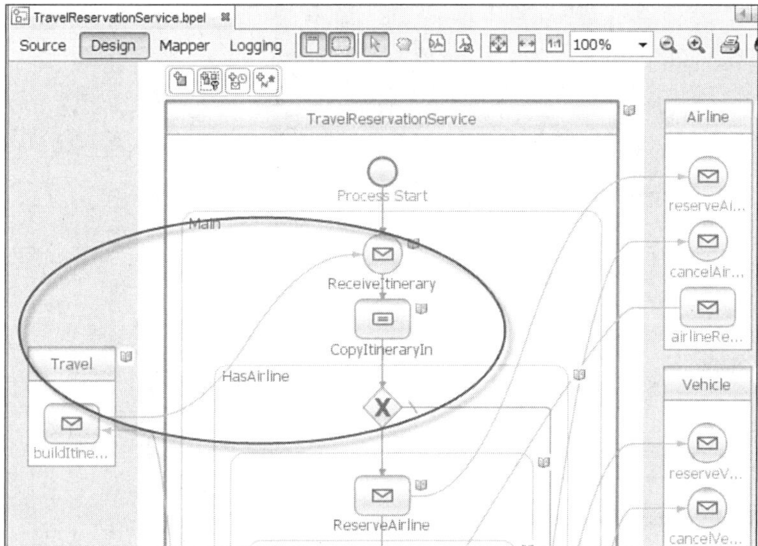

Figure 18.9 Client sends travel itinerary

Scroll down to see the *ReceiveItinerary* activity in the main sequence activity. The IF element in the *HasAirline* contains two assigned activities. If the client itinerary does not contain a pre-existing airline reservation, the itinerary will be sent to the Receive element *reserveAirline* in the Partner Link Airline. This is displayed in Figure 18.10.

Scroll down to see the Invoke element `ReserveAirline` on the diagram and the Receive element `ReserveAirline` in the Partner Link Airline on the right side. The airline reservation is created and a modified itinerary is sent back to the Receive element `AirlineReserved`.

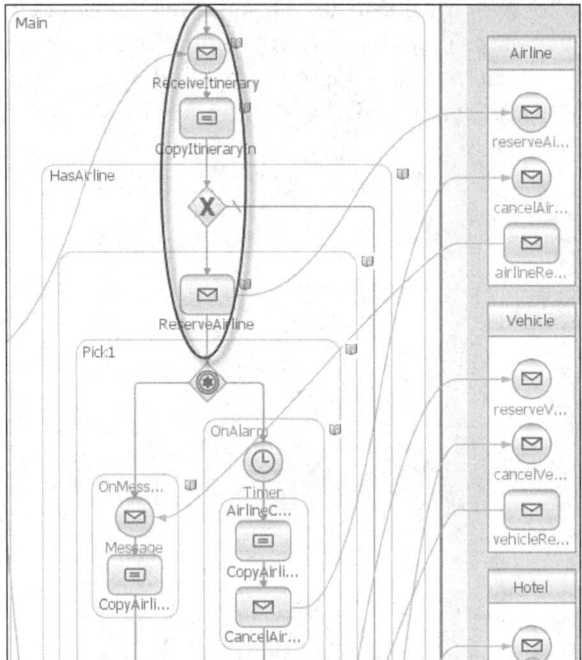

Figure 18.10 No airline reservation

TravelReservationService contains similar logic for the remaining items on the itinerary. Double-click the `TravelReservationService.bpel` tab again in the source editor window to reset the size of the editor.

Running the TravelReservationService Project

The application server in the NetBeans environment must be running in the background for compiling and deploying to take place. Complete the following steps to ensure the application server is running properly:

1. Click on the **Services** tab to open the Services window.
2. Right-click the **GlassFish V2** node. If the *Start* item in the context menu is disabled, the server is already running. If not choose **Start**. Refer to Figure 18.2.

As the project unfolds, Travel Reservation Service communicates with its partner services via its public interfaces. These interfaces are defined in partner-specific WSDL files.

The NetBeans IDE SOA pack includes a bundled EJB project called `Reservation PartnerServices`. The `ReservationPartnerServices` project contains a basic

EJB- and JMS-based implementation of the three partner services. These partner services are *Hotel Reservation Service*, *Vehicle Reservation Service*, and *Airline Reservation Service*. These partner web services must be deployed to the bundled GlassFish application server before you can test run the `TravelReservation Service` process.

To deploy the *ReservationPartnerServices* Application to the GlassFish V2 Server, follow these steps:

1. From the main menu, choose **Files > Open Project**.
2. Use the Open Project Wizard to navigate to the directory where the TravelReservationService was previously created.
3. Select **ReservationPartnerServices**. Click the **Open Project Folder** button.
4. In the Projects tab, right-click on the **ReservationPartnerServices** project node and choose **Undeploy** and **Deploy** from the context menu.
5. Wait until the `BUILD SUCCESSFUL` message appears in the Output window. Switch to the Services node, and expand **Servers > GlassFish V2 > Applications > EJB Modules**. If the node *ReservationPartnerServices* is there, *ReservationPartnerServices* are considered deployed successfully.
6. Expand **GlassFish V2 > Resources > JMS Resources > Connection Factories**. This should contain the `jms/ReservationCallbackProvider DestinationFactory` node.
7. Expand **GlassFish V2 > Resources > JMS Resources > Destination Resources**. If it contains the `jms/ReservationCallbackProviderBean` node, JMS deployment has succeeded.

As shown in Figure 18.11, *ReservationPartnerServices* has been successfully deployed.

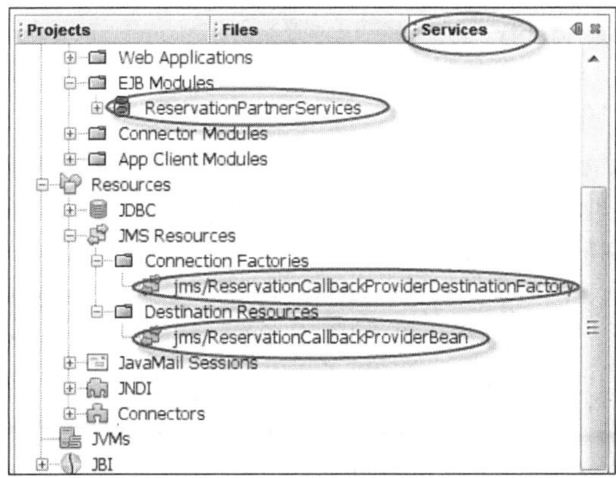

Figure 18.11 Deploying a ReservationPartnerServices application

Next, deploy the *TravelReservationServiceApplication* composite application to the GlassFish V2 server to make the service assembly available to the application server, allowing its service units to be run. To do this, perform the following operations,

1. Switch to the Projects tab in the left pane. Right-click on the **TravelReservationServiceApplication** project node and choose **Deploy Project** from the context menu.
2. The Select Server dialog pops up. Select **Sun GlassFish V2** as the target application server. Click the **OK** button to close the dialog.
3. Wait until the `BUILD SUCCESSFUL` message appears in the Output window. Then select the **Services** tab in the left pane. Expand the **GlassFish V2 > JBI > Service Assemblies** node. A new subnode is now added. If it is not listed, right-click on the **Service Assemblies** node and select the **Refresh** option.

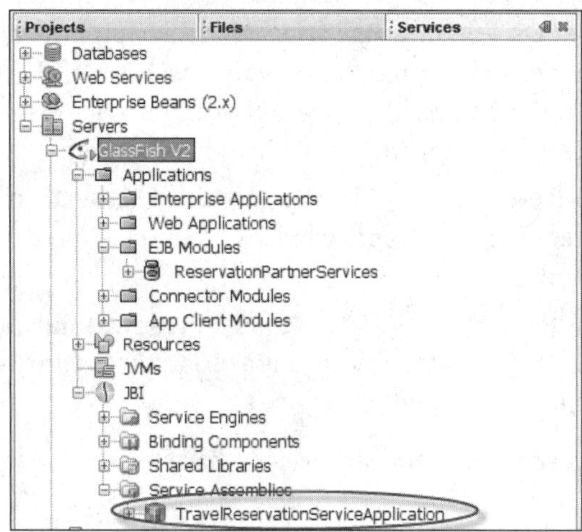

Figure 18.12 Deployed service assembly

Testing the TravelReservationApplication

Switch to the Projects tab in the left pane. Expand the **TravelReservationServiceApplication > Test node** and expand all the subnodes. Each test case contains two XML files: `Input.xml` for input and `Output.xml` for output. These XML files contain SOAP message data. Each one represents a different case that can test the *TravelReservationService* to exercise the process in slightly different ways. Each time the test is run, the current output is compared to the content of `Output.xml` as represented in Figure 18.13.

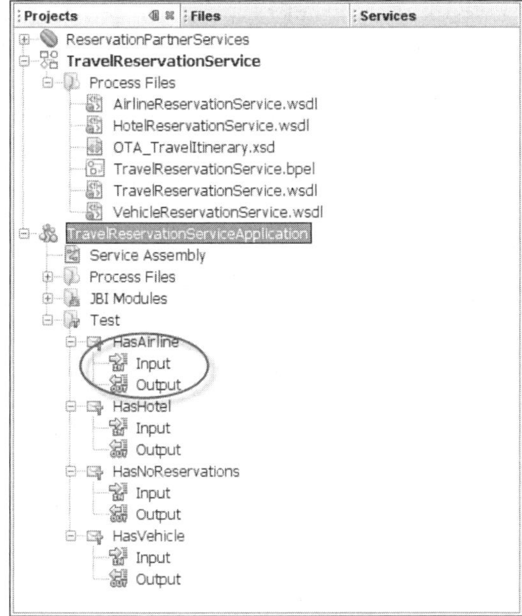

Figure 18.13 Test Cases of TravelReservationService Application

Right-click on the `HasNoReservations` node and select **Run** from the context menu. The IDE now sends the *HasNoReservations* SOAP message to the BPEL runtime. The IDE indicates if the test is successful. You can see the test results in the JUnit Test Results window, as shown in Figure 18.14.

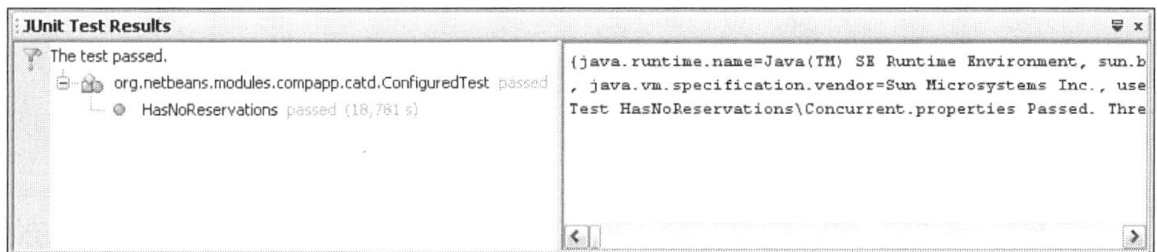

Figure 18.14 Running the TravelReservationService application

Debugging the TravelReservationService Project

NetBeans IDE provides an excellent debugging environment for debugging Enterprise applications. To invoke debugging, it must be enabled first; so enable the BPEL Debugger. Please note that the firewall must be disabled or appropriately configured for the BPEL runtime to start and run properly. Follow these steps to begin the debugging process:

1. Click on the **Services** tab to open the Services in the left pane.
2. Under the GlassFish V2 node, expand the JBI node, and then expand the Service Engines node. Right-click on the `sun.bpel.engine` node and select **Properties** from the Context menu.
3. In the Properties window, set the *DebugEnabled* property to `true`, write down the value of the DebugPort port, and then click the **Close** button, as shown in Figure 18.15.

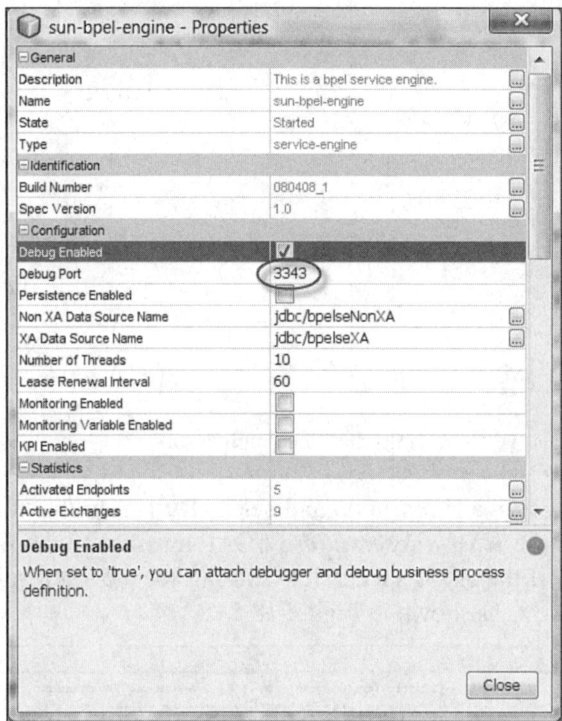

Figure 18.15 Engine Properties menu

4. Under the Services tab, select the **AppServer** node and **Stop the Application server**.
5. Select the **AppServer** node and right-click to select **Start in Debug** mode.
6. Wait until the server is restarted in debug mode. Then switch back to the Projects tab in the left pane, and select the `TravelReservation Service.bpel` node.
7. Click the **TravelReservationService.bpel** tab in the BPEL Editor *Design View* window. Switch to *Source View* by clicking on the **Source** tab. You can turn on the source line numbers by selecting **View > Show Line Numbers** in the main menu. Toggle the break point by clicking on lines 168 and 180, as shown in Figure 18.16.

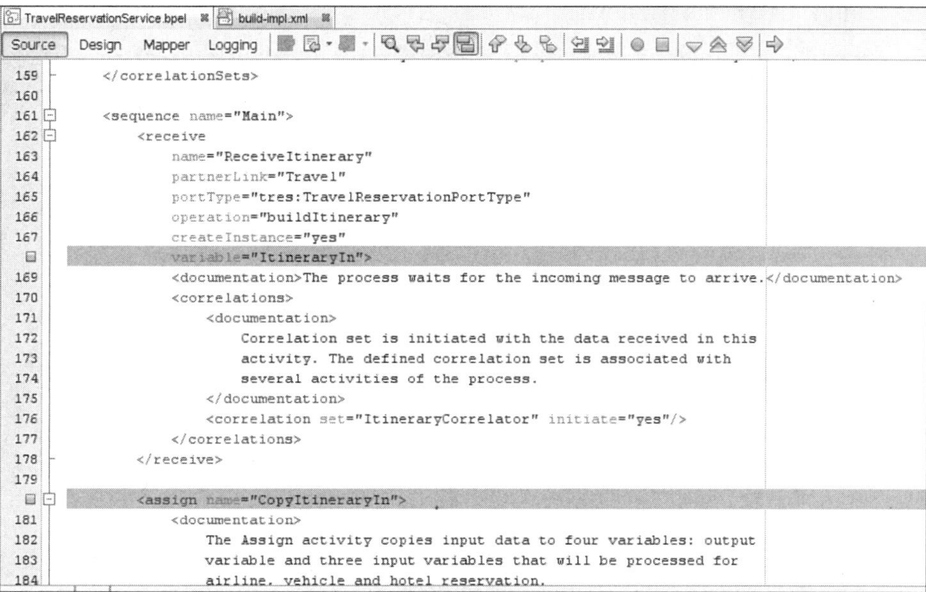

Figure 18.16 Set a break point from the source view.

In the BPEL Editor window, switch to the *Design view*. The break points that were set earlier are visible in the Design view as well, as shown in Figure 18.17.

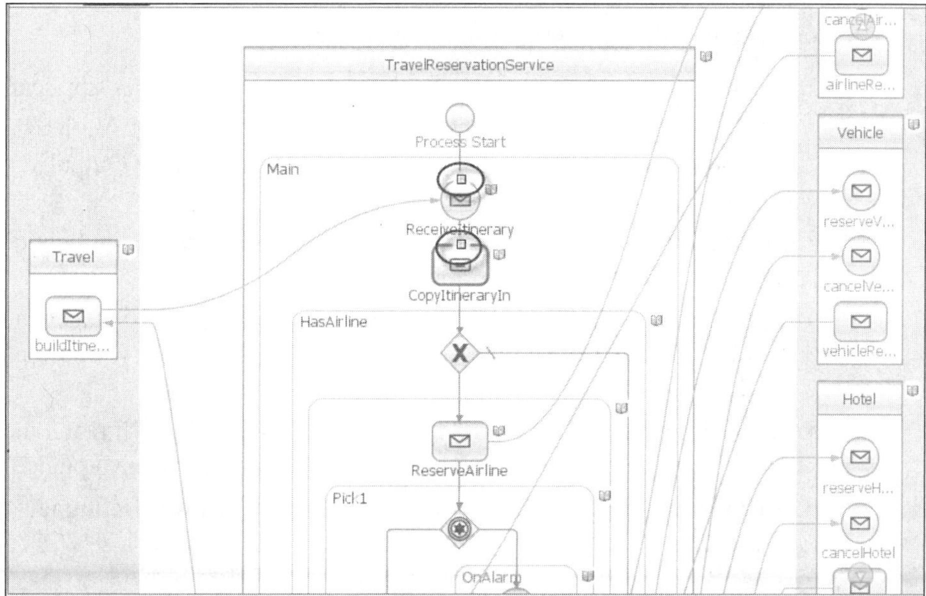

Figure 18.17 Viewing the break point from the Design view

As shown in Figure 18.18, break points can be also viewed from the Navigator and Breakpoints windows.

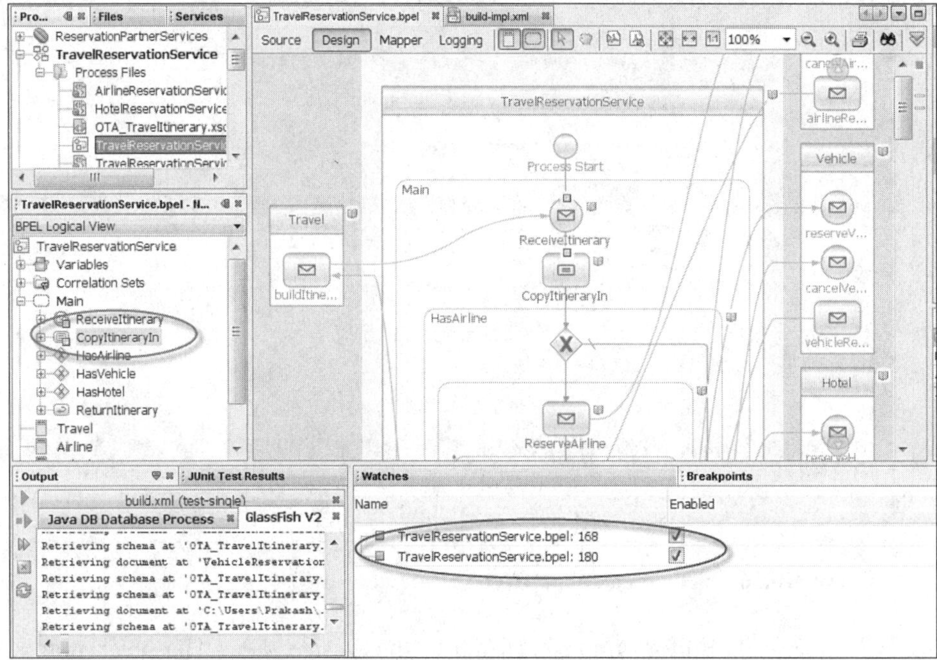

Figure 18.18 Break points in Design view

To complete the debugging session, follow these steps:

1. In the Projects window, select the *TravelReservationService* application node, right-click and choose *Debug (BPEL)* from the context menu.
2. Wait until the `BUILD SUCCESSFUL` message appears in the Output window.
3. Switch to the BPEL Debugger Console window to ensure the `Debug session started` message appeared.
4. Upon reaching the first break point, you can examine the changes in the BPEL Variables Debugging[3] window, in the BPEL Editor window, and in the Navigator window.
5. Click **Continue** (or a **Ctrl F5** key combination), and you'll reach the second break point. Notice that the BPEL variables are now updated.
6. To complete this debugger session, simply select **Finish Debugger Session**.

Summary

This case study profiled Silhouette Travels, a company that offers a network-accessible service for customers to submit travel itineraries. The reservation itinerary is filed with the travel reservation business process employed by Silhouette Travels. The goal is for each of the reservation services to confirm the reservation by sending a callback message to the business process.

The NetBeans IDE with SOA Pack was used to demonstrate the delivery of a specific use case of a travel reservation scenario under the SOA module of the NetBeans package. The structure and the function of the IDE, in terms of different panes, tabs, files, runtime, and project structures, were covered briefly.

The process or the workflow scenario of the travel reservation requirement was enunciated with the help of BPEL process modeling aspects of the NetBeans IDE in terms of two views: Design view and Source view. Debugging and testing of the BPEL process was also highlighted as part of the NetBeans development environment for the application built as per the paradigm of SOA. Both the Design view and the Source view of the process debugging were highlighted as part of the process modeling capabilities of the NetBeans IDE Enterprise Pack.

Endnotes

1. `www.netbeans.org/community/releases/67/install.html`
2. A palette such as this opens up in the right side of the main pane.
3. Note that the BPEL process can be debugged in two modes—visual debugging in Design view and source debugging in Source view—with the ability to switch between the two editor views.

References

Web References

AJAX

Jennifer Ball. "New Technologies for Ajax and Web Application Development: Project jMaki, Project Dynamic Faces, and Project Pohobs." http://java.sun.com/developer/technicalArticles/J2EE/webapp_1/

BPEL

Berry de Vos, Jos Zwiers. "What Is BPEL—Practical Usage." www. radikalfx.com/bpel/index.html

Matjaz B. Juric. "A Hands-On Introduction to BPEL." www.oracle.com/technology/pub/articles/matjaz_bpel1.html

Brenda M. Michelson. "Business Process Execution Language (BPEL) Primer." http://elementallinks.typepad.com/bmichelson/2005/09/view_bpel_proce.html

Stephen A. White. "Mapping BPMN to BPEL Example." www.bpmn.org/Documents/Mapping%20BPMN%20to%20BPEL%20Example.pdf

Wikipedia. "What Is Business Process?" http://en.wikipedia.org/wiki/Business_process

Wise Geek. "What Is BPEL?" www.wisegeek.com/what-is-bpel.htm

CICS

Wiki. "CICS." http://en.wikipedia.org/wiki/CICS and www.webopedia.com/TERM/C/CICS.html

Wiki. "What Is CICS?" www.wisegeek.com/what-is-cics.htm

Design Pattern

e-gov Belgium—Fedict. "e-gov Architecture Application Architecture." www.belgium.be/eportal/ShowDoc/fed_ict/imported_content/pdf/egov_Architecture_Application_Architecture_EN.pdf?contentHome=entapp.BEA_personalization.eGovWebCacheDocumentManager.fr

Sun Microsystems. "J2EE Design Pattern." www.sun.com/training/catalog/courses/SL-500.xml

ESB

Suresh Chande. "ESB: Enterprise Service Bus." www.cs.helsinki.fi/u/chande/courses/cs/WSA/presentations/L10_EnterpriseServiceBus.pdf

IBM. "The Enterprise Service Bus." www-306.ibm.com/software/info1/websphere/index.jsp?tab=landings/esbbenefits

Andrew Nash. "What Is This ESB Thing Anyway?" http://news/zdnet.com/2100-9593_22-5993412.html

Susana Schwartz. "Will MOM Catch the Bus?" www.intelligententerprise.com/showArticle.jhtml?articleID=49400885

Balwinder Sodhi. "Implementing Customizable ESB with Java." www.javaworld.com/javaworld/jw-08-2005/jw-0808-esb_p.html

Ron Ten-Hove. "Composite Materials." http://blogs.sun.com/rtenhove/entry/what_is_enterprise_service_bus

Wiki. "Enterprise Service Bus." http://en.wikipedia.org/wiki/Enterprise_Service_Bus

ESB Importance

Frank Teti. "Enterprise Service Bus: Yet Another Paradigm Shift or Better Orchestration of Old Technologies?" www.theserverside.com/tt/articles/article.tss?l=ESBParadigm

GDS

Bear Stearns. "Internet Travel: Point, Click, Trip: An Introduction to the Online Travel Industry, London: 1–99." www.mindbranch.com/Global-Distribution-Systems-R560-2103/

Samipatra Das. "Global Distribution Systems in Present Times." www. hotel-online.com/News/PR2002_4th/Oct02_GDS.html

Hibernate

"Hibernate." www.hibernate.org

Implementing SOA with Java EE 5

Gopalan Raj, Binod P. G., Rick Palkowic. "Implementing Service-Oriented Architectures (SOA) with the Java EE 5 SDK." http://java.sun.com/developer/technicalArticles/WebServices/soa3/

IMS

Frank Naudé. www.orafaq.com/glossary/faqglosi.htm, www.mainframes.com/ims.htm, www-306.ibm.com/software/data/ims/

IMS TM

Wiki. "Information Management System" http://en.wikipedia.org/wiki/Information_Management_System

J2EE Best Practices

Chris Richardson. "J2EE Design Decisions." www.javaworld.com/javaworld/jw-01-2006/jw-0130-pojo.html

J2EE Patterns

Sun Microsystems. "Business Delegate Pattern." http://java.sun.com/blueprints/patterns/.html

Sun Microsystems. "Transfer Object Design Pattern." http://java.sun.com/blueprints/patterns/html

J2EE Versus .NET

Chad Vawter, Ed Roman. "J2EE Versus Microsoft.NET: A Comparison of Building XML-Based Web Services." www.theserverside.com/tt/articles/pdf/J2EE-vs-DOTNET.pdf

Java EE 5 Developer Productivity

Arun Gupta, Jitendra Kotamraju, Vivek Pandey. "How We Migrated WS-IS Sample Application from JAX-RPC 1.1 to JAX-WS 2.0." http://weblogs.java.net/blog/arungupta/archive/javaone/BOF-9162.pdf

Raghu R. Kodali. "The Simplicity of EJB 3.0." http://java.sys-con.com/read/117755_1.htm

Ryan Lubke. "Does JSF Simplify Web Application Development?" http://blogs.sun.com/roller/page/rlubke?entry=does_jsf_simplify_web_application

Debu Panda. "Java Adventure Builder Migrated to Use EJB 3.0 and JSR-181." www.theserverside.com/news/thread.tss?thread_id=35777

Java Specification Request

"Common Annotations for the Java Platform." http://jcp.org/en/jsr/detail?id=250

"Enterprise JavaBeans 3.0." http://jcp.org/en/jsr/detail?id=220

"J2EE Application Deployment." http://jcp.org/en/jsr/detail?id=88

"J2EE Connector Architecture 1.5." http://jcp.org/en/jsr/detail?id=112

"J2EE Management." http://jcp.org/en/jsr/detail?id=77

"Java API for XML Registries 1.0 (JAXR)." http://jcp.org/en/jsr/detail?id=93

"Java API for XML-Based RPC (JAX-RPC) 1.1." http://jcp.org/en/jsr/detail?id=101

"Java API for XML-Based Web Services (JAX-WS) 2.0." http://jcp.org/en/jsr/detail?id=224

"Java Architecture for XML Binding (JAXB) 2.0." http://jcp.org/en/jsr/detail?id=222

"Java Authorization Contract for Containers." http://jcp.org/en/jsr/detail?id=115

"Java Data Object." http://jcp.org/en/jsr/detail?id=243

"Java Message Service API." http://jcp.org/en/jsr/detail?id=914

"Java Persistence API." http://jcp.org/en/jsr/detail?id=220

"Java Platform, Enterprise Edition 5 (Java EE 5)." http://jcp.org/en/jsr/detail?id=244

"Java Servlet 2.5." http://jcp.org/en/jsr/detail?id=154

"Java Transaction API (JTA)." http://jcp.org/en/jsr/detail?id=907

"JavaBeans Activation Framework (JAF) 1.1." http://jcp.org/en/jsr/detail?id=925

"JavaMail." http://jcp.org/en/jsr/detail?id=919

"JavaServer Faces 1.2." http://jcp.org/en/jsr/detail?id=252

"JavaServer Pages 2.1." http://jcp.org/en/jsr/detail?id=245

"JavaServer Pages Standard Tag Library." http://jcp.org/en/jsr/detail?id=52

"SOAP with Attachments API for Java (SAAJ)." http://jcp.org/en/jsr/detail?id=67

"Streaming API for XML." http://jcp.org/en/jsr/detail?id=173

"Web Service Metadata for the Java Platform." http://jcp.org/en/jsr/detail?id=181

jRuby

Wikipedia. "jRuby." http://en.wikipedia.org/wiki/Ruby

OTA

OTA home page. www.opentravel.org

Paradigm Shift

Wiki. "Paradigm Shift." http://en.wikipedia.org/wiki/Paradigm_shift and www.mc2consulting.com/riskdef.htm

Paradigm Shift in IT

Drik. www.bioss.sari.ac.uk/~dirk/essays/ParShiftsInfTech/index.html

Performance Benchmark

"SPEC jAppServer." www.spec.org/jAppServer

Portlet

Wikipedia. "Portlet." http://en.wikipedia.org/wiki/Portlet

Ruby

Wikipedia. "Ruby." http://en.wikipedia.org/wiki/JRuby

Sabre, GDS

Thomas Hoffman, Computerworld. "Case study: Sabre's Web Services Journey." www.javaworld.com/javaworld/jw-01-2007/jw-0108-sabre.html?page=1

SOA

David J. N. "SOA Realization: Service Design Principles." http://www-128.ibm.com/developerworks/webservices/library/ws-soa-design/

"SOA." www.webservicesolympus.com/soa/index.jsp?forum=40

SOA General

"SOA Learning Guide." http://searchwebservices.techtarget.com/generic/0,295582,sid26_gci1068517,00.html?Offer=WStsstxtsoalg87#SOA Definitions

SOAP

W3C. "SOAP Version 1.2 Part 0: Primer." www.w3.org/TR/soap12-part0/

W3C. "SOAP Version 1.2 Part 1: Messaging Framework." www.w3.org/TR/soap12-part1/

W3C. "SOAP Version 1.2 Part 2: Adjuncts." www.w3.org/TR/soap12-part2/

SOA Patterns

www.orchestrationpatterns.com

www.workflowpatterns.com

Dragos A. Manolescu. "Patterns for Orchestration Environments." September 8–12, 2004, Allterton Park, Monticello, Illinois. http://hillside.net/plop/2004/papers/dmanolescu0/PLoP2004_dmanolescu0_0.pdf

Tango

Harold Carr. "An Overview of Sun's Project Tango." http://weblogs.java.net/blog/haroldcarr/archive/2006/02/an_overview_of_1.html

Harold Carr. "Sun's Project Tango." http://java.sun.com/developer/technicalArticles/glassfish/ProjectTango/

Nicholas Kassem, Harold Carr. "Composable Web Services Using Interoperable Technologies from Sun's Project Tango." http://developers.sun.com/learning/javaoneonline/2006/webtier/TS-4661.pdf and http://searchwebservices.techtarget.com/tip/0,289483,sid26_gci1211905,00.html?track=NL-110&ad=562924& asrc=EM_NLN_495101&uid=1282904

Web Services

Qusay H. Mahmoud. "Developing Web Services with Java2 Enterprise Edition (1.4) Platform." http://java.sun.com/developer/technicalArticles/J2EE/j2ee_ws/

WSDL

W3C. "WSDL Version 2.0 Part 0: Primer." www.w3.org/TR/wsdl20-primer/

W3C. "WSDL Version 2.0 Part 1: Core Language." www.w3.org/TR/wsdl20/

W3C. "WSDL Version 2.0 Part 2: Adjuncts." www.w3.org/TR/wsdl20-adjuncts/

WSDL and UDDI

John Colgrave, Karsten Januszweski. "Using WSDL in UDDI Registry." www.oasis-open.org/committes/uddi-spec/bp/uddi-spec

XML

"Extensible Markup Language." http://xml.coverpages.org

W3C. "Extensible Markup Language." www.w3.org/XML/

Yahoo!

"Yahoo! Developer Network." http://developer.yahoo.com

Books

Design Patterns

Deepak Alur, John Crupi, Dan Malks (2003). *Core J2EE Patterns: Best Practices and Design Strategies*, 2nd Edition, Prentice Hall/Sun Microsystems.

Gregor Hohpe, Bobby Woolf. (2004). *Enterprise Integration Patterns: Designing, Building, and Deploying Messaging Solutions*. Addison Wesley.

ESB

David A. Chappell (2004). *Enterprise Service Bus: Theory in Practice*. O'Reilly Media, Inc.

J2EE

Deepak Alur, John Crupi, Dan Malks (2003). *Core J2EE Patterns: Best Practices and Design Strategies*, 2nd Edition. Sun Microsystems Press, Prentice Hall.

Nadir Gulzar (2003). *Practical J2EE: Application Architecture*. McGraw Hill/ Osborne.

B. V. Kumar, S. Sangeetha, S. V. Subrahmanya (2005). *J2EE Architecture*. Tata McGraw-Hill.

Java

Peter Van Der Linden (2000). *Just Java*, 4th Edition. Sun Microsystems Press, Addison Wesley.

Peter Van Der Linden (1997). *Not Just Java*. Sunsoft Press Java Series.

Java, XML

Brett McLaughlin (2000). *Java and XML*. O'Reilly.

MDA

Anneke Kleppe, Jos Warmer, Wim Bast (2003). *MDA Explained: Model Driven Architecture: Practice and Promise*. Pearson Education.

NetBeans

Tim Boudreau, Jesse Glick, Simeon Greene, Jack Woehr, Vaughn Spurlin (2002). *NetBeans: The Definitive Guide*. O'Reilly.

Patrick Keegan, Ludovic Champenois, Gregory Crawley, and Charlie Hunt (2006). *The NetBeans IDE Field Guide: Developing Desktop, Web, Enterprise, and Mobile Applications*, 2nd Edition. Prentice Hall Ptr.

Adam Myatt (2007). *Pro NetBeans IDE 5.5 Enterprise Edition*. Apress.

SOA

Thomas Erl (2005). *Service-Oriented Architecture: Concepts, Technology, and Design*. Prentice Hall PTR.

Derek Krafing, Karl Banke, Dirk Salma (2004). *Enterprise SOA: Service Oriented Architecture Best Practices*. The Codd Series.

Eric Newcomer, Greg Lomow (2005). *Understanding SOA with Web Services*. Addison Wesley.

Software Architecture

Paul Clements, Rick Kazman, Mark Klein (2002). *Evaluating Software Architecture: Methods and Case Studies*. Addison Wesley.

Web Services

Doug Kaye (2003). *Loosely Coupled: The Missing Pieces of Web Services*. RDS Press.

B. V. Kumar, S. V. Subrahmanya (2004). *Web Services: An Introduction*. Tata McGraw Hill.

XML

Frank P. Coyle (2002). *WML, Web Services, and the Data Revolution*. Pearson Education.

INDEX

E

I

J

K

L

M

Q

R

S

U

V

W

X–Y–Z

Addison-Wesley | Cisco Press | EXAM/CRAM | IBM Press | QUE | PRENTICE HALL | SAMS | Safari Books Online